Palgrave Advances in Bioeconomy: Economics and Policies

Series Editor
Justus Wesseler
Agricultural Economics and Rural Policy Group
Wageningen University
Wageningen, Gelderland, The Netherlands

More information about this series at
http://www.palgrave.com/gp/series/16141

Liesbeth Dries • Wim Heijman
Roel Jongeneel • Kai Purnhagen
Justus Wesseler
Editors

EU Bioeconomy Economics and Policies: Volume I

Editors
Liesbeth Dries
Agricultural Economics and Rural
Policy Group
Wageningen University
Wageningen, Gelderland
The Netherlands

Roel Jongeneel
Agricultural Economics and Rural
Policy Group
Wageningen University
Wageningen, Gelderland
The Netherlands

Justus Wesseler
Agricultural Economics and Rural
Policy Group
Wageningen University
Wageningen, Gelderland
The Netherlands

Wim Heijman
Agricultural Economics and Rural
Policy Group
Wageningen University
Wageningen, Gelderland
The Netherlands

Kai Purnhagen
Law and Governance Group
Wageningen University
Wageningen, Gelderland
The Netherlands

ISSN 2524-5848   ISSN 2524-5856   (electronic)
Palgrave Advances in Bioeconomy: Economics and Policies
ISBN 978-3-030-28633-0   ISBN 978-3-030-28634-7   (eBook)
https://doi.org/10.1007/978-3-030-28634-7

This Palgrave Macmillan imprint is published by the registered company Springer Nature
Switzerland AG.
The registered company address is: Gewerbestrasse 11, 6330 Cham, Switzerland

CONTENTS

CONTRIBUTORS

Willy Baltussen Consumer and Chain Unit, Wageningen Economic Research, The Hague, The Netherlands

Johan Bremmer Innovation- and Risk Management and Information Governance Unit, Wageningen Economic Research, The Hague, The Netherlands

Jeroen Candel Public Administration and Policy Group, Wageningen University, Wageningen, Gelderland, The Netherlands

Liesbeth Dries Agricultural Economics and Rural Policy Group, Wageningen University, Wageningen, Gelderland, The Netherlands

Emil Erjavec Agricultural Policy and Economics Department, University of Ljubljana, Ljubljana, Slovenia

Tomás García Azcárate Institute of Economics, Geography and Demography, Spanish National Research Council, Madrid, Spain

Wim Heijman Agricultural Economics and Rural Policy Group, Wageningen University, Wageningen, Gelderland, The Netherlands

Alexia Herwig Law and Governance Group, Wageningen University, Wageningen, Gelderland, The Netherlands

Roel Jongeneel Agricultural Economics and Rural Policy Group, Wageningen University, Wageningen, Gelderland, The Netherlands

Vincent Linderhof Green Economy and Landuse Unit, Wageningen Economic Research, The Hague, The Netherlands

Alan Matthews Department of Economics, Trinity College Dublin, Dublin, Ireland

Yuliang Pang University of Antwerp, Antwerp, Belgium

Kai Purnhagen Law and Governance Group, Wageningen University, Wageningen, Gelderland, The Netherlands

Huib Silvis Performance and Impact Agrosectors, Wageningen Economic Research, The Hague, The Netherlands

Coen van Wagenberg Consumer and Chain Unit, Wageningen Economic Research, The Hague, The Netherlands

Justus Wesseler Agricultural Economics and Rural Policy Group, Wageningen University, Wageningen, Gelderland, The Netherlands

LIST OF FIGURES

LIST OF TABLES

PART I

Introduction

CHAPTER 1

Introduction

Justus Wesseler, Liesbeth Dries, Wim Heijman,
Roel Jongeneel, and Kai Purnhagen

Over the past two decades, the European Union (EU) internal market policies in general, and the ones related to agriculture and the common agricultural policies in particular, have observed substantial changes. These include a move from direct production-related payments towards payments linked with environmental performance and rural development. The EU Common Agricultural Policy (CAP) is organized under two pillars, including cross-cutting issues. The first pillar includes the direct payments and market measures, and the second pillar includes the rural development policy. Rural development policy has become evermore important.

The increase in horizontal and vertical integration in the agriculture and food sector, the increase in intra-industry trade and the globalisation of trade but also in norms and values have linked the agricultural sector

J. Wesseler (✉) • L. Dries • W. Heijman • R. Jongeneel
Agricultural Economics and Rural Policy Group, Wageningen University,
Wageningen, Gelderland, The Netherlands
e-mail: justus.wesseler@wur.nl; liesbeth.dries@wur.nl; wim.heijman@wur.nl; roel.jongeneel@wur.nl

K. Purnhagen
Law and Governance Group, Wageningen University,
Wageningen, Gelderland, The Netherlands
e-mail: kai.purnhagen@wur.nl

© The Author(s) 2019   3
L. Dries et al. (eds.), *EU Bioeconomy Economics and Policies: Volume I*,
Palgrave Advances in Bioeconomy: Economics and Policies,
https://doi.org/10.1007/978-3-030-28634-7_1

more strongly with the food sector. Further, technical change has increased the portfolio for processing biomass not only into food and feed but also into a number of alternative bio-based products including bioenergy, bio-polymers and more (European Commission 2012). The development of bio-based industries provides new opportunities for agriculture and rural communities (Wesseler and von Braun 2017). Environmental concerns and climate change in particular have increased the demand for sustainable development-related policies as indicated in the circular economy (European Commission 2015) and bioeconomy strategy (European Commission 2018) documents.

As a result of these developments, assessing the agricultural sector and related policies in isolation may result in substantial biases from a technical change, a regional (Heijman et al. 2017), an organisational (Pascucci et al. 2015) as well as a legal perspective (Purnhagen 2013). One of the most striking examples is perhaps the debate about new developments in plant breeding. It has often been argued that the stringent regulatory policies on the approval of genetically modified organisms (GMOs) can be justified by concerns of EU consumers towards the technology, but that this will not have further implications for other sectors such as medicine. This argument falls short of the insight that such kind of policy is very likely to spill over to other sectors of the economy as well. Take patent applications for the gene-editing technology CRISPR-Cas that can be applied across several sectors as an example: The EU has only a share of about 7% of all patents, while the USA and China have a share of more than 40% according to a recent study (Martin-Laffon et al. 2019).[1] The shares for the medical sector are even lower, only about 3.5%, while for the agricultural sector they are about 8%. The results suggest that EU policies on GMOs can have substantial, in this case negative, spill-over effects on other sectors. The example further illustrates the complexity of EU bioeconomy policies.

Within the two volumes, we attempt to make a contribution to better understanding the complexity of EU bioeconomy policies. As mentioned above agricultural policies in the EU should not be assessed in isolation. We have given the book the name *EU Bioeconomy Economics and Policies* to explicitly stipulate the importance of the interconnectedness of the agricultural sector and related policies with up- and downstream sectors.

---

[1] Gene editing is considered to be the leading technology in biology for developing new solutions for a number of problems in agricultural production and human medicine as well as new products for the bio-based industry. CRISPR (clustered regularly interspaced short palindromic repeats) in combination with Cas proteins is a widely used technology for gene editing. (Doudna and Sternberg 2017).

The book is a follow-up on two earlier books on "*EU policy for agriculture, food and rural areas*" edited by Arie Oskam, Gerrit Meester and Huib Silvis (Oskam et al. 2011). This new edition has maintained some of the structure of the previous ones but has been largely revised and partly written afresh. Additional chapters on the EU bioeconomy and circular economy policies as well as on bioenergy policies have been added. The part on rural areas has been expanded by including tourism.

In general, the chapters are short and descriptive in nature to provide the reader with information about the current state of policies and underlying motivations. We believe this is an important part of applied policy analysis where a researcher needs to first get a basis of understanding of the state of the art of the current situation before moving into policy analysis and conclusions for policy recommendations.

While the chapters are rather policy descriptive, we have included two theory-oriented chapters. The first one, Chap. 2, stresses important aspects of applied policy analysis derived from economic theory and the second one, Chap. 7, volume 2 focuses on the economic theory of public goods, an important characteristic of rural amenities.

The two volumes are organized in six parts. Each part concentrates on specific policy areas except for Part I, which includes this introduction and the chapter on the economic theory of bioeconomy policies. Part II covers the institutional framework of the European Union. Part III covers agricultural policies, Part IV food policies, Part V rural policies and Part VI circular bioeconomy policies. Each part includes a chapter on the future developments derived from the individual chapters to provide the reader with some ideas about what to expect. Naturally, there are some overlaps between the different chapters caused by interlinkages of topics and policies.

REFERENCES

Doudna, J., and S. Sternberg. 2017. *A Crack in Creation: Gene Editing and the Unthinkable Power to Control Evolution.* Boston: Houghton Mifflin Harcourt.
European Commission. 2012. *Innovating for Sustainable Growth. A Bioeconomy for Europe.* Luxembourg: Publications Office of the European Union.
———. 2015. Closing the Loop—An EU Action Plan for the Circular Economy. COM (2015) 614 final. Brussels.
———. 2018. *A Sustainable Bioeconomy for Europe: Strengthening the Connection Between Economy, Society and the Environment.* Luxembourg: Publications Office of the European Union.

Heijman, W., J. Klijs, J. Peerlings, J. Rouwendal, and R.A. Schipper. 2017. *Space and Economics: An Introduction to Regional Economics.* Wageningen: Wageningen Academic Publishers.

Martin-Laffon, J., M. Kuntz, and A.E. Ricroch. 2019. Worldwide CRISPR Patent Landscape Shows Strong Geographical Biases. *Nature Biotechnology* 37: 601–621.

Oskam, A., G. Meesters, and H. Silvis, eds. 2011. *EU Policy for Agriculture, Food and Rural Areas.* 2nd ed. Wageningen: Wageningen Academic Publishers.

Pascucci, S., L. Dries, K. Karantininis, and G. Martino. 2015. Regulation and Organizational Change in the Governance of Agri-Food Value Chains. *British Food Journal* 117 (10). https://doi.org/10.1108/BFJ-07-2015-0268.

Purnhagen, K. 2013. *The Politics of Systematization in EU Product Safety Regulation: Market, State, Collectivity, and Integration.* New York: Springer.

Wesseler, J., and J. von Braun. 2017. Measuring the Bioeconomy: Economics and Policies. *Annual Review of Resource Economics* 9: 17.1–17.24.

CHAPTER 2

Bioeconomy Economics and Policies

Justus Wesseler, Roel Jongeneel, and Kai Purnhagen

2.1   INTRODUCTION

Policies supporting the development of the bioeconomy in the European Union (EU) have as an objective the improvement of overall well-being or in the words of the European Commission "ensuring the prosperity of its citizens" (European Commission 2018, p. 4). Defining the improvement of overall well-being is a non-trivial exercise. Arrow et al. (2012) present a general framework for measuring improvement in well-being. According to this framework, improvements are possible if well-being, measured as the discounted sum of current and future well-being, as a result of a policy change is larger than well-being without the policy change while opportunity costs including irreversibility effects need to be taken into consideration. This framework requires a proper description of the current situation and possible alternatives. In general, more than one policy alternative exist

J. Wesseler (✉) • R. Jongeneel
Agricultural Economics and Rural Policy Group, Wageningen University, Wageningen, Gelderland, The Netherlands
e-mail: justus.wesseler@wur.nl; roel.jongeneel@wur.nl

K. Purnhagen
Law and Governance Group, Wageningen University, Wageningen, Gelderland, The Netherlands
e-mail: kai.purnhagen@wur.nl

© The Author(s) 2019   7
L. Dries et al. (eds.), *EU Bioeconomy Economics and Policies: Volume I*,
Palgrave Advances in Bioeconomy: Economics and Policies,
https://doi.org/10.1007/978-3-030-28634-7_2

for improving well-being. Among the different alternatives, the best one should be selected (Coase 2006). One of the challenges among several is that a change in policy is not costless or, to put it differently, the current state we observe is efficient. One important problem is that overall improvements not only generate winners, those that lose can in principle be compensated as those losses are less than the gains. While compensation in principle is possible, implementing compensation is more complicated. This starts with defining what should be considered as being a loss and is further complicated by the fact that losses, in many cases, differ by person. Moreover, the implicit allocation of property rights may be a factor in the felt need for compensation of the losers. Overall, this requires a very detailed knowledge about the current situation, including a detailed analysis of current policies and the possible consequences of change.

Definition of the bioeconomy

The bioeconomy covers all sectors and systems that rely on biological resources (animals, plants, micro-organisms and derived biomass, including organic waste), their functions and principles. It includes and interlinks: land and marine ecosystems and the services they provide; all primary production sectors that use and produce biological resources (agriculture, forestry, fisheries and aquaculture); and all economic and industrial sectors that use biological resources and processes to produce food, feed, bio-based products, energy and services (excluding biomedicines and health biotechnology added in a footnote). (EC 2018, p. 4)

The forgoing raises the question about how policy makers and policy analysts know? Hayek (1944) is very critical about the possibility of policy makers in solving the information problem. Policies providing individual freedom secured by individual rights have a strong potential for improving well-being and, in general, are considered to be a better alternative over policies not following a rights-based approach (Easterly 2014). Still, the challenge remains over what decisions are left to the individual and what decisions are transferred to other higher orders.

Differentiating policies in ex ante and ex post widely understood by including legal frameworks such as constitutions provide a framework about what kind of changes are possible. Competition about legal frameworks between countries is expected to deliver better outcomes over time (Buchanan and Tullock 1962). Countries where policy adjustments are less costly are expected to grow faster than others. Time in this context is an important factor. In a dynamic world where new information is generated continuously, timing of policy adjustment is a challenge (Wesseler and Zhao 2019). Studies on long-run economic growth show regional aspects such as location seem to matter more than policies. Easterly (2014) and Acemoglu et al. (2019) find support for the hypothesis that long-run economic growth is supported by democracy more than other forms of governance.

The economics of bioeconomy policies are further complicated by the political economy of policy decisions. Interest groups try to influence policy outcomes by rent-seeking. The policy choices finally made largely depend on these influences (Schmitz et al. 2010). For policy analysis, identification of the different interest groups and their objectives is an important part of the research agenda. Modelling these choices ex ante can provide important insights about likely policy outcomes as well as the distribution of benefits and costs among different groups. Those groups less involved/less organised in the policy debates are often those who have to pay the price (Petit 2019).

The lobby activities are also often driven by the character of the goods involved. Private goods such as most of the food products are characterised by rivalry and high degree of competition. Market forces drive prices close to those characterised by the textbook example for polypolistic markets. Other goods such as agricultural landscapes, clean air and clean water are examples of public goods. In theory, private incentives might not be large enough to provide a sufficiently large enough amount of those goods that would maximise social welfare. Government interventions can correct the imbalance via different policies. This is widely done for public goods of the bioeconomy. Prominent examples include nature reserves, manure policies to protect groundwater resources and animal welfare regulations. Assessing the benefits and costs of government interventions for adjusting the provision of public goods is a non-trivial exercise. Identifying the optimal level is an impossible task. The models used are a simplification of reality. Nevertheless, illustrating trade-offs of policy choices and identifying possibilities for improvement is feasible. For applied policy analysis, a description of the current state of nature is an important first step that allows to identify possibilities for improvement as well as an analysis of suggested policy changes. The models need to consider the uncertainties related to policy changes as well as possible irreversibility effects as they are unavoidable but not to be neglected parts of reality (Wesseler and Zhao 2019).

2.2   THE IMPORTANCE OF IRREVERSIBILITY

There is a strong link between uncertainty and irreversibility. Uncertainty only becomes relevant in connection with irreversibility. If a decision being made under uncertainty is completely reversible, uncertainty does not matter. The "mistake" been made can be corrected ex post without additional costs. Uncertainty causes additional costs, because in the case of an unfavourable outcome, reversing the outcome results in additional costs. In this sense, every decision is irreversible as we cannot move back in time (Fisher 2000). The important aspect is time. Depending on the time length considered, that is, time length of decision-making is not infinitesimal small anymore, the importance of irreversibility and what to consider as irreversible will be smaller or larger.

This is illustrated by the following example. A farmer cultivates crops. Within the cropping season, the application and quantity of pest and disease control can be timed. During the cropping season, the expenses for pest and disease control are sunk. They cannot be reversed economically speaking. They will be "reversed" at the end of the cropping season when the farmer sells his harvest. Analysing the investment into pest and disease control within the cropping season needs to consider the irreversibility effect as this can have an effect on timing and quantity (Ndeffo Mbah et al. 2010). Analysing the investment into a control technology such as a sprayer to be used over several years, where the benefits result from higher crop yields due to pest and disease control realised at the end of the season, does not need to treat pest and disease control as irreversible but the investment into the control technology.

The above is just one illustrative example. The combination of uncertainty and irreversibility and effects on benefits and costs matter for policy analysis as well as summarised in a recent review by Wesseler and Zhao (2019) and we argue are fundamental for policy analysis.

2.3   LEGAL ENVIRONMENT

The description of the current state to be able to predict future states and related outcomes with respect to policy changes is complicated by the legal environment of the EU. EU policies are characterised by minimum and maximum harmonisation. Minimum harmonisation provides member states with a high amount of flexibility to implement policies, while maximum harmonisation simply said applies to all member states. Minimum harmonisation allows for several different responses as it provides flexibility. The observed responses provide a good overview about what member state policy makers consider efficient responses. In general, those policies are considered to be less costly as differences between member states are taken into account by member states themselves following the principle of subsidiarity and might be even further strengthened at member state level by further delegating responses to lower level even to the individual (source). Examples include, relative to the previous programming period, gained flexibility by member states under the CAP reform (CAP 2014–2020) regarding the implementation of the new CAP regulations, particularly in relation to the implementation of the new direct payment regulation.

2.3.1   Ex ante and Ex post Policies

Many of the EU policies are not directly targeted towards increasing farm household income but targeted towards public goods such as clean air and water, nature conservation, or animal welfare. Differences in transaction costs provide arguments for government intervention via regulatory policies and support for the provision of those goods. In principle, if the legal system would work perfectly, the market would internalise externalities ex ante, and in cases where this would not happen because of uncertainties, ex post liability via courts would correct outcomes (Shleifer 2010). In a similar vein, Rothbard (1982) has expressed a strong view based on individual property rights and ex post tort law. The protection of individual property rights serves as a policy guide. This requires a well-functioning legal system. But legal systems have also their shortcomings. Judges face an information problem. Deep pockets, asset constraints and more limit the efficiency of policy strategies solely based on ex post liability (Shleifer 2010) and provide arguments for combining ex ante policies with ex post liability policies. As Shavell (1984) and Kolstad et al. (1990) show, a combination of ex ante policies and ex post liabilities often results in less costly solutions with uncertainty about potential outcomes as the main reason. In many cases, a combination of ex ante regulations and ex post liabilities provides the incentives for delivering public goods. Ex ante regulations include a wide range of policy instruments including price policies such as positive and negative taxes (subsidies), quantity policies such as quotas and also production constraints such as standards and prohibitions. Ex post

Table 2.1   Policy analysis framework

	Private	*Non-private*
Reversible	Ex ante and ex post differentiated by benefits and costs and	
Irreversible	stakeholder	

Source: Based on Demont et al. (2005)

liabilities include payment for damages based on negligence, trespassing and several forms of liability (e.g. joint, several, joint and several).

This adds another important dimension to be considered from a policy analysis perspective. Policies need to be differentiated into ex ante and ex post policies. In addition, uncertainty is important and needs to be considered as already mentioned above, and hence real option methodology can be applied for policy analysis (Wesseler and Zhao 2019).

Table 2.1 summarises the main dimensions we consider to be relevant for policy analysis. They include a differentiation of benefits and costs by stakeholder into ex ante and ex post further differentiated by private and non-private and reversible and irreversible.

Recently, the use of nudges has been added to the policy toolset. Nudges are used to steer behaviour in a specific direction to improve outcomes at almost no costs. Examples include the order of food in canteens to increase fruit consumption (source) or the change from an "opt-in" to an "opt-out" policy. The use of nudges while widely accepted as a policy tool is constrained by what is legally possible.

2.4   POLICY ANALYSIS AT THE MICRO-LEVEL

A large share of bioeconomy policies such as the common agricultural policy is mainly targeted at farms. At the micro-level, the theory of the farm household has become a powerful tool for assessing implications of policy changes. Following Schmitt (1989a, b) the main points of the theory can be summarised as in Fig. 2.1. The horizontal axis shows the time available to the farm household and can be allocated between farm and off-farm work, while the vertical axis shows household income. Farm income shows first increasing and then decreasing marginal returns to labour. Off-farm labour is introduced with constant marginal return to labour for simplicity. The optimal allocation of labour between farm and off-farm work and leisure time is identified by adding the indifference curve of the household for leisure and labour. The optimal allocation of

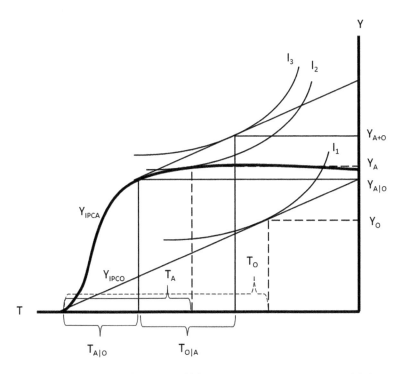

Fig. 2.1 Combination of on- and off-farm income. Note: Y: income, T: time, I_i: indifference curves between labour and leisure, Y_{IPCA}: income possibility curve agriculture, Y_{IPCO}: income possibility curve off-farm, Y_A: income on-farm work only, Y_O: income off-farm work only, $Y_{A|O}$: income from agriculture, when working off-farm, Y_{A+O}: combined income from agriculture and off-farm work, T_A: labour time working agriculture only, T_O: labour time working off-farm only, $T_{A|O}$: labour time agriculture when working also off-farm, $T_{O|A}$: labour time off-farm when working in agriculture as well. (Source: Authors based on Schmitt 1989b)

time is shown by point a, where T_a is spent for farm work, T_{off} for off-farm work and T_L for leisure. A number of modification of the model exists including different forms of labour organisation including family and non-family labour, transaction costs, financial markets and more (Beckmann 1997; Benjamin 1992; Nakajima 1986; Phimister and Roberts 2006). From a policy perspective, the important issue is that farm household income may not only depend on income from agriculture and that changes in agricultural policies need to consider potential implications not only for farm but also off-farm income. Further, farm household income may not only be affected by changes in agricultural policies but also by other policies and, in particular, labour market policies. Hence, there is not one but many "optimal" farm sizes, at least as many as the number of farm households as every household will be different and more as the "optimal" farm size within a farm household will differ if over time endogenous and exogenous factors change (and as they always will).

The farm household model mentioned provides the first step for policy analysis. Information about farm household income over time allows to test the implications of bioeconomy polices on farm households. This is relevant for policies with the objective of increasing farm household income.

There are a number of other factors that affect farm household income as a result of policies not directly targeted towards farm households. This includes, among others, the organisation of markets. Concentration of market power in the upstream and downstream sectors has been a continuous concern. Maintaining competition in the upstream and downstream sectors by monitoring and regulating mergers and acquisitions has been an important policy tool. Concerns have been raised related to technology policies that reduce competition in the market. The approval time and direct costs of new technologies have long been a concern such as the use of genetically modified organisms or biological control mechanisms in agriculture (Smart et al. 2017; Fredericks and Wesseler 2019) as they not only reduce access to new technologies but also support concentration among companies (OECD 2018).

2.5   Conclusion

In conclusion, bioeconomy policies have the objective to improve future well-being. Often, more than one policy exist for improvement. For assessing whether a policy indeed improves future well-being, a detailed description of the current state of nature is required, which addresses to what extent the policy change effects ex ante and ex post results and its reversible and irreversible benefits and costs. The benefits and costs of not only the target group but also other non-target groups need to be considered. We argue that the descriptive analysis of policies and policy changes is as such an important part of applied policy analysis.

REFERENCES

Acemoglu, D., N. Suresh, and P. Restrepo. 2019. Democracy Does Cause Growth. *Journal of Political Economy* 127 (1): 47–100.

Arrow, K.J., P. Dasgupta, L.H. Goulder, K.J. Mumford, and K. Oleson. 2012. Sustainability and the Measurement of Wealth. *Environment and Development Economics* 17 (3): 317–353.

Beckmann, V. 1997. *Transaktionskosten und institutionelle Wahl in der Landwirtschaft: zwischen Markt, Hierarchie und Kooperation.* Berlin: Sigma.

Benjamin, D. 1992. Household Composition, Labor Markets, and Labor Demand: Testing for Separation in Agricultural Household Models. *Econometrica* 60 (2): 287–322.

Buchanan, J., and G. Tullock. 1962. *The Calculus of Consent: Logical Foundations of Constitutional Democracy.* Ann Arbor: University of Michigan Press.

Coase, R. 2006. The Conduct of Economics: The Example of Fisher Body and General Motors. *Journal of Economics & Management Strategy* 15 (2): 255–278.

Demont, M., J. Wesseler, and E. Tollens. 2005. Irreversible Costs and Benefits of Transgenic Crops: What Are They? In *Environmental Costs and Benefits of Transgenic Crops*, Wageningen UR Frontis Series, ed. J. Wesseler, vol. 7, 113–122. Dordrecht: Springer.

Easterly, W. 2014. *The Tyranny of Experts: Economists, Dictators, and the Forgotten Rights of the Poor.* New York: Basic Books.

European Commission. 2018. *A Sustainable Bioeconomy for Europe: Strengthening the Connection Between Economy, Society and the Environment.* Luxembourg: Publications Office of the European Union.

Fisher, A. 2000. Introduction to Special Issue on Irreversibility. *Resource and Energy Economics* 22: 189–196.

Fredericks, C., and J. Wesseler. 2019. A comparison of the EU and US Regulatory Frameworks for the Active Substance Registration of Microbial Bio Control Agents. *Pest Management Science* 75 (1): 87–103.

Hayek, F. 1944. *The Road to Serfdom.* Chicago: The University of Chicago Press.

Kolstad, C., T.S. Ulen, and G.V. Johnson. 1990. Ex Post Liability for Harm vs. Ex Ante Safety Regulation: Substitutes or Complements. *American Economic Review* 80 (4): 888–901.

Nakajima, C. 1986. *Subjective Equilibrium Theory of the Farm Household.* Amsterdam: Elsevier.

Ndeffo Mbah, M.L., G. Forster, J. Wesseler, and C. Gilligan. 2010. Economically Optimal Timing of Crop Disease Control Under Uncertainty: An Options Approach. *Journal of the Royal Society Interface* 7 (51): 1421–1428.

OECD. 2018. *Concentration in Seed Markets: Potential Effects and Policy Responses.* Paris: OECD Publishing.

Petit, M. 2019. Another Reform of the Common Agricultural Policy: What to Expect. *EuroChoices* 18 (1): 34–38.

Phimister, E., and D. Roberts. 2006. The Effect of Off-Farm Work on the Intensity of Agricultural Production. *Environmental & Resource Economics* 34: 493–515.

Rothbard, M. 1982. Law, Property Rights, and Air Pollution. *Cato Journal* 2 (1): 55–99.

Schmitt, G. 1989a. Farms, Farm Households, and Productivity of Resource Use in Agriculture. *European Review of Agricultural Economics* 16: 257–284.

———. 1989b. Simon Kuznets' "Sectoral Shares in Labor Force": A Differential Explanation of His (I+S)/A Ratio. *American Economic Review* 79 (5): 1262–1276.

Schmitz, A., C.B. Moss, T.G. Schmitz, H.W. Furtan, and H.C. Schmitz. 2010. *Agricultural Policy, Agribusiness, and Rent-Seeking Behaviour.* 2nd ed. Toronto: University of Toronto Press.

Shavell, S. 1984. A Model of the Optimal Use of Liability and Safety Regulations. *The Rand Journal of Economics* 15 (2): 271–280.

Shleifer, A. 2010. Efficient Regulation. NBER Working Paper No. 15651.

Smart, R., M. Blum, and J. Wesseler. 2017. Trends in Genetically Engineered Crops' Approval Times in the United States and the European Union. *Journal of Agricultural Economics* 68 (1): 182–198.

Wesseler, J., and J. Zhao. 2019. Real Options and Environmental Policies – The Good, the Bad, and the Ugly. *Annual Reviews in Resource Economics* 11: 21.1–21.16.

PART II

Institutional Framework

CHAPTER 3

European Integration: A Historical Overview

Kai Purnhagen

3.1 Introduction

The cradle of the European Union (EU) we know today stands in the rubble left from the Second World War (Afilalo et al. 2014, at 283). The National Socialists' excessive nationalism, whose roots were laid already centuries ago on the battleground of the African continent (Pakenham 1991, at 21), had destroyed Europe, leaving the strong desire for a European Union of States based on formal equal treatment (Craig 2017, at 12; Afilalo et al. 2014, at 284–285). Such a Union should ensure lasting peace by overcoming the destructive nationalism in favour of an ever-closer Union (Lipkens 1985). In his speech in Zurich in September 1946, Winston Churchill called for a United States of Europe coalition modelled on the United States of America. The past had taught that international peace treaties were no effective means to keep peace in Europe on a sustainable basis (Afilalo et al. 2014, at 285). The establishment of a supranational rather than an international legal system aimed at facilitating and deepening trade between its members appeared to be a more viable concept. Put simply, the EU was founded on the principle that whoever trades

K. Purnhagen (✉)
Law and Governance Group, Wageningen University,
Wageningen, Gelderland, The Netherlands
e-mail: kai.purnhagen@wur.nl

© The Author(s) 2019
L. Dries et al. (eds.), *EU Bioeconomy Economics and Policies: Volume I*,
Palgrave Advances in Bioeconomy: Economics and Policies,
https://doi.org/10.1007/978-3-030-28634-7_3

with each other does not fight! (Afilalo et al. 2014, at 285) Since such a supranational order cannot be realized primarily by a national policy, law has a special function as an instrument (Weiler 1981; id. 1991). The core idea of EU integration is hence, as is still seen in Art. 3 (1) TEU today, the safeguarding and maintenance of peace through economic integration based on the rule of law. See Table 3.1 for a summary.

3.2   THE EARLY YEARS: THE FOUNDATION OF THE EUROPEAN COAL AND STEEL COMMUNITY

What we know today as European Union grew out of an organization known as the European Coal and Steel Community (ECSC). The ECSC summoned the coal and steel industries of Germany and France, both important industries of war, to ensure their joint supervision and allow other European states to participate (Craig 2017, at 13). This move respected the French security interests connected to a resurgent Germany (Craig 2017, at 13). It also enabled Germany to reintroduce itself as part of the international community (Craig 2017, at 13). This move was not only determined by altruistic motives, but had rather been part of a strategy to counterbalance the rising Russian dominance of Eastern Europe and the emergence of the Cold War (Craig 2017, at 13). On 18 April 1951, Germany, France, Italy and the Benelux countries signed the Treaty, establishing the ECSC in Paris. It entered into force on 23 July 1952 and lasted for a period of 50 years. As of 23 July 2002, the area of the EC Treaty was officially applicable to the coal and steel sectors. Despite the fact that the Treaty had been limited to the sectors of coal and steel only, the drafters of the Treaty saw the potential of it being a first step towards further European integration (Duchêne 1994, at 139).

3.3   TOWARDS EUROPEAN ECONOMIC UNITY: THE FOUNDATION OF THE EUROPEAN ECONOMIC COMMUNITY

The proposals for the enlargement of the Community to establish a European Political Community (EPC) and a European Defense Community (EDC) of 1954 failed at the French National Assembly (Pinder 1998). As a reaction, the Belgian Prime Minister Paul-Henri Spaak published a report in 1956, which had already contained the basic plan for an institution that

Table 3.1 Historical overview

1946	Winston Churchill calls for a "kind of United States of Europe" at Zurich University
1949	France, UK and the Benelux countries set in place a Council of Europe
1951	Treaty of Paris signed by Belgium, France, Germany, Italy, Luxembourg, the Netherlands, establishing the European Coal and Steel Community (ECSC)
1957	Treaties of Rome signed to establish the European Economic Community (EEC) and the European Atomic Energy Community (Euratom)
1958	First session of European Parliamentary Assembly in Strasbourg. Robert Schuman elected its President
1962	The Parliamentary Assembly changes its name to the European Parliament
1972	A majority of Norwegian voters against joining the EU
1973	Denmark, Ireland and the UK join the European Communities
1974	Establishment of the European Council, the European Regional Development Fund and the economic and monetary union. Introduction of direct elections to the European Parliament
1978	Establishment of the European Monetary System
1979	First direct elections to the European Parliament
1981	Greece joins the European Community
1984	Draft Treaty on the establishment of the European Union passed by the European Parliament
1985	Treaty of Rome amended and integration by drawing up a Single European Act revitalized
1986	Spain and Portugal join the Community, Single European Act signed
1992	Maastricht Treaty on the European Union is signed
1993	Single European Market enters into force
1995	Austria, Finland and Sweden join the European Union. Schengen Agreement comes into force between Belgium, France, Germany, Luxembourg, the Netherlands, Portugal and Spain
1997	Amsterdam Treaty signed
1998	Establishment of the European Central Bank
2000	Formal proclamation of the Charter of Fundamental Rights of the European Union
2001	Treaty of Nice signed
2002	Euro coins and notes enter circulation in the 12 participating Member States
2004	Cyprus, the Czech Republic, Estonia, Hungary, Latvia, Lithuania, Malta, Poland, the Slovak Republic and Slovenia join the European Union. The Heads of State and Government and EU foreign ministers sign the Treaty establishing a Constitution for Europe
2005	French and Dutch voters reject ratification of the European Constitutional Treaty
2007	Bulgaria and Romania join the EU
2009	Lisbon Treaty in Force
2013	Croatia joins the EU
2016	In a referendum 51.9% of UK voters vote for leaving the EU
2017	UK files for formal intention to withdraw from the EU

was later to become the European Atomic Energy Community (Euratom) (Craig 2017, at 14). The Treaty establishing the European Economic Community (EEC) on 25 March 1957, however, realized parts of the EDC and the EPC, this time in the framework of an economic enlargement. The main objective of the EEC was the gradual establishment of a common market (Craig 2017, at 14). It includes a common customs tariff vis-à-vis third countries and the free movement of goods, services and labour between Member States. Germany, France, Italy and the Benelux countries formed Member States of the EEC. The same day the same partners signed the Treaty on Euratom in Rome, which deals with the peaceful use of nuclear energy. Both contracts are called "The Treaties of Rome." They entered into force on 1 January 1958 and, unlike the ECSC, did not have a fixed time limit.

As an addition to the Treaties of Rome, the parties signed an Agreement on Common Institutions for the European Communities. This Treaty ensured that the ECSC, EEC and the Euratom share a parliamentary assembly, a Court of Justice and an Economic and Social Committee (Craig 2017, at 15). The merger agreement, which entered into force on 1 July 1967, also created a Commission and a Council. Despite these common institutions, the autonomy of the three communities remained. The communities increased by accessions of Denmark, Great Britain, Ireland (1973), Greece (1981), Portugal and Spain (1986) to 12 members (so-called South Extension). Greenland left the Communities in 1985 following a referendum. In this period, tensions between an intergovernmental view of the Community, as exercised in particular by the French President Charles de Gaulle's empty chair politics, primarily governed EU politics (Craig 2017, at 16–17). The Single European Act (EEA), which entered into force on 1 July 1987, marked a turnaround and put the completion of the internal market as a major goal back on the table of European integration. It "still ranks as one of the most significant Treaty revisions in the history of the EU" (Craig 2017, at 18). Art. 13 EEA (now Art. 28 para. 2 TFEU) defined the internal market as "one (s) area without internal frontiers in which the free movement of goods, persons, services and capital (…) is guaranteed." Measures to achieve the internal market no longer had to be adopted unanimously in the Council but only by a qualified majority. The legislative competence of the European Parliament (EP) has been strengthened by the introduction of the cooperation procedure.

Informal European Political Cooperation (EPC) between Member States in the field of foreign policy has been enshrined in the Treaty. The competences of the Communities have been extended in the fields of social policy, research and technological development, environmental policy and common foreign policy.

3.4   TOWARDS A POLITICAL UNION: THE TREATY ON EUROPEAN UNION

The Treaty on the European Union (TEU), the so-called Treaty of Maastricht, which entered into force on 1 November 1993, founded the EU (Corbett 1993; Curtin 1993). The EU was the umbrella organization for the three European Communities (ECs) and two other policy areas: the Common Foreign and Security Policy (CFSP) and the Police and Judicial Cooperation in Criminal Matters (PJCC). The EU had no legal personality. The EEC was renamed the European Community (EC) because, in addition to economic cooperation, the Community also regulated other policies. It also adopted the gradual introduction of Economic and Monetary Union, introduced citizenship of the Union and strengthened the EP's position through the co-decision procedure. In 1995, the EU increased to 15 members through the accession of Finland, Austria and Sweden. On 1 January 1999, the monetary union was partially realized by the introduction of the Euro. The Treaty of Amsterdam, which entered into force on 1 May 1999, involved the EP in other areas of legislation (Craig 2017, at 22–24). Furthermore, the appointment of the President of the Commission was conditional on the EP's approval. Measures such as setting the maximum seats of the EP should prepare the EU for the following enlargements. The institutional rules were amended to reflect the EU's role to become an actor at the international level (Lenaerts and Smijter 1999/2000).

The first European Convention, chaired by Roman Herzog, drafted the Charter of Fundamental Rights (CFR), which was proclaimed in Nice on 7 December 2000 (de Búrca 2001). It contains a written catalogue of EU fundamental rights enshrined at the Union level. Although the CFR was not formally legally effective initially, it was applied in practice by the European courts.

3.5   TOWARDS A GLOBAL PLAYER: THE FIRST BIG ENLARGEMENT TO THE EAST

With the first big enlargement to the East on 1 May 2004 by the accessions of Estonia, Latvia, Lithuania, Malta, Poland, Slovakia, Slovenia, the Czech Republic, Hungary and Cyprus, the EU grew from 15 to 25 Member States. The Treaty of Nice, which entered into force on 1 February 2003, reflected this enlargement by introducing institutional change to the Treaties (Barents 2001). It introduced in particular rules on the weighing of votes in the Council, the distribution of seats in the EP and the composition of the Commission. It also established the qualified majority procedure as a regular voting procedure. The second enlargement to the East took place on 1 January 2007, with the accession of Bulgaria and Romania, bringing the EU up to the current size of 27 Member States. The Member States signed a Treaty, establishing a Constitution for Europe (TCE) in 2004, which was intended to reform the existing treaty. It had two main objectives: (1) should it modernize the EU in terms of decision-making and (2) should it prepare the EU to become more of a national union, for example, by introducing a flag and an anthem. However, following negative referendums in their countries, France and the Netherlands did not ratify the TCE (Dehousse 2006). As a result, the TCE never went into force.

3.6   PICKING UP THE PIECES OF THE FAILED CONSTITUTION: THE TREATY OF LISBON

After the failure of the TCE, the Treaty of Lisbon came into force on 1 December 2009, which picked up the pieces left behind by the TCE (Craig 2017, at 26). As such, the Treaty of Lisbon adopts numerous reform proposals of the TCE, but largely dispenses nation-state elements. The EU, which is the legal successor to the EC, is granted legal personality. The EU incorporated the former purely intergovernmental PJCC. The CFSP remains intergovernmental and independent. The introduction of the "ordinary legislative procedure" (formerly co-decision procedure) as a regulatory procedure strengthened the position of the EP. The former TEC was slightly modified and renamed as the "Treaty on the Functioning of the European Union" (TFEU). A reference in Art. 6 TEU declared the CFR as legally binding. Since then, the CFR has been binding on the institutions of the Union and on the Member States in their actions within the scope of Union law, or when they are implementing EU law into national legal systems. On 1 July 2013, Croatia joined the EU as its 28th member.

3.7   First Signs of Disintegration: The Brexit Process

On 23 June 2016, in a referendum in the UK, 51.9% of voters voted for the UK to leave the EU (so-called Brexit) (Craig 2016; Peers and Harvey 2017). The referendum is binding neither under the law of the UK nor under the EU law. The UK notified in writing to the European Council on 29 March 2017 the intention to withdraw from the EU pursuant to Art. 50 para. 2 sentence 1 TEU. Subsequently, a two-year negotiation phase started, which has been extended several times, since the UK and the EU could not agree on the terms of leaving the EU.

3.8   Assessment

After a period of steady deepening and widening of the EU, the European integration project has been witnessing with Brexit its first serious illustration of its limits regarding both deepening and widening. Likewise, UK's failure to execute its divorce with the EU in a meaningful way sent a signal to other members of the EU. The European integration process has succeeded in a way that, even if one wanted, the legal and economic ties with the rest of the EU have become so strong that Member State interest can only be executed in concert with the interest of other Member States. In this sense, Brexit has also illustrated the success of the EU integration project.

Either way, Brexit has for sure left its footprint on the integration of the EU. This has likely influenced the EU integration process in two ways: it illustrated to the EU that when arguing for further integration, this cannot be facilitated against the will of its peoples. Hence, the EU needs to realize that indeed a legitimacy crisis demands a rethinking of how politics is conducted and explained. Member States and political parties need to realize that populism at the cost of the EU may fire back; hence political campaigns at the costs of the EU integration process are likely to become increasingly unpopular. The integration process will certainly continue, but more mindful of the effect it creates with the everyday life of people.

It is very likely to slow down and become defiant towards Member State and individual's interest (Purnhagen 2020).

REFERENCES

Afilalo, A., D. Patterson, and K. Purnhagen. 2014. Statecraft, the Market State and the Development of European Legal Culture. In *Towards a European Legal Culture*, ed. G. Helleringer and K. Purnhagen, 277. München/Oxford/Baden-Baden: Beck/Hart/Nomos.

Barents, R. 2001. Some Observations on the Treaty of Nice. *Maastricht Journal of European and Comparative Law* 8: 121.

Corbett, R. 1993. *The Treaty of Maastricht*. London: Longman.

Craig, P. 2016. Brexit: A Drama in Six Acts. *European Law Review* 41 (4): 447–668.

———. 2017. Development of the EU. In *European Union Law*, ed. Catherine Bernard and Steve Peers, 2nd ed. Oxford: Oxford University Press, Chapter 2.

Curtin, D. 1993. The Constitutional Structure of the Union: A Europe of Bits and Pieces. *Common Market Law Review* 30: 17–69.

de Búrca, G. 2001. The Drafting of the Charta of Fundamental Rights. *European Law Review* 26: 126.

Dehousse, R. 2006. The Unmaking of a Constitution: Lessons from the European Referenda. *Constellations* 3: 151.

Duchêne, F. 1994. *Jean Monnet: The First Statesman of Interdependence*. London: Norton.

Lenaerts, K., and E. de Smijter. 1999. The European Union as an Actor under International Law. *Yearbook of European Union Law* 19 (1): 95–138.

Lipgens, W., ed. 1985. *Documents of the History of European Integration*. Florence: European University Institute.

Pakenham, T. 1991. *The Scramble for Africa*. New York: Avon Books.

Peers, S., and D. Harvey. 2017. Brexit. The Legal Dimension. In *European Union Law*, ed. Catherine Bernard and Steve Peers, 2nd ed. Oxford: Oxford University Press, Chapter 27.

Pinder, J. 1998. *The Building of the European Union*. Oxford: Oxford University Press.

Purnhagen, K. 2020. From Supranationality to Managing Diversity—A (Re-)new(ed) Paradigm for the Establishment of the Internal Market? In *Internal Market 2.0*, ed. Inge Govaere and Sacha Garben. Oxford: Hart. Forthcoming.

Weiler, J. 1981. The Community System. The Dual Character of Supranationalism. *Yearbook of European Law* 1 (1): 257–306.

———. 1991. The Transformation of Europe. *Yale Law Journal* 100 (8): 2403–2483.

CHAPTER 4

European Agriculture and the Bioeconomy: A Historical Overview

Kai Purnhagen and Alan Matthews

4.1 INTRODUCTION

Articles 38–44 (Title III) of the Treaty on the Functioning of the European Union (TFEU) govern the European Union (EU)'s Common Agricultural Policy (CAP). Despite the fact that already in 1956, the Spaak report emphasized that it is "inconceivable that any common market should be established in Europe which did not include agriculture" (Spaak committee 1956), agricultural regulation has developed largely in topical isolation from other provisions of the internal market (Usher 2001). Within the EU internal market, such agricultural exceptionalism is based on the view that applying the rules of the free market to agricultural products would result in an inefficient allocation of resources, particularly with respect to farmers' incomes (Schmitt 1990). The continuous possibility of "imminent

K. Purnhagen (✉)
Law and Governance Group, Wageningen University,
Wageningen, Gelderland, The Netherlands
e-mail: kai.purnhagen@wur.nl

A. Matthews
Department of Economics, Trinity College Dublin, Dublin, Ireland
e-mail: Alan.Matthews@tcd.ie

© The Author(s) 2019   27
L. Dries et al. (eds.), *EU Bioeconomy Economics and Policies: Volume I*,
Palgrave Advances in Bioeconomy: Economics and Policies,
https://doi.org/10.1007/978-3-030-28634-7_4

market failure" in agricultural markets hence required constant market intervention (Schmitt 1990), which serves as the economic justification of why the agricultural market in the EU has been ruled throughout its history by a CAP. The economic design of this market is hence intertwined with the design of its underlying policy.

4.2   Policy Design of the Common Agricultural Policy in Historical Context

Historically, the Common Agricultural Policy (CAP) of the EU is rooted in the price support measures that have been established since the end of the nineteenth century in Germany and other Western countries. These measures were geared towards protection of producers in some agricultural sub-sectors, taking into account the national importance of agricultural production on the one hand and the specificities of agricultural markets on the other (Tracy 1989). When, after the Second World War, negotiations on the formation of the European Economic Community began, negotiators agreed that, despite the agreed specialty of the agricultural market, the markets for agricultural products should be part of the common market (Fietz 2012). However, the six founding members had also established complicated income support welfare state systems for the agricultural population, which were aptly called the "agricultural welfare state" (Sheingate 2001). Article 38 of the Treaty of Rome thus laid down the establishment of a common market for agricultural products and Article 39 set up a CAP, which was subsequently largely decoupled from the rules of the other common markets (Purnhagen 2019). Contrary to conventional wisdom, these provisions do not form any legal obligation to prioritise farmers' income over other objectives of the CAP (Purnhagen and Schebesta 2017). However, from the historical context, it becomes clear that the CAP has essentially been established as an income policy for the agricultural producers (Knudsen 2009). Accordingly, Article 39 (1) also establishes the increase in income for the "agricultural community" as one of the five objectives of the CAP.

The policy design pursued by the CAP in accordance with the Treaty's 1957 objective has changed radically in the subsequent years. In the course of the establishment of the CAP, in the 1960s sectoral, different systems were established to ensure a relatively high price level, ranging from market intervention to price support to volume regulation through quotas.

Under the influence of the highly controversial Mansholt Plan, investment promotion programmes for the "modernization" of agriculture were not introduced until 1972 as a "second pillar" of the CAP (Grant 1997; Knudsen 2009). The combination of production incentives through market support and increased efficiency through "modernization" has led to chronic overproduction since the late 1970s, price erosion, criticism in the context of the world trade order and repeated budget crises in the European Community (Grant 1997). At the same time, there has been massive criticism of the negative environmental impact of the CAP (SRU 1985). As a response, since 1989, voluntary agri-environmental programmes have been increasingly introduced in the framework of the CAP (Buller et al. 2000). The so-called MacSharry reform of 1992 brought about a radical reorganization of the instruments of the CAP with the introduction of an area-related single payment ("first pillar") partially decoupled from production, which was justified as compensation for significant price reductions. This reform was intended to bring income support to agriculture in line with WTO rules, which were then agreed in 1994. Direct payments were compulsory with the requirement that 15% of the land be taken out of production. With the Agenda 2000 adopted in 1999, the programme's support for investment modernization, agri-environmental measures and regional rural development (Leader) have been combined into an Integrated Rural Development Policy, the current "Second Pillar." The so-called 2003 Fischler reform brought about a substantial decoupling of direct payments from production and their mandatory link with compliance with a number of regulatory requirements (cross compliance, a somewhat popular option for Member States in Agenda 2000). The most recent CAP reform of 2013 links the payment of one-third of direct payments with conditions to provide 5% of farmland as an ecological priority area, crop rotation and permanent greenland conservation (so-called greening of the first pillar).

4.3   Rise of Bioeconomy Policies

Since the beginning of the 2010s, EU agricultural production and agricultural policy have increasingly been framed as part of the EU's bioeconomy strategy. The bioeconomy concept emerged from a vision of replacing fossil-based feedstocks for energy and materials with bio-based ones. Through the application of advanced life sciences, biomass could be converted into materials, chemicals and fuels. The bioeconomy was rooted in the development of industrial biotechnologies which promised cleaner energy sources and greener industrial processes (less pollution, less emissions and less waste).

Since then, the bioeconomy concept has evolved beyond biotechnology. It is advocated as a way of reconciling economic growth and environmental goals. It is seen as a way of addressing global challenges, such as climate change, energy security, food security and resource depletion, and is closely linked with concepts such as the circular economy and green growth. As discussed in the EU's updated bioeconomy strategy published in 2018:

> We live in a world of limited resources. Global challenges like climate change, land and ecosystem degradation, coupled with a growing population force us to seek new ways of producing and consuming that respect the ecological boundaries of our planet. At the same time, the need to achieve sustainability constitutes a strong incentive to modernise our industries and to reinforce Europe's position in a highly competitive global economy, thus ensuring the prosperity of its citizens. To tackle these challenges, we must improve and innovate the way we produce and consume food, products and materials within healthy ecosystems through a sustainable bioeconomy. (European Commission 2018a)

The EU produced its first Bioeconomy Strategy and Action Plan in 2012 (European Commission 2012). The Strategy defined the bioeconomy as "the production of renewable biological resources and the conversion of these resources and waste streams into value-added products, such as food, feed, bio-based products as well as bio-energy." The major aim of the strategy was "to pave the way to a more innovative, resource efficient and competitive society that reconciles food security with the sustainable use of renewable [biological] resources for industrial purposes, while ensuring environmental protection."

Taken together, the EU bioeconomy is a substantial part of the European economy. In 2015, the bioeconomy had a turnover of €2.3 trillion and employed 18 million people in the EU. It generated 4.2% of the EU's gross domestic product (GDP) and employed 8.2% of the labour force. Agriculture and food processing are the main sectors in the bioeconomy. The food, drink and tobacco industry accounted for half of the total turnover and agriculture for a further 17%. Other important sectors include forestry, fisheries and aquaculture, manufacture of wood products and furniture, manufacture of bio-based chemicals, manufacture of bio-based textiles, manufacture of liquid biofuels and production of bio-electricity. Employment in the "traditional" sectors such as agriculture, fishing and aquaculture, bio-based textiles and manufacture of wood products has been falling, while employment has increased in bio-based chemicals, forestry and bio-based electricity over the period 2009–2015 (Joint Research Centre 2018).

Agricultural production and agricultural policy in the EU are now embedded in the wider context of the knowledge-based bioeconomy. This gives rise to significant policy questions and choices, given the potential trade-offs between food security, the supply of biomass for industrial purposes and environmental protection.

What is the most effective use of EU funds to support the development of the bioeconomy and to reap its potential to create jobs and growth, particularly in rural and coastal areas? How can competing demands for biomass, for example, between food and energy, be reconciled and can biomass supply be increased sufficiently to meet the foreseeable demand? While a transition to production based on renewable biomass holds out the promise of a more sustainable production system, this is not guaranteed as biological resources can also be over-exploited. How should the environmental consequences of biomass production be considered when advocating the expansion of the bioeconomy?

The remainder of this chapter discusses the development of EU bioeconomy policy and what it means for agricultural policy.

4.4   POLICY EVOLUTION

The EC Bioeconomy Strategy and Action Plan was developed by the Commission's DG Research and Innovation in 2012 in the context of the Europe 2020 Strategy (European Commission 2010). The Europe 2020 strategy is the EU's agenda for growth and jobs for the decade up to 2020. It emphasizes smart, sustainable and inclusive growth to overcome the structural weaknesses in Europe's economy, improve its competitiveness and productivity and underpin a sustainable social market economy.

The Strategy's opening sentence sets out the overall challenge in stark terms. "In order to cope with an increasing global population, rapid depletion of many resources, increasing environmental pressures and climate change, Europe needs to radically change its approach to production, consumption, processing, storage, recycling and disposal of biological resources (European Commission 2012)." Promoting the bioeconomy was a key element to contribute to the sustainable, smart and green economic growth of Europe, while comprehensively addressing societal challenges: ensuring food security, managing natural resources sustainably, reducing dependence on non-renewable resources, mitigating and adapting to climate change as well as creating jobs and maintaining European competitiveness.

The Strategy and Action Plan reflected the recognition that major research and innovation investments were necessary to sustainably address the supply side and to increase productivity, reducing losses and tapping into new biomass resources, such as waste and aquatic resources. However, the Strategy went beyond research and innovation, pointing to the need for a coherent policy framework to ensure best use was made of available biomass resources and to avoid conflicts arising from competing uses, including ecosystems services and climate mitigation potential. Also, actions to enhance markets and competitiveness were deemed essential to realize the jobs and growth potential of the bioeconomy (European Commission 2017a).

The wide scope of the Strategy means that it interacts with and links to many different policy areas. It seeks to develop the knowledge base for sustainable increases in primary production. It requires changes in production and consumption patterns and the development of healthier and more sustainable diets. It aims to limit food waste and losses. It foresees ecosystem-based management of natural resources to reverse declining biodiversity. Dependence on fossil sources of energy should be reduced and the transformation to a low-carbon society facilitated. It aims to capitalize on the advances in life sciences and biotechnologies to support the creation of new value chains and bio-based products as the basis for continued growth in the EU industrial base.

The strategy's Action Plan focused on three areas of action: generating the investments needed at the EU and national levels as well as by the private sector; improved coherence of policies and encouraging greater public engagement and supporting the development of markets for bio-based products, for example, through the use of public procurement and by developing standards and the circular economy.

The Commission undertook a review of the 2012 Bioeconomy Strategy in 2017 and noted several successes in its implementation (European Commission 2017a). EU research and innovation funding dedicated to the bioeconomy was doubled in the Horizon 2020 research programme. A Bio-based Industries Joint Undertaking was set up under Horizon 2020 as a private-public partnership in research and development activities. This €3.7 billion joint initiative between the EU and the Bio-based Industries Consortium manages research, demonstration and deployment projects along entire value chains including primary production of biomass, processing industry and final use. Public money from the Horizon 2020 research programme leverages investments by private sources in processes and products that contribute to the aims of the bioeconomy. Public engagement had increased, for example, through the creation of a Bioeconomy Stakeholders Panel, and several Member States and regions have published their own bioeconomy plans. An important initiative was the creation of the Bioeconomy Knowledge Centre within the Joint Research Centre, which is the Commission's science and knowledge service. This acts as a central repository of bioeconomy-relevant data, information and analysis.

The review noted that the policy context in which the bioeconomy operates had changed significantly since 2012. Major developments within the EU included the presentation of the Circular Economy package and Action Plan in 2015 and the Energy Union package with a forward-looking climate policy also in 2015. At the global level, the EU has committed to the United Nations 2030 Agenda for Sustainable Development and its 17 Sustainable Development Goals, including the 2015 Paris Agreement on climate action. The scope of the 2012 Strategy and Action Plan and the relevance and focus of its objectives and actions needed to be revised considering these developments. The review noted that the relevance of a sustainable, circular bioeconomy was further underlined by these developments.

In October 2018, the Commission launched its updated bioeconomy strategy. While the 2012 Strategy had a strong industry and jobs focus, the sustainability dimension is much more to the fore in the 2018 update. It emphasizes the necessity of a sustainable bioeconomy to build a carbon-neutral future in line with the climate objectives of the Paris Agreement. It highlights that the sustainable bioeconomy is the renewable segment of the circular economy, by turning bio-waste and residues into valuable resources and creating the innovations and incentives to help retailers and consumers cut food waste. It notes that the bioeconomy can contribute to restoring ecosystems by achieving plastic-free seas and oceans and preventing land degradation. However, it underlines that a sustainable bioeconomy can also support the modernization and strengthening of the EU industrial base as well as job creation.

4.5   The Bioeconomy and the CAP

The Commission's updated bioeconomy strategy noted that specific interventions would be developed under the Common Agricultural Policy to support inclusive bioeconomies in rural areas. The aim is to better link national bioeconomy strategies and national strategic plans under the Common Agricultural Policy.

The Commission's Communication on the CAP after 2020 *The Future of Food and Farming* noted that new rural value chains, such as renewable energy, the emerging bioeconomy, the circular economy and ecotourism, can offer good growth and job potential for rural areas (European Commission 2017b). The Commission's legislative proposal for the CAP after 2020, published in June 2018, also took note of emerging opportunities for action in the bioeconomy, renewable energy and the circular economy (European Commission 2018b). One of the nine specific objectives that Member States should address in their national CAP strategic plans is promoting employment, growth, social inclusion and local development in rural areas, including bioeconomy and sustainable forestry.

References

Buller, H., G.A. Wilson, and A. Hol, eds. 2000. *Agri-Environmental Policy in the European Union*. Farnham: Ashgate.

European Commission. 2010. *Europe 2020: A Strategy for Smart, Sustainable and Inclusive Growth*. Brussels: European Commission, COM(2010) 2020.

———. 2012. *Innovating for Sustainable Growth: A Bioeconomy for Europe*. Brussels: European Commission, COM(2012) 60.

———. 2017a. *Staff Working Document on the Review of the 2012 European Bioeconomy Strategy*. Brussels: European Commission, SWD(2017) 374.

———. 2017b. *The Future of Food and Farming*. Brussels: European Commission, COM(2017) 713.

———. 2018a. *A Sustainable Bioeconomy for Europe: Strengthening the Connection between Economy, Society and the Environment: Updated Bioeconomy Strategy*. Brussels: European Commission.

———. 2018b. *Regulation of the European Parliament and of the Council; Establishing Rules on Support for Strategic Plans to Be Drawn up by Member States under the Common Agricultural Policy (CAP Strategic Plans) and Financed by the European Agricultural Guarantee Fund (EAGF) and by the*

European Agricultural Fund for Rural Development (EAFRD) and Repealing Regulation (EU) No 1305/2013 of the European Parliament and of the Council and Regulation (EU) No 1307/2013 of the European Parliament and of the Council. Brussels: European Commission, COM(2017) 713.

Fietz, R. 2012. Die GAP-Reform 2014 aus dem Blickwinkel der betroffenen Landwirte in Deutschland. In *Die Gemeinsame Agrarpolitik vor neuen Herausforderungen*, ed. J. Martinez. 19-ff. Baden-Baden: Nomos.

Grant, W. 1997. *The Common Agricultural Policy.* New York: St. Martins.

Joint Research Centre. 2018. *European Commission's Knowledge Centre for Bioeconomy: Brief on Jobs and Growth of the Bioeconomy 2009–2015.* Brussels.

Knudsen, A.C.L. 2009. *Farmers on Welfare: The Making of Europe's Common Agricultural Policy.* Ithaca: Cornell University Press.

Purnhagen, K.P. 2019. The End of Agricultural Exceptionalism in EU Free Movement Law and Competition Law after Lisbon? Wageningen Working Papers of Law and Governance 3/2019.

Purnhagen, K.P., and H. Schebesta. 2017. A Case Moving at the Frontiers of Market Access, Freedom of Goods, the Common Agricultural Policy and Science in Court. *European Law Review* 42 (3): 420–433.

Schmitt, G. 1990. Landwirtschaft ein Ausnahmebereich? Ein alte Frage und eine neue Antwort. *Ordo* 41: 219–220.

Sheingate, A.D. 2001. *The Rise of the Agricultural Welfare State.* Princeton/Oxford: Princeton University press.

Spaak Committee. 1956. *The Brussels Report on the General Common Market (Spaak Report).* Luxembourg: Information Service High Authority of The European Community for Coal and Steel.

SRU. 1985. *Umweltprobleme der Landwirtschaft: Sachverständigenrat für Umweltfragen.* Stuttgart/Mainz: Kohlhammer Verlag.

Tracy, M. 1989. *Government and Agriculture in Western Europe 1880–1988.* 3rd ed. London: Harvester Wheatsheaf.

Usher, J. 2001. *EC Agricultural Law.* 2nd ed. Oxford: Oxford University Press.

WEBSITES

The composition and activities of the Bioeconomy Stakeholders Panel. are described on its website available at: https://ec.europa.eu/research/bioeconomy/index.cfm?pg=policy&lib=pane

The Bioeconomy Knowledge Centre's. website is available at: https://biobs.jrc.ec.europa.eu/

Information on the Circular Economy Package and related actions. is available on the DG ENVI website at http://ec.europa.eu/environment/circular-economy/index_en.htm

Information on the Energy Union. is available at https://ec.europa.eu/energy/en/topics/energy-strategy-and-energy-union/building-energy-union

CHAPTER 5

EU Institutions and Decision-Making Processes

Kai Purnhagen

5.1 Introduction

The European Union (EU) institutions are listed in Art. 13 Treaty on European Union (TEU). Art. 14 et seq. TEU lists the essential legal framework conditions of the individual bodies. These provisions are then further substantiated in Art. 223 et seq. Treaty on Functioning of the European Union (TFEU). The decision-making procedures are summarized in Fig. 5.1.

5.2 The European Council

5.2.1 Function

The Council is the political governing body of the EU. In this function, he submits the general political objectives and priorities of the EU. These guidelines set a political framework for the action of both the Commission

K. Purnhagen (✉)
Law and Governance Group, Wageningen University,
Wageningen, Gelderland, The Netherlands
e-mail: kai.purnhagen@wur.nl

© The Author(s) 2019   37
L. Dries et al. (eds.), *EU Bioeconomy Economics and Policies: Volume I*,
Palgrave Advances in Bioeconomy: Economics and Policies,
https://doi.org/10.1007/978-3-030-28634-7_5

and of the Council. However, these guidelines are not legally binding, as the European Council has no legislative competence under Art. 15 (1) (2) TEU. The main tasks are as follows: The Council…

- … has important powers in contract amendments (Art. 48 TEU).
- … is a kind of 'emergency brake': in certain particularly sensitive policy areas, where the ordinary majority legislative procedure in the Lisbon Treaty applies, a Member State can make a referral to the European Council, and therefore on a point-by-point basis to demand a return to unanimity.
- … is instrumental in important personnel decisions: nomination of the President of the Commission (Art. 17 VII TEU); Decision on the rotation procedure by which the members of the Commission are to be appointed (Art. 17 V UAbs 2 EUV i.V. Art. 244 TFEU); Appointment of the High Representative of the Union for Foreign Affairs and Security Policy (Art. 18 I TEU); Appointment of the members of the Executive Board of the ECB (Art. 283 II TFEU).

5.2.2   Composition, Leadership and Place of Origin

Art. 15 (2) TEU stipulates that the European Council is composed of the Heads of State and Government of the Member States as well as the President of the European Council and the President of the Commission. The High Representative of the Union for Foreign Affairs and Security Policy is taking part in his work. Accordingly, besides the voting Heads of State or Government of the Member States, the non-voting Presidents of the European Council and of the Commission are part of the European Council. The High Representative of the Union for Foreign Affairs and Security Policy participate in its work (Art. 15 (2) sentence 2 TEU). Members of the Commission or national governments may also be called in (Art. 15 (3) TEU). The President of the European Council leads according to Art. 15 para. 6 lit. a) TEU the chair and is according to Art. 15 (5) TEU elected by the voting members of the European Council. The presidency changes every two and a half years. Since the first EU East enlargement, the meetings are held exclusively in Brussels.

5.2.3   *Procedure*

According to Art. 15 (3) sentence 1 TEU, the European Council meets twice a half-year when convened by its President. If required, extraordinary meetings shall be convened. Resolutions of the European Council are usually in consensus. Details of the decision-making procedure are laid down in Art. 235 TFEU and the Rules of Procedure of the European Council. The results of the meetings are summarized in a report by the President, which he according to Art. 15 para. 6 lit. d) TEU has to submit to the European Parliament (EP).

5.3   COUNCIL OF THE EUROPEAN UNION

The Council of the EU is the most important legislative body of the EU next to the EP.

5.3.1   *Function*

According to Art. 16 (1) TEU, the Council acts as legislator together with the European Parliament and exercises its budgetary powers together with it. Its tasks include policy-making and coordination under the Treaties.

- Legislation: With the EP, the Council is the EU's main legislative body. In the internal market, the Council can act only on the initiative of the Commission. In the ordinary legislative procedure, the Council has a veto position.
- Budgetary powers: The Council adopts the EU annual budget, in cooperation with the EP, on the basis of a preliminary draft by the Commission.
- Definition and coordination: The Council coordinates Member State economic policies (Art. 121 (1) TFEU) and sets out the Union's economic policy (Art. 121 (2) TFEU). For this purpose, the Council issues, according to Art. 121 para. 2 UAbs. 3 TFEU, a recommendation setting out the foundations of the economic policies of the EU and the Member States. Although these recommendations are not legally binding, the Council can still impose sanctions in accordance with Art. 121 (4) TFEU if a Member State

does not agree with the principles set out in the recommendation. The Council, acting in agreement with the President of the Commission, assigns the members of the Commission. The Council can request that a member of the Commission is removed from office by the European Court of Justice (ECJ) for serious misconduct. It also appoints the members of the Court of Auditors (Art. 286 (2), second sentence, TFEU), the Committee of the Regions (Art. 301a (2) TFEU) and the Economic and Social Committee (Art. 305 (2) TFEU). The Council is the highest authority of all EU officials and employees. It sets out the salaries, allowances and pensions of key personnel and the remuneration paid in respect of all EU staff. The Council negotiates and concludes for the EU contracts with third countries or international organizations.

5.3.2   Composition, Leadership and Place of Origin

Pursuant to Art. 16 (2) TEU, the Council is composed of one representative from each Member State at ministerial level who is authorized to bind the government of the Member State he represents and to vote. The power of representation arises from national law.

Example: In Germany, the following persons are authorized to represent: –each Federal Minister, each Minister of State, insofar as the focus is exclusively on the legislative powers of the Länder in the areas of education, culture or broadcasting. In such a case, the Federal Government has its representation powers gem. Art. 23 para. 6 GG i.V.m. § 6 (2) of the Law on Cooperation between the Federation and the Länder in matters of the European Union to the Ministers of the States, – any Secretary of State who is a civil servant or a Parliamentary Secretary, although they are not, as required by law, in the rank of Minister. However, this legally not unproblematic practice is tolerated.

The Presidency of the Council rotates between Member States. Each Member State holds the Presidency for six months, aiming for balance between large and small countries. An exception to this rule applies to the Foreign Affairs Council, in which Art. 18 (3) TEU is always chaired by the High Representative of the Union for Foreign Affairs and Security Policy. The Council is located in Brussels. However, he holds his meetings in the months of April, June and October in Luxembourg.

5.3.3 *Procedure*

The Council meets in various compositions, deviating according to the respective area under discussion. The representatives of the specialized ministries familiar with the subject forms the Council. Thus, for example, matters of monetary policy are discussed in the Council of Ministers of Finance Ministers (ECOFIN); for other topics, there are other specialized councils. If no specific subject area is the subject of the Council negotiations and thus the topic cannot be assigned to a special Council of Ministers, the Council of General Affairs will deal with the subject. The decisions are taken by vote in the Council. Whether a vote succeeds depends on whether a majority is achieved. The EU law has different requirements for when a 'majority' is reached, which can be determined according to the following examination scheme:

Step 1: Unanimity or Qualified Majority?
Pursuant to Art. 16 (3) TEU, the Council takes its decisions by qualified majority, as long as the Treaties do not specify otherwise. This means that in some particularly sensitive areas, such as the Common Foreign and Security Policy, as well as tax, asylum and immigration policies, the decisions of the Council need to be taken unanimously. Each Member State can veto these areas. However, if a qualified majority is required, then step 2 determines what kind of qualified majority is needed.

Step 2: Single, Double or Further Qualified Majority?
As a rule, decisions will only be taken by a qualified majority. The definition of a qualified majority arises from Art. 16 (4) TEU and Art. 238 (2) and (3) TFEU. In this procedure, a qualified majority must fulfil two criteria: At least 55% of the Member States each have to represent 65% of the population. At least four Member States can achieve a blocking minority. If, on an exceptional basis, the Council does not act on a proposal from the Commission or the High Representative of the Union for Foreign Affairs and Security Policy, Art. 16 (4) UBAs. 3 i.V.m. Art. 238 (2) TFEU requires a quota of 72% for a majority of the Member States. If not all Member States have the right to vote, the determination of the qualified majority only applies to the Member States having voting rights and the populations they represent. Examples include decisions in the area of enhanced cooperation (Art. 330 (3) TFEU) or the Eurogroup (Art. 136 (2) TFEU).

5.4   THE EUROPEAN PARLIAMENT

The EP is the legislative authority in the EU, together with the Council of the EU. In addition, the EP also has a controlling or advisory function. The Treaty of Lisbon has significantly strengthened the role of the EP.

5.4.1   Function

According to Art. 14 (1) TEU, the European Parliament, together with the Council, acts as legislator and exercises the budgetary powers together with the EP. The EP exercises political control and advisory functions according to the Treaties. It elects the President of the Commission.

- Legislation: In recent years, with each new revision of the Treaties, the EP has secured more influence in the legislative process. Meanwhile, the EP is in terms of legislation on an equal footing with the Council. This development is the result of efforts to reduce the alleged democratic deficit of the EU.
- Budgetary powers: The EP determines the EU annual budget in cooperation with the Council and on the basis of a preliminary draft by the Commission.
- Control and advisory role: The EP's oversight and advisory role is primarily for the Commission. In this context, it not only elects the President of the Commission (Art. 14 (1) (3) TEU), but the entire Commission can only begin its work after its endorsement by the EP (Art. 17 (7) (3) TEU). This measure has proven to be a particularly powerful tool of the EP to enforce concessions from the Commission and the Member States. During the work of the Commission, the EP exercises its supervisory and advisory role primarily through the right of inquiry granted to it under Art. 230 TFEU and when discussing the Commission's overall report under Art. 233 TFEU. In addition, as a last resort, it may force the resignation of the Commission by a vote of no confidence under Art. 17 (8) TEU. The EP can also initiate a committee of inquiry which examines infringements of EU law or other maladministration in the application of that law.

5.4.2 *Composition, Leadership and Place of Origin*

According to Art. 14 TEU, the European Parliament is made up of representatives of EU citizens. The members of the EP are elected by universal, direct, free and secret ballot for a term of five years. Their number may not exceed 750, plus the President. Citizens represented taking the principle of digressive proportionality into account, whereas each Member State needs to be represented by a minimum of six members. No Member State receives more than 96 seats. The extreme cases here are Germany with 96 seats (or one seat per 559,000 inhabitants) and Malta with six seats (or one seat per 67,000 inhabitants). The President and the Bureau are appointed for the term of office of Parliament (2.5 years) by the members of Parliament. The EP is located in Strasbourg. However, additional plenary sessions are held in Brussels, where the EP committees also meet. The General Secretariat is located in Luxembourg.

5.4.3 *Procedure*

The EP decides by a majority of the votes cast.

5.5   THE EUROPEAN COMMISSION

The European Commission, together with the Council of the EU and the European Council, is the 'government' of the EU. It is responsible as an essential executive body for the execution of the Treaties. As guardian of the Treaties, the Commission also oversees compliance with European law in the Member States. Finally, with its right of initiative for legislative acts, it holds a key position in the EU legislative process.

5.5.1 *Function*

According to Art. 17 (1) TEU, the Commission promotes the general interests of the Union and takes appropriate initiatives to that end. It ensures the application of the Treaties and the measures adopted by the institutions by virtue of the Treaties. It monitors the application of Union law under the control of the Court of Justice of the European Union. The Commission executes the budget and manages the programmes. It carries out coordination, executive and administrative functions in accordance with the Treaties. Except in the common foreign and security policy and in the other cases provided for in the Treaties, it represents the Union's externally. It launches the annual and multiannual programmes of the Union with the aim of achieving interinstitutional agreements.

The Commission's main tasks are therefore as follows:

- Legislation: The Commission has the legislative initiative. Under Art. 17 (2) TEU, a legislative act of the Union may in principle only be adopted on a proposal from the Commission.
- Executive Body: The Commission implements the laws of the Union. Her in-house administrations and largely independent external agencies are available for this purpose. The Commission carries out the budget.
- Monitoring function: The Commission, as 'guardian of the Treaties,' has a supervisory role in the 'application of EU law' (Art. 17 (1) (3) TEU). In order to exercise its supervisory role vis-à-vis the Member States, the Commission has the power to file for an infringement procedure. It may also act in relation to persons by imposing sanctions, for example, in competition law.

5.5.2   Composition, Leadership and Place of Origin

Pursuant to Art. 17 (4) TEU, the Commission is made up of a national of each Member State, its President and the High Representative of the Union for Foreign Affairs and Security Policy. A possibility of reducing the number of members of the Commission for reasons of rationality provided for in Art. 17 (5) TEU has so far not been used. Overall, the Commission consists of the President, the Vice-Presidents, one of whom is the EU's High Representative for Foreign Affairs and Security Policy, and the other members of the Commission, each of whom has a specific department. The term of office of the commission runs in parallel to the term of office of the EP (five years).

1. The President

The President is nominated by the European Council and subsequently elected by the EP. He is represented by the Vice-President appointed by him from the Members of the Commission. the High Representative serves as another Vice-President. The President has the competence to set the guidelines of the Commission. The President also decides on the internal organization of the Commission.

2. The High Representative for Foreign Affairs and Security Policy

The High Representative of the Union for Foreign Affairs and Security Policy is appointed by the European Council. He is the 'foreign minister' of the EU. As such, he leads the foreign and security policy of the EU and presides over the Foreign Affairs Council. The latter ensures a personal merger of the institutions of the Commission and of the Council, which represents a breakthrough of the principle of institutional balance. He is at the same time one of the Vice-Presidents of the Commission.

3. Other Members of the Commission

The Council, in agreement with the President, determines all other members of the Commission. Members of the Commission are independent above all of the influence of their home state.

4. Confirmation by Parliament and termination

The EP must conform to the Commission in its entirety. This right has proved to be a powerful instrument of the EP, with which it can compel both the Commission and the Member States to make concessions. The membership in the commission ends after expiry of the five-year term of office or by death, voluntary, by force, that is, by resignation or impeachment by the ECJ. The Commission is located in Brussels.

5.5.3   Procedure

The Commission decides by a simple majority. At the top of the administrative structure, the Commission is the final decision-maker in most administrative matters. Each member of the Commission will be assisted by a Cabinet to assist the Member in his essential leadership functions. The Cabinet is similar to the personal office of a minister. In terms of content, each Member has a field of expertise comparable to that of the German ministers. Each department has a Directorate-General presided over by a member of the Commission. The actual programmatic work takes place in these Directorates-General.

5.6   Legislation in the European Union

Based on the Treaties, EU institutions can enact more specialized laws governing specific market areas, so-called secondary legislation. Whether EU institutions can initiate such secondary legislation depends on whether the Treaties assign the EU with a competence. This competence norm also determines the legislative procedure to apply. Finally, when secondary legislation has been adopted, implementing or delegating acts may provide further rules on their operation.

5.6.1   *The Principle of Conferral*

The EU acts according to Art. 5 (1), 2 TEU according to the principle of conferral. This means that it can only act within the scope of the powers assigned to it by its Member States. This is an expression of the EU's lack of *Kompetenz-Kompetenz*, that is, its inability to create its own competences. Accordingly, each act of the EU is based on a previously conferred competence norm, which must be selected and specified by the legislator on the basis of objective and judicial criteria with regard to the aim and content of the act (European Court 1993). If he fails to comply with this requirement, the act is void (European Court 1994).

5.6.2   *The Legislative Procedures*

When a competence has been assigned Union institutions can act according to the legislative procedure foreseen in the respective competence norm. The legislative procedures are listed in an overview in Art. 289 TFEU and can be divided into the ordinary and the special legislative procedure, as well as other legislative procedures. The procedures are significantly different due to the different participation rights of the EP. Which procedure is to be used depends on the respective competence standard.

5.6.2.1   *The Ordinary Legislative Procedure*

The ordinary legislative procedure as foreseen in Art. 289 (1) in conjunction with Art. 294 TFEU is the regulatory procedure, which has the greatest weight in terms of quantity and quality. The EP has full voting rights and can also prevent a legal act from coming into force. The individual steps of the ordinary legislative procedure are expressly and clearly formulated in Art. 294 TFEU.

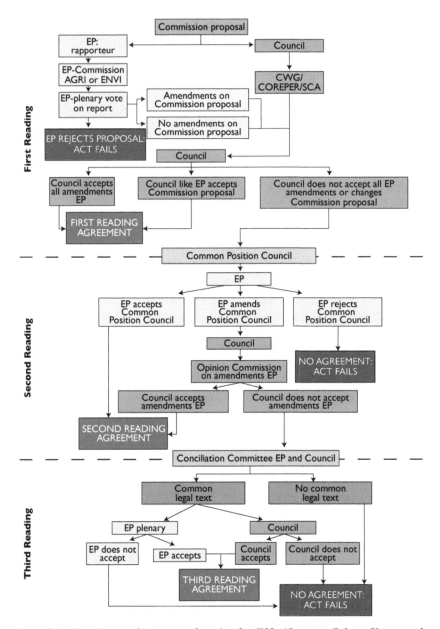

Fig. 5.1 Decision-making procedure in the EU. (Source: Gebert Kunst and Thomas van Rijn. 2011. EU Institutions and decision-making process, In: *EU Policy for agriculture, food and rural areas,* ed. A. Oskam, G. Meester and H. Silvis, 68 Wageningen Academic Publishers, 2nd ed.)

5.6.2.2 The Special Legislative Procedure

The special legislative procedure as stipulated in Art. 289 (2) TFEU is not governed by a single standard comparable to Art. 294 TFEU. The EP can only be heard in this framework and refuse to give its consent, but not prevent the act. Ultimately, only the Council has the power to make decisions, which can adopt the Commission's proposal with the appropriate majority, depending on the standard of competence.

5.6.2.3 Other Legislative Procedures

Under other legislative procedures, institutions can usually legislate without the involvement of the EP. This procedure is the most used in the field outside of the internal market.

5.6.3   Implementing, Delegated Acts and Special Acts

Implementing acts, delegating acts and special acts can further specify the rules within secondary legislation (Fig. 5.2).

According to Art. 290 TFEU, Parliament and Council can empower the Commission to regulate in certain areas, provided the prerequisites spelled out in Art. 290 TFEU are met (so-called delegated acts). Furthermore, the Commission can be empowered to regulate the requirements for the implementation of a certain act (so-called implementing act). The rules and principles governing the exercise of the Commission's implementation of such an act are laid down in the 'Comitology Decision' (European Parliament and Council 2011). According to the comitology decision, the control procedure works as such.

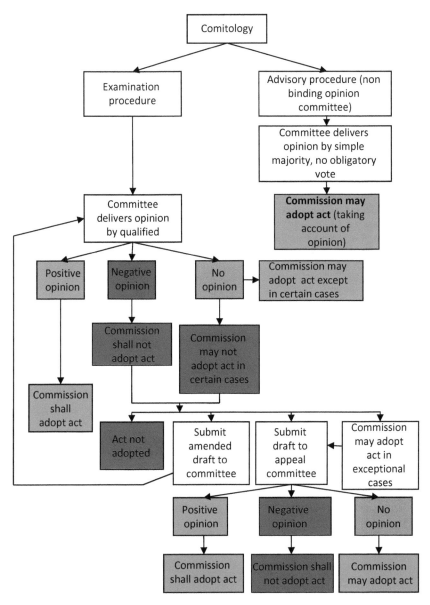

Fig. 5.2 Comitology procedure in the EU. (Source: Gebert Kunst and Thomas van Rijn. 2011. EU Institutions and decision-making process, In: *EU Policy for agriculture, food and rural areas,* ed. A. Oskam, G. Meester and H. Silvis, 72 Wageningen Academic Publishers, 2nd ed.)

References

European Court. 1993. Judgment of the Court of 17 March 1993; Commission of the European Communities v Council of the European Communities. European Court Reports 1993 I-00939. Case C-155/91.

———. 1994. Judgment of the Court of 28 June 1994; European Parliament v Council of the European Union. European Court Reports 1994 I-02857. Case C-187/93.

European Parliament and Council. 2011. Regulation (EU) No 182/2011 of the European Parliament and the Council of 16 February 2011; Laying Down the Rules and General Principles Concerning Mechanisms for Control by Member States of the Commission's Exercise of Implementing Powers. *Official Journal of the European Union* 55: 13–18.

Kunst, Gebert, and Thomas van Rijn. 2011. EU Institutions and Decision-Making process. In *EU Policy for Agriculture, Food and Rural Areas*, ed. A. Oskam, G. Meester and H. Silvis, 2nd ed., 68, 72 Wageningen Academic Publishers.

CHAPTER 6

EU Budgetary Politics and Its Implications for the Bioeconomy

Jeroen Candel

6.1 Introduction

The Multiannual Financial Framework (MFF) decision-making process belongs to the most discordant and tedious of EU policymaking. Negotiations about the European budget trudge along consecutive summits and are one of *the* occasions of 'high politics', in which the member states' heads of government are in the driver's seat (Peterson 1995). Although being a separate policy process, decisions about the MFF have major implications for the various more substantive fields of EU policymaking. This particularly applies to the reforms of the Common Agricultural Policy (CAP), which has traditionally been allocated a large, albeit decreasing, part of the EU budget. Not only do the outcomes of the MFF negotiations directly shape the budget available for policy interventions, the budgetary process also has more *indirect* effects by affecting power constellations and the overall willingness to reform. The former particularly shows in the distinction between net contributors and

J. Candel (✉)
Public Administration and Policy Group, Wageningen University,
Wageningen, Gelderland, The Netherlands
e-mail: jeroen.candel@wur.nl

© The Author(s) 2019   51
L. Dries et al. (eds.), *EU Bioeconomy Economics and Policies: Volume I*,
Palgrave Advances in Bioeconomy: Economics and Policies,
https://doi.org/10.1007/978-3-030-28634-7_6

receivers, as well as the increased role of the European Council in setting out sectoral policy contours.

In the MFF negotiations for the period 2021–2027, Brexit and the emergence of new political priorities, such as climate change, migration, and stimulating economic growth, have put considerable pressure on the budgets of traditional distributive policies, most notably the CAP and the Cohesion Fund. At the same time, the political coalition backing the status quo in agricultural and rural development spending remains unchangeably strong, and favours an increase of the overall EU budget rather than a radical redistribution.

This chapter will explain some of the main processes and controversies in EU budgetary policymaking. While putting the emphasis on the development of the Multiannual Financial Framework and its implications for the domains covered in this book, the EU's *annual* budgetary process will be briefly described as well. In the same vein, whereas most attention is given to the big spending policies, most notably the CAP, other efforts relevant to the bioeconomy will also be touched upon.

6.2   The European Financial Frameworks

6.2.1   MFF Overall Ceiling and Resources

The EU's Multiannual Financial Framework is bound by an overall ceiling of EU expenditures. This 'own resources ceiling' is calculated as a percentage of the EU's estimated Gross National Income (GNI; 1.20% in 2018), based on the latest economic forecasts. This overall ceiling is one of the main sources of political disagreement within and between the institutions in the MFF negotiations. In the most recent reform round, setting out the MFF for the period 2021–2027, the Commission has proposed to increase the own resources ceiling to 1.29%. The main reasons for this proposed rise are the departure of the UK, which has been a net contributor to the budget, and the desire to strengthen financial abilities to deal with new concerns. The member states have been divided about this proposal. Whereas France's President Macron has favoured an 'expansionary' budget, many smaller Northern member states have organized themselves in a 'Hanseatic League' under Dutch leadership that has voiced strong objections against a budget increase (Khan 2018).

The Treaty of Lisbon prescribes that the EU's annual expenses should be in balance with the revenue that comes in through the own resources

(Article 310 of the TFEU). Currently, three types of own resources exist (Council decision 2013/335):

- Traditional own resources (14.7% of revenue in 2017), the largest part of which consist of customs duties raised on imports from outside of the EU.
- Own resources based on value added tax (VAT; 12.1% in 2017): a uniform rate of 0.3% is levied on the harmonized VAT base of each member state. As calculating these levies has proven rather cumbersome, the Commission has proposed a simplified system, the share of which in the overall own resources would increase.
- Own resources based on GNI (56.3% in 2017): member state transfers based on a standard percentage of their GNIs.

For the budget period 2021–2027, the Commission has proposed to diversify these sources of revenue by introducing: (i) national contributions on the basis of the amount of non-recycled plastic packaging waste in each member state, (ii) a 20% share of the auctioning revenue of the European Emissions Trading System, and (iii) a 3% call rate applied to the new Common Consolidated Corporate Tax Base (European Commission 2018b). Past attempts to diversify and increase sources of own revenue, however, stranded as a result of unwillingness among member states' governments, which have favoured keeping a finger on the pulse.

6.2.2 Expenses

The expenses of the Union are divided into six 'categories of expense' (or 'headings'), each with a specific 'commitment appropriation', that is, a maximum annual amount of expenditure. These categories transcend individual policies or domains and reflect broader political objectives. The allocation of the budget across these categories thus provides a good indication of shifts in political priorities. Table 6.1 provides an overview of the allocations under the 2014–2020 MFF as well as the proposals for the 2021–2027 MFF (European Commission 2018c).

Every year, by 1 September, the Commission proposes an *annual* draft budget, which is bound by the agreements made under the MFF. The budget is structured in titles, chapters, articles, and items. Titles entail the various policy domains, which are all under the responsibility of one of the Commission's directorate-generals. Chapters cover the administrative

Table 6.1   Expense categories under the 2014–2020 and 2021–2027 Multiannual Financial Frameworks

Expense categories	2014	2020	Total 2014–2020	Proposed for 2021–2027 (different categories)
Smart and inclusive growth	60,283	69,004	450,763	Single market, innovation and digital:
Competitiveness for growth and jobs	15,605	21,079	125,614	166,303
Economic, social, and territorial cohesion	44,678	47,925	325,149	Cohesion and values: 391,974
Sustainable growth:	55,883	50,558	373,179	Natural resources and environment: 336,623
natural resources of which market-related expenditure and direct payments	41,585	37,605	277,851	of which market-related expenditure and direct payments: 254,247
Security and citizenship	2053	2469	15,686	Migration and border
Global Europe	7854	8794	58,704	management: 30,829
Administration	8218	9417	61,629	Security and defence:
Compensations	27	0	27	24,323
				Neighbourhood and the world: 108,929
				European public administration: 75,602
Total appropriations for commitments	134,318	140,242	959,988	1,134,583

Source: European Commission (2013)

expenditure within these domains and include the spending programmes, such as the Cohesion Fund. Articles and items correspond to general and specific objectives pursued.

Financial allocations for policies relevant to the bioeconomy fall under various headings and associated spending programmes. The most relevant programmes and associated budgets under the 2014–2020 MFF include (all under current prices):

- The Common Agricultural Policy Pillar I, part of the 'Sustainable Growth: Natural Resources' heading: €312,735 million.
- Rural Development (CAP Pillar II), part of the 'Sustainable Growth: Natural Resources' heading: €95,577 million.
- The European Maritime and Fisheries Fund, part of the 'Sustainable Growth: Natural Resources' heading, which supports the implementation of the Common Fisheries Policy: €7405 million.

- The Horizon2020 Framework Programme for Research and Innovation, part of the 'Competitiveness for growth and jobs' heading: €79,401 million, of which € 3851 million is allocated to the 'societal challenge' of 'food security, sustainable agriculture and forestry, marine, maritime and inland water research, and the bioeconomy'.
- Expenditure relating to the food chain, animal health, and animal welfare and relating to plant health and plant reproductive material, part of the 'Security and citizenship' header: €1892 million.
- The Health Programme, part of the 'Security and citizenship' header, part of which is used for prevention measures related to unhealthy dietary habits and obesity: €449 million.

This overview shows that CAP expenditure is by far the largest part of all expenditure related to the bioeconomy. Meanwhile, expenditure under the other programmes is relatively modest when compared to member state budgets. The relative asymmetry between the 'rapid and sustained expansion of regulation' (Thatcher 2001) and budgetary resources is why the EU is commonly referred to as a 'regulatory state' (Majone 1996; Eberlein and Grande 2005).

6.2.3   Decision-Making Process

The Multiannual Financial Framework is adopted in the form of a regulation,[1] following a special legislative procedure in which the Council decides by unanimity following on the Parliament's consent, for which an absolute majority in the EP is required. Although the European Council does not have a formal role in the procedure, it is *the* institution in which most of the bigger controversies are fought out and a final deal is brokered by the heads of government (Laffan and Linder 2015). More humdrum negotiations are held within different configurations of the Council of the EU. The general coordination across budgetary chapters lies within the hands of the General Affairs Council, which is mainly made up of European (sometimes Foreign) Affairs ministers. The Agricultural Council negotiates the agricultural budget and has traditionally proven to 'be locked into a clientelist relationship with farmers and generally favour[ing] higher agri-

[1] The own resources system is embedded in a separate Council decision. However, both proposals are negotiated as a single package for the post-2020 MFF.

cultural spending' (ibid., p. 226). That said, in the last MFF reform round, many of the actual agricultural spending decisions were taken by the European Council, which gave strong signals to the Agricultural Council about the position to be taken in trialogue negotiations with the Parliament (Matthews 2013; see 4.3). Lastly, the Economic and Financial Affairs Council generally tries to exert budgetary discipline (Laffan and Linder 2015), while also being responsible for negotiating budgetary instruments under the Economic and Monetary Union, such as the European Investment Stabilisation Function.

Although the MFF and CAP are decided upon in separate procedures, in practice, they have become strongly linked. The CAP post-2013 reform round showed that the institutions, particularly the EP, were unwilling to start the CAP trialogues until the MFF heading numbers had been agreed upon, which proved to work strongly in favour of those in favour of the status quo (Matthews 2014).

The *annual* budget is decided on through an annual budgetary cycle. The European Commission sends a draft budget to the Council and EP by 1 September. Subsequently, the Council adopts its position, including amendments, by 1 October, after which the Parliament has 42 days to come with its own position and amendments. If both institutions have divergent positions, a Conciliation Committee is formed, which needs to reach an agreement on a joint text within 21 days, which is then submitted to the Council and Parliament for approval again. The EP traditionally sees its budgetary rights as one of its key methods of asserting influence, as a result of which it often takes an assertive role vis-à-vis the Council in negotiations about financial allocations to specific programmes.

6.3   AGRICULTURAL SPENDING OVER TIME

As shown above, agriculture has traditionally been one of the few EU spending policy domains. That said, whereas agricultural expenditures (in current prices) increased from approximately €10 billion in 1980 to almost €60 billion in 2018, its share of the EU budget has dropped from between 60% and 70% in the late 1980s to about 35% in 2020, and will most likely further decrease after 2020. As will be shown below, this relative decrease is not just explained by an increase of the overall EU budget, but just as much by a process of capping the CAP budget that started in the 1980s. Meanwhile, agricultural spending has to be distributed across 28 member states in 2018, versus only 12 member states in the early

1990s. Another important change is the introduction of the second pillar, which led to a partial modulation of spending on income support to funding new priorities.

In the first decades of its existence, the CAP's budget increased steadily as a result of the coupled support system, which incentivized ever-continuing production increases. Between 1982 and 1986, the budget rose on average by as much as 15% a year, which led to great pressure on European politicians to curb agricultural expenditure. In addition, the European community developed from a net agricultural importer to a net exporter, as a result of which the agricultural budget could no longer be financed from import duties (Bos 2011).

A first measure to control the growth of the budget was the introduction of the milk quota in 1984. Four years later, the Commission pushed a system of 'budget stabilizers' through, which entailed a cut in prices in case farmers would exceed a maximum guarantee quantity, which was set for various major commodities. Nevertheless, these new measures insufficiently succeeded in bringing down the policy's costs, as production continued to grow and ministers 'could not face up to the cuts that were involved' (Sheehy 1999).

The stabilization of the agricultural budget really took off from the MacSharry reforms in 1992, which started the process of gradually decoupling support from production. This had two budgetary implications (Bos 2011). First, the new system of direct income support was more predictable compared to the coupled system that was linked to market developments, making it easier to stay within the budget. Second, it shifted the burden from consumers, who had to pay artificially high prices before, to the taxpayers, who fund the EU budget.

The strong link between the MFF and CAP became particularly apparent from 1999, when the European Council bypassed a deal by the ministers of agriculture of two weeks earlier and lowered the annual ceiling for agriculture expenditure (for an extensive discussion of this reform, see: Ackrill 2000). Next, the European Council decided in 2002 to limit the nominal increase of Pillar I expenditure to a maximum of 1% per year until 2014. The pressure on the budget available for market measures and income support was further intensified by the introduction of the second pillar in the Agenda-2000 reform, accompanied by voluntary and later (2003) compulsory modulation, and the accession of ten new member states, which led to a process of gradually redistributing resources from older to newer member states.

The most recent reform round of 2010–2013 saw this trend reinforced even further. Following on member state governments' financial problems resulting from the global economic crisis that started in 2008, the European Council decided to further curb the agricultural budget; not through a dramatic cut, but by refusing an inflation correction for the 2014–2020 period (Swinnen 2015a).

Based on the Commission's proposals, this development is expected to continue in the agricultural budget for the period after 2020. That said, the member states remain divided. While some member states have been favouring CAP budget cuts for a long time, others take an opposing view. Greek Prime Minister Tsipras even went as far as arguing that the proposed cuts are a 'gift to far-right populists and Eurosceptics' (ANA 2018). The Parliament has also strongly resisted a further decline of the budget, adopting a resolution on 14 November 2018, stating that the financing of the Common Agricultural Policy for the EU-27 should be maintained at the level of the 2014–2020 budget in real terms.

6.4   Hot Potatoes in Agricultural Budgetary Policymaking

Beside the size of the overall budget, there have been various other sources of controversy in recent EU agricultural budgetary policymaking. This section will concisely elaborate some of these hot potatoes.

6.4.1   External Convergence and Net Balances

The debate about 'external convergence'[2] revolves around the question of how to make the distribution of resources between member states 'fairer', which the Commission (2015) interprets as levelling out direct payments per hectare between older and newer member states. Concretely, this is done by gradually increasing the national envelopes of member states of which the average payment (in euro per hectare) is below 90% of the EU's average, whereas the envelopes of member states receiving more than the average are levelled down. This will close about one-third of the gap between current levels of payments and the '90% of the EU average' level

---

[2] As contrary to 'internal convergence', which is about levelling out hectare payments *within* member states.

by 2020. Although the Commission has strongly pushed for this principle of equal pay per hectare, it has met considerable resistance from governments and farmer groups in the older member states. These latter actors argue that an equal hectare premium ignores differing production costs, such as land prices and labour costs, across member states and thus have a fundamentally different perspective on what can be considered a 'fair' distribution of resources. A relatively strong coalition of member states under Italian leadership has emerged in the Agricultural Council, aiming to block a further harmonization (ToekomstGLB.nl 2018).

Although a bit of a political taboo, the discussion on external convergence also relates to member states' position as either a net contributor or receiver, as it touches upon the more fundamental question of the desired level of redistribution of resources from richer to poorer member states. In this respect, there are large differences in terms of whether member states 'gain' or 'lose' from the agricultural budget. On his influential blog, Alan Matthews (2015) calculated these differences by first looking at CAP inflows less each member state's contribution to the CAP budget.[3] This showed that 12 member states were net contributors in 2014, of which Germany on its own covered 43% of the net contributions. After Germany, the biggest net contributors were The Netherlands, the UK, Italy, and Belgium, while Poland, Greece, Spain, and Romania benefited the most. Subsequently, he corrected this calculation for countries' size, by relating the net transfers to the size of each country's GNI. This shows a slightly different picture (Fig. 6.1), in which The Netherlands, Belgium, Luxembourg, and Croatia[4] were the biggest contributors, while Bulgaria, Hungary, Latvia, and Greece received most. Beside influencing the public debates *within* these countries (cf. Carrubba 1997), these positions also affect the political constellations of power in EU decision-making, as net contributor countries 'may think that they have bought themselves more 'weight' behind their opinions and the right to disagree with the majority of countries' (Mattila 2004).

---

[3] Including both the European Agricultural Guarantee Fund (EAGF) and the European Agricultural Fund for Rural Development (EAFRD).

[4] Matthews notes that for Croatia this may be 'due to slow disbursement of committed rural development funds'.

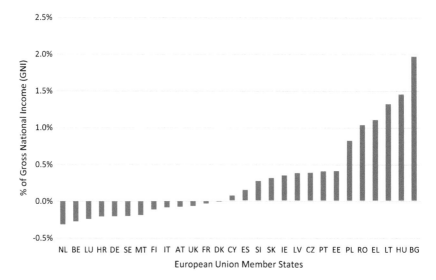

Fig. 6.1 Net gainers and losers from CAP expenditure, 2014 (% GNI). (Source: Matthews 2015)

6.4.2   Co-financing

A second debate revolves around the issue of co-financing. Co-financing has been used for decades in structural policy and the rural development pillar of the CAP. In these areas, the EU contributes to national programmes on the basis of a 'co-financing rate', a percentage of the total programme cost that is bound to a maximum threshold. These co-financing rates are specified for each operational programme. For rural development programmes, the maximum co-financing rates lay between 53% and 85% for the period 2014–2020, whereby the higher rates apply to the 84 'convergence regions' in which per capita GDP lies below 75% of the EU average.

The assumption behind co-financing schemes is that it makes member states 'more cost-conscious, leading to prudent implementation of the funds and hence greater efficiency' (Bos 2011). It is questionable whether this expectation is always met; in a recent report on cohesion policy, the European Court of Auditors (2018a) concluded that member state governments often apply for money in a rush at the end of a programme period, 'making use of the money becom[ing] an end in itself, rather than a means of achieving policy objectives' (European Court of Auditors 2018b).

In spite of these considerations, which may apply to the distribution of EU resources, in general, calls for expanding co-financing to the first pillar have come to find increased resonance. Analysts and commentators have argued that with the shift from price to direct income support, the rationale for organizing these payments at EU level has disappeared, as income and social policy are member state competences (Grethe 2008; Bos 2011). The use of co-financing may then be used to facilitate a transition towards a re-nationalization of payments, or as a second-best alternative (SER 2006). Alan Matthews (2018) has recently listed four more potential benefits of co-financing Pillar I payments:

- National co-financing of Pillar I payments requires member state governments to take greater ownership of agricultural policy, thus improving efficiency.
- National co-financing of Pillar I payments puts Pillar I and Pillar II spending on an equal footing, which would make it more attractive for member states to transfer funds from Pillar I to Pillar II.
- National co-financing of Pillar I payments allows the EU to use its budget to drive member state expenditure in the direction of priorities with higher European value added.
- National co-financing of Pillar I payments would free up EU budget resources, which could be used to deal with the budgetary effects of Brexit and/or for new priorities.

In spite of these expected merits, there has been strong resistance against such a policy change. After the European Commission (2017) mentioned co-financing the first pillar as a future possibility in a reflection paper, various ministers of agriculture immediately rejected the idea. The Irish Minister of Agriculture Michael Creed, for example, argued the introduction of co-financing in the first pillar 'would be a retrograde step which could undermine the Single Market and lead to nationalisation of agricultural policy' (Cadogan 2018). Similar voices of concern have been raised by various groups in the EP, farmer interest groups, and the Committee of the Regions, which added that co-financing the first pillar would place 'a burden on the budgets of regions and disadvantag[e] the poorest EU member states' (European Committee of the Regions 2017). Consequently, although the idea has in the past been met with sympathy in *some* countries, most notably the UK and the Netherlands, the coalition against it seems too strong for any policy change to occur in the near future.

6.4.3   *The Role of the European Council*

A third controversy involves the increased role of the European Council (and General Affairs Council) in agricultural policymaking, which became particularly visible in the post-2013 CAP reform. Although the heads of government do not play a formal role in the CAP reform processes, the simultaneous MFF decision process allowed them to assertively appropriate authority over several key CAP elements by including them in the MFF 'negotiation box' (Swinnen 2015b). These elements included the overall size of the CAP budget, internal and external convergence, greening, and rural development allocations per member state. The Parliament has strongly resisted this procedure, claiming the European Council has curbed the EP's co-decision rights: as different from the ordinary legislative procedure that applies to the CAP regulations, the Parliament only has the right of consent over the MFF regulation, thus not being able to propose amendments (Matthews 2014).

In addition, the insistence of the EP to wait with the CAP negotiations until the overall budget would be known considerably impacted the leverage of the various coalitions involved. Matthews (ibid.) argues that this choice has worked to 'strongly favour those holding to a status quo-oriented position on the reform proposals (for example, farm groups) while disadvantaging those who sought a more radical change in the orientation of the CAP (for example, environmental groups seeking a greater focus on environmental public goods)', as the latter could no longer wield the argument that the budget might face significant cuts in the absence of a genuine reform.

6.5   OTHER BUDGETARY DEVELOPMENTS RELEVANT TO THE BIOECONOMY

Apart from the heavily polarized debate on agricultural expenditure, there have been various other, albeit relatively minor, budgetary debates and developments that are relevant to furthering the European bioeconomy. This section will briefly reflect on the most important of these.

One of the major developments in this respect is the scaling up of climate policy ambitions, resulting from the 2015 UNFCC Paris Agreement. Following on these ambitions, the Commission (2018a) has set the objective of using 25% of the 2021–2027 MFF for 'climate mainstreaming' (up from 20% in the 2014–2020 budget), referring to the alignment of sectoral policy efforts with the Paris Agreement. Although this commitment may seem ambitious, the majority of these funds are already-existing allocations to traditional policies, such as the CAP, for which policy legacies have proven very resilient in the light of desires to incorporate sustainability concerns (cf. Feindt et al. 2019; Greer 2017; OECD 2017). Compared to the CAP and cohesion policy, with questionable climate impacts, the budget of the LIFE Programme for the Environment and Climate Action, which may be expected to have much more direct and positive impacts, remains modest, with €5.4 billion proposed for the next EU budget.

A central pillar of these climate ambitions is the 'clean energy transition', under the 'Clean energy for all European package' (COM/2016/860 final), setting new ambitious targets for renewable energy and cross-border electricity interconnections. The Commission has proposed to double funding compared to the 2014–2020 MFF, largely through the Cohesion Fund and a (proposed) new European Fund for Strategic Investments. That said, a substantial financing gap to achieve the energy transition goals remains (Williams et al. 2018). For that reason, as response to the Commission's MFF proposals, the European Parliament has called for an additional €4.8 billion through setting up a new Energy Transition Fund. As with all budgetary proposals, final expenditure will depend on the outcomes of inter-institutional bargaining in the MFF decision-making process.

The bioeconomy is also expected to continue to play a central role in the Horizon research framework for 2021–2027; a considerable €10 billion to support research and innovation in 'food, agriculture, rural development and the bioeconomy' is foreseen (European Commission 2018a).

Lastly, two more minor (expected) budgetary developments involve allocations to food safety and fisheries and marine policy. Regarding the former, the budget for the European Food Safety Authority (EFSA) is expected to increase, allowing the agency to perform more verification studies, inter alia (Michalopoulos 2018). For the European Maritime and Fisheries Fund, a slight decrease of funding is expected. The proposed budget under the MFF for 2021–2027 is €6.1 billion (current prices), which would imply stable funding compared to the 2014–2020 period in current prices, but a decrease of approximately 15% when applying a 2% annual deflator (Scholaert 2019).

The overall picture that emerges is that of a gradual increase of budgetary allocations to objectives related to the bioeconomy and adjacent fields. In addition, there seems to be an increasing *diversification* of funds and interventions, possibly resulting in an instrument mix that is better fitted to realize ambitious overarching objectives (cf. Candel, and Biesbroek 2016). At the same time, many of these budgetary proposals may prove more ambitious in wording than in fostering genuine policy change.

6.6   CONCLUSION

Budgetary reforms remain among the most contentious of EU policy processes. Indeed, there are probably no better EU-level examples of Harold Lasswell's (1958) famous definition of politics as 'who gets what, when and how' than the MFF and CAP budgetary negotiations. The many different actors and associated interests involved, and consequent lengthy rounds of bargaining, have made the budget cycle into the high mass of EU decision-making. It is only through the interplay of an extensive regime of institutional procedures and structures on the one hand, and formidable political and diplomatic skills on the other, that a final compromise can be struck at all.

This also explains why budgetary allocations have changed only incrementally over time. New overarching priorities *have* emerged, resulting in new EU funds and programmes, but these remain relatively modest compared to the big spending programmes. Meanwhile, the CAP's Pillar I has proven remarkably resilient, in spite of considerable pressures to scale down traditional agricultural expenditure. Consequently, in most fields, the EU continues to rely on its regulatory and norm-setting powers, rather than treasury-based instruments, for steering the Union towards desired directions.

The idea of further developing and investing in the bioeconomy has come to find broad resonance in recent budgetary proposals. It remains to be seen whether this resonance will result in a coherent set of policy objectives and supportive instrument mix or whether the 'bioeconomy' is first and foremost a handy label to provide new legitimacy to existing policy frameworks and spending programmes (cf. Candel 2016). In any case, the concept's centrality in the MFF proposals makes that it is here to stay for the next decade, which will make it a powerful discursive device for actors trying to push sectoral policies into more sustainable directions (cf. Lyngaard and Nedergaard 2009).

REFERENCES

Ackrill, R.W. 2000. CAP Reform 1999: A Crisis in the Making. *Journal of Common Market Studies* 38: 343–353.
Ana. 2018. Tsipras Says CAP and Regional Policy Cuts a 'Gift' to Anti-Europeans. Last modified at December 31, 2018. https://www.euractiv.com/section/agriculture-food/news/tsipras-says-cap-and-regional-policy-cuts-a-gift-to-anti-europeans/
Bos, M. 2011. The EU Budget. In *EU Policy for Agriculture, Food and Rural Areas*, ed. A. Oskam, G. Meester, and H. Silvis, 2nd ed. Wageningen: Wageningen Academic Publishers.
Cadogan, S. 2018. Creed Warns Against National Co-financing of Direct Farm Payments. Last modified at January 5, 2018. https://www.irishexaminer.com/breakingnews/farming/creed-warns-against-national-co-financing-of-direct-farm-payments-821224.html
Candel, J.J.L. 2016. Putting Food on the Table: The European Union Governance of the Wicked Problem of Food Security. PhD Dissertation, Wageningen University.
Candel, J.J.L., and G.R. Biesbroek. 2016. Toward a Processual Understanding of Policy Integration. *Policy Sciences* 49: 211–231.
Carrubba, C.J. 1997. Net Financial Transfers in the European Union: Who Gets What and Why? *The Journal of Politics* 59: 469–496.
Eberlein, E., and E. Grande. 2005. Beyond Delegation: Transnational Regulatory Regimes and the EU Regulatory State AU. *Journal of European Public Policy* 12: 89–112.
European Commission. 2013. The Multiannual Financial Framework 2014–2020—Frequently Asked Questions. Last modified at November 19, 2013. http://europa.eu/rapid/press-release_MEMO-13-1004_en.htm
———. 2015. Glossary of Terms Related to the Common Agricultural Policy. Last modified at April, 2015. https://ec.europa.eu/agriculture/glossary_en
———. 2017. *Reflection Paper on the Future of EU Finances.* Brussels: European Commission.
———. 2018a. *A Modern Budget for a Union that Protects, Empowers and Defences: The Multiannual Financial Framework for 2021–2027.* Brussels: European Commission. COM(2018) 321 final.
———. 2018b. *Modernising the EU Budget's Revenue Side.* Brussels: European Commission. https://ec.europa.eu/commission/sites/beta-political/files/budget-proposals-modernising-budget-revenue-side-may2018_en.pdf

———. 2018c. *Proposal for a Council Regulation Laying Down the Multiannual Financial Framework for the Years 2021 to 2027*. Brussels: European Commission.

European Committee of the Regions. 2017. Reform of the Common Agricultural Policy: Local and Regional Leaders Call for a Fair, Sustainable and Inclusive CAP. Last modified at July 12, 2017. https://cor.europa.eu/en/news/Pages/Reforme-de-la-Politique-Agricole-Commune.aspx

European Court of Auditors. 2018a. *Commission's and Member States' Actions in the Last Years of the 2007–2013 Programmes Tackled Low Absorption but Had Insufficient Focus on Results*. Luxembourg: European Court of Auditors.

———. 2018b. Using Cohesion Funds Money Should Not Become an End in Itself. Last modified at September 12, 2018. https://www.eca.europa.eu/en/Pages/NewsItem.aspx?nid=10396

Feindt, P.H., C.J.A.M. Termeer, J.J.L. Candel, and Y. Buitenhuis. 2019. *Assessing How Policies Enable or Constrain the Resilience of Farming Systems in the European Union: Case Study Results—SURE-Farm Report*. Berlin/Wageningen: SURE-Farm.

Greer, A. 2017. Post-Exceptional Politics in Agriculture: An Examination of the 2013 CAP Reform. *Journal of European Public Policy* 24: 1585–1603.

Grethe, H. 2008. Agricultural Policy: What Roles for the EU and the Member States? In *Subsidiarity and Economic Reform in Europe*, ed. G. GelauffF, I. Grilo, and A. Lejour. Berlin: Springer.

Khan, M.R. 2018. New 'Hanseatic' States Stick Together in EU Big League. Accessed at January 17, 2019. https://www.ft.com/content/f0ee3348-f187-11e8-9623-d7f9881e729f

Laffan, B., and B. Linder. 2015. The Budget: Who Gets What, When, and How? In *Policy-Making in the European Union*, ed. H. Wallace, M. Pollack, and A.R. Young. Oxford: Oxford University Press.

Lasswell, H.D. 1958. *Politics: Who Gets What, When, How?* New York: Meridian.

Lyngaard, K., and P. Nedergaard. 2009. The Logic of Policy Development: Lessons Learned from Reform and Routine within the CAP 1980–2003. *Journal of European Integration* 31: 291–309.

Majone, G. 1996. *Regulating Europe*. London: Routledge.

Matthews, A. 2013. Implications of the European Council MFF Agreement for the Agricultural Environment. Last modified at February 26, 2013. http://capreform.eu/implications-of-the-european-council-mff-agreement-for-the-agricultural-environment/

———. 2014. *The Impact of the Simultaneous MFF Negotiations on the European Parliament's Influence on the 2013 CAP Reform*. Dublin: The Institute for International Integration Studies.

———. 2015. Gainers and Losers from the CAP Budget. Last modified at November 17, 2015. http://capreform.eu/gainers-and-losers-from-the-cap-budget/

————. 2018. *National Co-financing of CAP Direct Payments*. Stockholm: Swedish Institute for European Union Studies.

Mattila, M. 2004. Contested Decisions: Empirical Analysis of Voting in the European Union Council of Ministers. *European Journal of Political Research* 43: 29–50.

Michalopoulos, S. 2018. EU Agriculture Ministers to Decide on EFSA's Budget, Sources Say. Last modified at October 31, 2018. https://www.euractiv.com/section/agriculture-food/news/eu-agriculture-ministers-to-decide-on-efsas-budget-sources-say/

OECD. 2017. *Evaluation of Agricultural Policy Reforms in the European Union: The Common Agricultural Policy 2014–20*. Paris: OECD.

Peterson, J. 1995. Decision-Making in the European Union: Towards a Framework for Analysis. *Journal of European Public Policy* 2: 69–93.

Scholaert, F. 2019. *European Maritime and Fisheries Fund 2021–2027*. Brussels: European Parliament Research Service.

SER. 2006. *Co-financing of the Common Agricultural Policy*. The Hague: Sociaal Economische Raad.

Sheehy, S. 1999. A Long, Long History of Agricultural Reform. *The Irish Times*, February 22.

Swinnen, J., ed. 2015a. *The Political Economy of the 2014–2020 Common Agricultural Policy: An Imperfect Storm*. London: Rowman and Littlefield International.

————. 2015b. *The Political Economy of the 2014–2020 Common Agricultural Policy: Introduction and Key Conclusions*. London: Rowman & Littlefield International.

Thatcher, M. 2001. European Regulation. In *European Union: Power and Policy-Making*, ed. J. Richardson. London: Routledge.

Toekomstglb.nl. 2018. Italië tegen gelijktrekken hectarepremies. Last modified at September 25, 2018. https://toekomstglb.nl/italie-tegen-gelijktrekken-hectarepremies/

Williams, R., I. Eichler, N. Gottmann, H. Förster, and A. Siemons. 2018. *Energy and the MFF—Study for the ITRE Committee*. Brussels: European Parliament.

CHAPTER 7

WTO Rules on Domestic Support for Agriculture and Food Safety: Institutional Adaptation and Institutional Transformation in the Governance of the Bioeconomy

Alexia Herwig and Yuliang Pang

7.1 INTRODUCTION

Governance of the bioeconomy is multilevel. It comprises supranational rules of European Union's (EU) law and international rules such as WTO law. These rules of international trade influence the competitiveness of the bioeconomy, the potential and rewards for innovation, the encouragement of transformation of the sector and its growth or decline. The legal institutional embedding of markets has important ramifications on the creation, shaping and performance of markets. As a result of new dynamics created, further institutional change can be fueled. In this chapter, we are interested in dynamic relationships of institutional adaptation and institu-

A. Herwig (✉)
Law and Governance Group, Wageningen University,
Wageningen, Gelderland, The Netherlands
e-mail: alexia.herwig@wur.nl

Y. Pang
University of Antwerp, Antwerp, Belgium
e-mail: yuliang.pang@uantwerpen.be

© The Author(s) 2019
L. Dries et al. (eds.), *EU Bioeconomy Economics and Policies: Volume I*,
Palgrave Advances in Bioeconomy: Economics and Policies,
https://doi.org/10.1007/978-3-030-28634-7_7

tional transformation of WTO law that result from changes induced through WTO law in the governance of the bioeconomy in the area of agricultural subsidies and of sanitary measures.

We submit that the legal obligations imposed through WTO law have led to adaptation of the supranational level of EU law, which was over time fed back to the international level and which has considerably transformed the gist of the agreements and often lessened or changed their trade-liberalizing effect. Non-WTO international rules further promote this trend. We surmise that positive stimuli for innovation in the agricultural sector therefore came mainly from internal regulatory effects rather than from competition through internationally traded goods. This is surprising given that domestic regulation is often perceived as an exception to trade liberalization.

Specifically, in the case of agricultural subsidies, the tightening of disciplines on domestic and export subsidies that occurred as a result of the WTO Uruguay Round Agreements in 1994 made it all the more rational for the EU to reform its Common Agricultural Policy (CAP) toward making support contingent on cross-compliance and meeting other green criteria of production. According to the EU's preferred notion of agricultural multifunctionality, agriculture has to be financially stimulated to produce public goods such as environmental protection and climate change mitigation, suggesting that the function of agriculture expanded beyond the production of food and feed to the production of public policy benefits (Potter and Thomson 2011).

It bears noting that pursuant to the WTO's Agreement on Agriculture (AoA) Green Box category, subsidies designed to stimulate agriculture to produce public goods and other positive externalities can be given without limitation as to quantity. Given the availability of the Green Box as well as WTO case law in *Canada-Dairy, EU Sugar* and *US-Cotton,* which tightened disciplines on export subsidies, the EU was prompted into offering to eliminate all export subsidies—an offer which the other WTO Members eventually took up in Nairobi in 2015. The move to Green Box subsidies is further promoted by international law obligations to combat climate change including through afforestation or measures to produce biofuels. These developments have transformed the Agreement on Agriculture from one in which subsidies are disciplined in quantitative terms to one in which subsidization is no longer disciplined in quantitative terms. The potential for growth and innovation in the bioeconomy therefore comes not so much from limits on domestic support and trade-induced greater competitiveness but from the opening created for transitioning agriculture to a CO_2 neutral or CO_2 negative sector of the economy, thereby stimulating innovation and the knowledge economy.

Similar developments can be observed under the Agreement on Sanitary and Phytosanitary Measures. The way the Agreement had been interpreted initially in EC-Hormones seemed strict because the Appellate Body required a specific, exposure-dependent risk assessment and rejected any influence of the precautionary principle on setting the quantum of proof for a risk assessment. By way of institutional adaptation, the EU scaled up the scientific backing of its foodstuff regulation up and sought to streamline its precautionary risk management policies through the creation of the European Food Safety Authority (EFSA) in 2002 just four years after the initial *EC-Hormones* decision (European Parliament and Council 2002). Moreover, the fact that market access and subsidy disciplines had been negotiated under the Agreement on Agriculture with an in-built liberalization agenda with uncertainty over its interpretation arguably increased the importance of Sanitary and Phytosanitary (SPS) measures as barriers to trade or potential instruments of protection. However, it became clear in the later Continued Suspension case that the Agreement on Sanitary and Phytosanitary Measures was much less strict. In fact, the Appellate Body gave considerable leeway to WTO Members to adopt measures inspired by the precautionary principle notwithstanding an existing risk assessment underlying a relevant international standard (World Trade Organization 2008a, b). In the final analysis, the Hormones and Continued Suspension sequence of cases indicates that the Sanitary and Phytosanitary Agreement is ultimately often not about substantive scientific constraints on national policies, let alone trade liberalization, but rather a procedural obligation of further scientific investigation, which provides stimuli for the development of a knowledge bioeconomy.

7.2   THE AGREEMENT ON AGRICULTURE

The WTO litigation process is being increasingly used in cases involving agricultural subsidies and other central aspects of farm policies. The link between the legal and the political aspects of the dispute settlement process is highlighted by these actions. The recent US-Cotton and EU-Sugar cases in particular demonstrate the close links between negotiations, litigation and changes in domestic farm programs. Other significant cases, such as those relating to Chilean price bands and to Canadian dairy policy, further represent a trend whereby the scope for domestic agricultural policies is becoming defined as much through the WTO legal rulings as through multilateral negotiations.

The Agreement on Agriculture (AoA) is one of the multilateral agreements on trade in goods concluded in the Uruguay Round, which is regarded as the most important milestone toward fully integrating agriculture into the rule-based multilateral trading system.

The AoA includes the following three pillars: market access, domestic support and export competition.

7.2.1   The Rules of the Agreement on Agriculture

7.2.1.1   Market Access

"Market access" means the terms and conditions under which agricultural products could be imported into the territory of a WTO Member. The Uruguay Round resulted in a systemic change away from various non-tariff border measures, including quotas and import restrictions, and toward a tariff-only regime. The legal basis of "tariff-only" regime in the AoA is laid down in Article 4.2, which requires that Members shall not maintain, resort to or revert to any measures of the kind, which have been required to be converted into ordinary customs duties. On the basis of tariff binding, WTO Members have been committed to reduce both the traditional tariffs and those new ones resulting from the tariffication process, with developed Members and developing Members having a different average tariff cut of 36 per cent and 24 per cent or a 15 per cent and 10 per cent reduction, respectively, per tariff line.

As an essential part of the tariffication package, Members were allowed in the Uruguay Round to establish the Tariff Rate Quota (TRQ) system as a way to safeguard at least the previous market access realities by a minimum or current import access commitment for all tariffied products in their Schedules (McMahon and Desta 2012).

The term "TRQ" can be defined from more than one dimension. As an economic term, a TRQ means a two-tiered tariff, and involves the interactions between three elements: in-quota tariff, quota volume, and out-of-quota tariff (OECD 2002). It is a combination of an import tariff and an import quota in which imports below a specified quantity enter at a low (or zero) tariff and imports above that quantity enter at a higher tariff (Deardorff 2014, 423). The TRQ system is a product of compromise in the Uruguay Round, which decides that it serves dual functions. On the one hand, it has been designed as a market access instrument to achieve minimum market access opportunities; on the other hand, it might be used as an instrument of protection in practice as a substantial proportion of agricultural production in developed Members is protected by TRQ.

The legal basis of the SSG provisions is Article 5 of the AoA, which allows certain Members to take recourse to temporary duty increases, above the bound levels, on specified agricultural products against import price or quantity surges on the basis of two preconditions.

7.2.1.2 Domestic Support

The term of "domestic support" has been put to use for the first time by the AoA without giving a proper legal definition. The WTO itself defines "domestic support" as "(sometimes 'internal support') in agriculture, any domestic subsidy or other measure which acts to maintain producer prices at levels above those prevailing in international trade; direct payments to producers, including deficiency payments, and input and marketing cost reduction measures available only for agricultural production". Although domestic support as a legal concept is used only in the AoA, it means essentially the same as the more familiar concept of domestic subsidies or agricultural subsidies.

WTO Members have provided various kinds of domestic support to their agricultural producers for the same or different purposes, which have brought about different consequences for international agricultural trade. Therefore, the first mission of the AoA is to allow Members to differentiate and categorize their various domestic support measures. Four distinct kinds of domestic support measures, namely Green Box measures, Blue Box measures, Development Box 6.2 measures and Amber Box measures are often mentioned. Although the AoA does not identify any boxes or colors, it identifies specific legal criteria for three of these categories. A domestic support measure qualifies for inclusion in a particular category by meeting that category's criteria. It is universally understood that Annex 2 defines Green Box measures and Article 6.5 defines Blue Box measures, which are payments tied to production-limiting programs. Article 6.2 of the AoA defines "S&D box" or Development Box measures. Amber Box measures are thus the residual subset of measures that do not meet the criteria for any of the Green Box, Blue Box or Development Box measures (see Table 7.1).

The legal basis of the Green Box measures is Annex 2 of the AoA, which stipulates that "domestic support measures for which exemption

Table 7.1   Categories of domestic support policies

Green Box: policies that have no or at most minimal trade-distorting effects and which meet given criteria (can include domestic food aid and environmental programs); support not subject to limit
Blue Box, certain payments made under production-limiting programs; support not subject to limit
Article 6.2, subsidies that meet certain criteria; support not subject to limit
Amber Box, policies not qualifying for above categories (includes market price support, payments related to current production or prices, and input subsidies); support subject to limit

Source: Own presentation-based WTO documents

from the reduction commitments is claimed shall meet the fundamental requirement that they have no, or at most minimal, trade-distorting effects or effects on production". The key element in distinguishing Green Box measures from any other domestic support measure is that they have no or minimal trade-distorting effects on trade and production. Beside this fundamental requirement, Green Box measures shall conform to two basic criteria: (1) they must be provided through publicly funded government programs (including government revenue foregone) not involving transfers from consumers; (2) they must not have the effect of providing price support to producers. Moreover, Green Box measures must meet policy-specific criteria that can be of many kinds. These specific criteria for relevant measures leave open the interpretation that among these measures are a number that could have more than a minimal effect on production.

Annex 2 gives the policy-specific Green Box criteria under 12 headings. The measures under these headings can be classified into two groups: the first one is programs involving expenditures on public services, such as research, training, marketing, promotion, infrastructure, domestic food aid or public stockholding for food security purposes; the second one is programs involving direct payments to producers. The latter can be further broken down into two sub-groups: income guarantee and security programs (natural disasters, government financial contributions to crop insurance, etc.) and programs to adjust structures and environmental programs (European Parliament n.d.). The common shorthand for the measures exempted as Green Box compliant is that they are not trade distorting. However, Annex 2 does not define "trade-distorting effects or effects on production" nor is there jurisprudence within the WTO on its legal meaning (Meléndez-Ortiz et al. 2009, 29). A major concern surrounding

Green Box subsidies is that payments may not respect the fundamental requirement described in paragraph 1 of Annex 2 of the AoA.

Domestic support measures that are not exempted from limit(s) on support are often referred to as Amber Box measures, without any such phrase being used in the AoA. The legal basis for these measures rests on Article 6.1 of the AoA, which states that the domestic support reduction commitments of each Member contained in Part IV of its Schedule shall apply to all of its domestic support measures in favor of agricultural producers with the exception of domestic measures, which are not subject to reduction in terms of the criteria set out in Article 6 and in Annex 2 of the AoA. The criteria in Article 6 are the Blue Box criteria in Article 6.5, and the Article 6.2 criteria for development box.

"Aggregate Measurement of Support" (AMS) is the legal terminology provided in the AoA to quantify Members' support under non-exempt domestic support measures, which is the centerpiece of Members' commitments in the domestic support pillar (McMahon 2016, 67). Article 1 (a) of the AoA defines the AMS as "the annual level of support, expressed in monetary terms, provided for an agricultural product in favor of the producers of the basic agricultural products or Non-Product-Specific support (NPS support) provided in favor of agricultural producers in general, other than support provided under programs that qualify as exempt from reduction under Annex 2 of this Agreement".

The AMS is to be calculated on a product-specific basis for each product receiving any type of non-exempt support, while non-product-specific support is to be aggregated into one number, which is to be included in the Total AMS. Therefore, the Total AMS is a sum of a number of components: all the AMSs. The definition of Total AMS refers to aggregate measurements of support in the plural. This is often overlooked in analysis that treats "the Product Specific AMS (PS AMS) as the single sum of all PS AMSs. Annex 3 of the AoA specifies how to calculate an AMS. Annex 4 specifies how to calculate an Equivalent Measurement of Support (EMS) as an alternative, if it is not practical to calculate an AMS.

Support under non-exempt domestic support measures is subject to reduction commitments, that is, a limit applies, or limits apply. As a result of the Uruguay Round negotiations, Members entered in their Schedules (Part IV, Section I, headed Domestic Support: Total AMS Commitments) their "Annual and Final Bound Commitment Levels". For most Members this entry is nil (or blank or zero), for other Members each yearly level is a specified amount. The Member's entry, whether nil or otherwise, constitutes the maximum amount of certain AMS support that the Member may provide. The Annual and Final Bound Commitment Levels are derived from reductions, with some adjustments, from the Base Total AMS. The Final Bound Commitment Level results from reducing the Base Total AMS, while also accommodating adjustments associated with support reductions from the year 1986. The reduction of developed Members with a Base Total AMS was 20 per cent, carried out over six years from 1995, while the reduction of developing Members with a Base Total AMS was 13.3 per cent over ten years. A Member's Current Total AMS (CTAMS) must not exceed the scheduled annual and final Bound Total AMS (BTAMS) (Article 6.3) (McMahon 2016, 69). Current Total AMS is the level of support actually provided during any year, measured in a particular way. It is the sum of all AMSs, except any AMS that does not exceed a threshold amount.

Under Article 7.2(b), a Member without a BTAMS (or with BTAMS of nil, zero or blank) is subject to limits on its individual AMSs. Those limits are at the same levels as the threshold amounts on AMSs for Members with a BTAMS. This means that having a BTAMS in its Schedule makes a difference in terms of a Member's policy space for AMS support, that is, support under non-exempt measures. The legal basis of the *de minimis* level domestic support is laid down in Article 6.4 of the AoA. In the current context, the *de minimis level* concerns the exemption of relatively small AMSs from a Member's CTAMS. An AMS, whether for a basic agricultural product or the non-product-specific AMS, that is no larger than its *de minimis* level can be exempted from the calculation of CTAMS.

The *de minimis* level is a given percentage times the value of production of the individual basic agricultural product (the given percentage times the value of total agricultural production in the case of the non-product-specific AMS). The percentage is 5 per cent for developed Members and 10 per cent for developing Members. When China and Kazakhstan acceded to the WTO, they committed to a *de minimis* percentage of 8.5 per cent. The exemption of *de minimis* AMSs from the calculation of CTAMS means that, for a Member with a BTAMS, the *de minimis* level is effectively a *de minimis* threshold. An AMS is allowed to be larger than its *de minimis* level but then it must be included in its entirety in the CTAMS. The *de minimis* level operates differently for a Member with a nil BTAMS: no AMS is allowed to exceed its *de minimis* level, which is thus effectively a *de minimis* limit on each individual AMS (Article 7.2(b)).

The Blue Box exemption results from one of the important compromises, the so-called Blair House Accord (Healy et al. 1998), brokered between the United States and the EU in order to save the Uruguay Round. It was originally designed to accommodate subsidies provided by the EU under the 1992 MacSharry reform of the Common Agriculture Policy (CAP) and by the United States under the deficiency payments programs in its 1990 Farm Bill (McMahon 2016, 86). The Blue Box payments were not subject to reductions, but support was not to exceed the 1992 levels. Thus, the Blue Box became the way in which the reformed CAP became consistent with the Uruguay Round constraints. The notifications by the EU to the WTO reflect this compromise (Orden et al. 2001, 64). The legal basis of Blue Box is Article 6.5 of the AoA, namely "direct payments under production-limiting programs".

The legal basis of development programs is Article 6.2 of the AoA. It identifies three types of government measures of assistance under which support shall not be required to be included in a Member's calculation of its CTAMS. As part of the special and differential treatment in the AoA, this exemption is available only to developing Members. The measures are (1) investment subsidies generally available to agriculture; (2) agricultural input subsidies generally available to low-income or resource-poor producers; and (3) domestic support to producers to encourage diversification from growing illicit narcotic crops.

7.2.1.3 Export Competition

The WTO defines export competition as follows: in Doha Round agriculture—export subsidies and the "parallel" issues, which could provide loopholes for governments' export subsidies—export finance (credit, guarantees and insurance), exporting state trading enterprises, and international food aid (World Trade Organization n.d.). Export subsidies (European Commission n.d.) refer to subsidies contingent on export performance, including the export subsidies listed in detail in Article 9 of the AoA. Paragraph 3 of Article 3, Article 8 and Article 10 of the AoA establishes a prohibition on export subsidies in excess of the budgetary outlay and quantity and levels of commitment specified in the Members' Schedules. However, two important WTO cases have established close links between export subsidies and domestic support as well as market access, which indicate that we cannot evaluate the effects of export subsidies in isolation. The Canadian-Dairy case shows the close link between domestic support and export subsidies since an over-quota domestically subsidized farm product, which could only be exported and was sold at a price less than the cost of production, was regarded as having benefited from an export subsidy (Horn and Mavroidis 2007, 237). The EU-Sugar case brings to light the subtle relationship between market access and export subsidies as the practice of the EU for re-exporting those sugars imported under its preferential agreements with former colonies to the world market was deemed as a de facto export subsidies to domestic sugar producers. The latest advances in this regard are the 2015 Nairobi Ministerial Decision on Export Competition, which specifies that Developed Members shall immediately eliminate export subsidies, except for some agricultural products; meanwhile based on the Special and Differential Treatment, Developing Members shall eliminate their export subsidy entitlements by 2018. In addition, they will keep the flexibility to cover marketing and transport costs for agricultural exports until the end of 2023. The least-developed countries (LDCs) and net food-importing developing countries (NFIDCs) will enjoy additional time to cut export subsidies (Díaz-Bonilla and Hepburn 2016).

7.2.2   Institutional Transformation of the Agreement on Agriculture

7.2.2.1   Adaptation by the EU
Pushed by the impending disciplines on domestic support, the EU began reforming its Common Agricultural Policy in the direction in which it was pushed by the Agreement on Agriculture, that is to say, away from direct income support and toward Green Box measures on which the agreement imposes no quantitative limit. Already in the 1992 Mac Sharry reforms, the EU started decoupling income support from production, and in the 2000 reforms, started to link financial support to rural development and environmental protection objectives (Anania and d'Andrea 2012). The 2003 Fischler reform of the CAP introduced cross-compliance whereby direct payments (Pillar I of the CAP) were made conditional on compliance with several EU directives linked to environmental protection and food safety. Non-income-related agricultural support under Pillar II also contained criteria linked to the production of environmental benefits and rural development. The 2007 Health Check achieved the decoupling of all support, modulation of income support into payments linked to rural development and limits on the price support provided through buying in

of surplus production. As a result of the 2007 reform, direct support declined from 39 per cent of gross farm receipt to 19 per cent. Following the most recent 2013 reform of the CAP, 30 per cent of payments are now linked to the production of positive environmental externalities by farmers. These reforms together seem to introduce a shift toward a greener, more multifunctional agriculture because the decline in direct income support made the multifunctional subsidies more important in line with the incentive provided by the Green Box to continue subsidization of agriculture, albeit for the production of public goods.

Nevertheless, limitations remain. Under Pillar I, the amount of positive environmental externalities a farm produces has no influence on the amount of payments it receives. Payments under Pillar II are linked to income forgone by farmers as foreseen by Annex 2 paragraph 12 (b) of the Green Box, meaning that payments have to rise in line with price increases of agricultural production. Anania thus criticizes the reforms of the CAP as remaining in substance unchanged as a form of price support with just a gloss of a greener, more multifunctional agriculture because the conditions of the green payment are too easy to meet (Anania and d'Andrea 2012). Some Green Box subsidies stimulate retirement of resources or of farmers or can be used to foster the establishment of alternative markets for agricultural production such as biofuels (World Trade Organization 2019). They have the effect of reducing output or stimulating novel demand, which will translate into increased prices for agricultural products. There is thus an in-built ratchet on amounts of support in the Agreement on Agriculture.

What we indeed witness are ever-increasing public expenditures on domestic support—albeit now under the Green Box—a phenomenon called box shifting—from the Amber to the Green Box (see Table 7.2).

The rising amount of domestic support raises the question whether the domestic support programs still meet the general criteria that all Green Box measures must meet, namely that they have no or at most minimal trade-distorting effect and no price supporting effect (World Trade Organization 2019). The legal issue is whether indirect effects on prices or trade are caught by this condition or only direct effects. At least as regards resource and farmer retirement support, it would be difficult to argue, in our view, that the indirect effect they may produce on agricultural prices of other producers by reducing output could be a form of price support or trade distortion because the purpose of these subsidies would thereby be negated. Might the level of support provided then tilt the balance against

Table 7.2   Total domestic support of the EU in 2001–2012 (Unit: Million Euro)

	Green	Blue	CTAMS	PS AMS	NPS AMS	DB	Total
2001	20,661.2	23,725.9	39,281.3	468.1	573.5	0.0	84,710.0
2002	20,404.3	24,726.5	28,490.4	1003.7	938.1	0.0	75,563.0
2003	22,074.1	24,781.7	30,880.2	901.4	1052.1	0.0	79,689.5
2004	24,390.6	27,236.6	31,214.3	955.3	1086.5	0.0	84,883.3
2005	40,280.2	13,445.2	28,427.1	191.7	1059.3	0.0	83,403.5
2006	56,529.8	5696.7	26,632.1	445.4	1407.0	0.0	90,711.0
2007	62,610.2	5166.1	12,354.2	1536.9	852.0	0.0	82,519.4
2008	62,825.4	5347.8	11,795.5	328.8	757.5	0.0	81,055.0
2009	63,798.1	5323.6	8764.0	803.7	598.1	0.0	79,287.5
2010	68,051.5	3141.8	6501.8	692.3	700.8	0.0	79,088.2
2011	70,976.8	2981.1	6858.9	311.8	690.9	0.0	81,819.5
2012	71,140.0	2754.2	5899.1	986.1	794.5	0.0	81,573.9

Source: Yuliang Pang, data based on notifications of the EU to the WTO

Green Box support under the general criteria? Again, an implicit quantitative limitation of Green Box support is difficult to sustain based on the legal text because Annex 2 refers to the Green Box support as support for which exemption from reduction commitments is claimed and then sets out the general and specific criteria. The exemption from the reduction commitments are therefore the result of meeting the criteria rather than part of the criteria themselves.

7.2.2.2   Institutional Transformation of the Agreement on Agriculture via the Link to Climate Change

While the foregoing analysis suggests that the Green Box provides an important loophole out of the disciplines on domestic support without any strict criteria on multifunctional environmental and climate change benefits, this assessment has to be nuanced. In the case of climate change mitigation, countries have collectively committed to keep global temperature increases below 2 °C in the 2015 Paris Agreement on Climate Change.

The agreement adopts a decentralized approach in that it invites state parties to indicate their nationally determined contributions to reaching this goal (United Nations 2015, Article 4). Nationally determined contributions include mitigation measures and may include adaptation measures which result in emission reductions such as conversion of agricultural land into sink (United Nations 2015, Article 4.7) for which a party may give

Green box subsidies. Parties shall use the accounting guidelines of the International Panel on Climate Change (IPCC) (United Nations 2015, Article 4.14). Parties shall also promote environmental integrity, transparency, accuracy, completeness, comparability and consistency, and ensure the avoidance of double counting (United Nations 2015, Article 4.13). The decision on the adoption of the Paris Agreement further specifies that parties must make methodologies they use for accounting for emissions, reductions and for determining that their contributions are fair and ambitious transparent and that they should use quantifiable information (United Nations 2016).

The Paris Agreement also adopts a compliance rather than an enforcement approach because how well countries meet their nationally determined contributions is reviewed through a facilitative, non-punitive and non-adversarial expert compliance committee and where shortcomings are detected, countries receive guidance and support to meet their targets (United Nations 2015, Article 15.2).

The most recent Conference of the Parties (COP) of December 2018 succeeded in an agreement on a rule book with indicators for accounting for climate change mitigation and monitoring. Significantly, countries failed to agree on guidelines for market mechanisms under Article 6 during COP 24 because of division over how to prevent double counting of emission reductions.[1] Arguably, this makes nationally confined measures such as subsidies to agriculture for emission reductions more important as a nationally determined contribution, especially if one takes account of the fact that the EU has committed itself in its first nationally determined contribution to achieve a reduction of 40 per cent in GHG emissions by 2030 (Latvia Presidency of the Council of the European Union 2015). The rulebook partly achieves environmental integrity insofar as developed and developing countries alike have to use the same set of reporting standards unless a country clearly lacks capacity (Latvia Presidency of the Council of the European Union 2015). But insofar as reporting rules do not distinguish between long- and short-term emissions (and savings), which affect the climate differently, the rules still fall short of achieving true environmental integrity.

By 2020, countries also have to ratchet their nationally determined pledges upwards, and the five-year global stocktake under the Paris Agreement keeps a check on whether the nationally determined contributions together are effective at stemming temperature increases (United

---

[1] Carbon Brief, n. 24.

Nations 2015, Article 14.1). More climate change mitigation efforts are therefore needed in the future and these may include economic stimuli in the form of income support to farmers for climate change mitigation, for instance, in order to reforest agricultural land, convert it to wetlands or replace GHG intensive farming with crop growing.

As regards climate change mitigation in the land use sector and accounting for reductions in emissions, the EU has committed itself to set up a new framework on how to include the land use sector in mitigation before 2020.[2] Until then, Member States of the EU have to account for changes in the land use sector on the basis of Decision 529/2013 (European Parliament and Council 2013). This decision sets out definitions of afforestation, reforestation and forest with detailed criteria on the area planted with trees, their minimum height in meters, crown cover and the density of trees (European Parliament and Council 2013, Article 2). It also stipulates expressly that Member States have to include biomass, soil organic carbon and harvested wood in their calculations (European Parliament and Council 2013, Article 4). Annex IV indicatively lists the kind of actions Member States may carry out in the land use sector such as selection of better crop varieties, extending crop rotations, better nutrient management, improving grazing land management and selecting more appropriate species. Some of these may overlap with Green Box subsidy measures.

Where WTO members thus choose to engage in climate change mitigation through income support to agriculture, they must follow the COP rulebook and in particular account not in terms of budgetary outlays but in terms of CO_2 equivalents. The expert compliance committee of the Paris Agreement verifies that emission reductions from changes in agricultural land use actually generate the level of reductions claimed and can make concrete suggestions for improvement. The rulebook and committee therefore indirectly tighten the disciplines of the Agreement on Agriculture's Green Box with more robust environmental criteria. Moreover, the agreement reached at the COP 24 may be used as a rule of international law binding in the relations between the parties in the sense of Article 31.3(c) of the Vienna Convention on the Law of Treaties for a contextual interpretation of the Green Box reference to objective criteria for environmental protection.

---

[2] European Union (EU) Nationally Determined Contributions, supra n. 30.

The loophole that the Green Box may have presented therefore gradually gets narrower through more precise international law obligations pertaining to climate change. While worries abound that environmental protection and trade liberalization objectives conflict under WTO law, the example of the Agreement on Agriculture in its interface with climate change and other international environmental law shows that this non-WTO international law contributes to the real stimulation of the bioeconomy through the innovations it induces via a regulatory change and in particular the generation of technical expert knowledge related to accurate accounting for emissions and reductions.

7.3   THE SPS AGREEMENT

7.3.1   Early and Strict Interpretation

The first case adjudicated under the SPS Agreement was the EC-Hormones case. In it, the US and Canada challenged the EU's ban on the sale of meat from cattle fattened through the use of natural and synthetic sex hormones for growth promotion. The EU lost the case because it had failed to base its ban on a risk assessment as required by Article 5.1 (World Trade Organization 1998a).

The Codex Alimentarius Commission had set an international standard authorizing maximum residue levels of these growth hormones in beef. The EU thus adopted a stricter level of protection than that enshrined in the Codex standard. According to Article 3.1, WTO members should base their protective regulations against food-borne risks on standards of the Codex. Article 3.3 allows them to adopt more protective measures, but they must provide a scientific justification or act in accordance with Article 5 (World Trade Organization 1998b, Article 3.3). According to Article 5.1, members should base their SPS measures on a risk assessment. The Appellate Body interpreted this as meaning that the risk assessment must reasonably support and sufficiently warrant the protective SPS measure in question (World Trade Organization 1998a, para. 186, 189, 193).

The EU had provided general evidence about the carcinogenic nature of natural and synthetic sex hormones. However, what the ban on beef targeted were not the sex hormones themselves but rather metabolites found in the beef when ingested by humans. For the ban on beef to be based on a risk assessment, the risk assessment had to be specific to the incriminated substance and exposure through meat (World Trade

Organization 1998a, para. 200). The EU had tried to argue that the SPS Agreement and in particular Article 5.1 should be interpreted with the help of the precautionary principle, which at that time had already been enshrined in several international treaties. It argued that the precautionary principle had become a customary international law and should have hence been taken into account in the interpretation of the SPS Agreement (World Trade Organization 1998a, para 16). The Appellate Body rejected this argument. It found that even if the precautionary principle had acquired the status of customary international law, it still would have to interpret and apply the provisions of the SPS Agreement (World Trade Organization 1998a, para. 124).

Because the EU did not lift the ban, Canada and the US obtained authorizations to levy additional tariffs on imports from the EU in the amount of US$117 million and Can$ 11 million (World Trade Organization 2008a, b). It bears noting that the EU had not tried to defend its ban as a provisional Article 5.7 measure taken because scientific evidence was insufficient. The interpretation of the SPS Agreement thus seemed strict because it required a high degree of epistemic validation and precise information. It also seemed strict because the Appellate Body seemed to view the precautionary principle as external to WTO law and at any rate as different from risk assessments. The decision in *EC-Hormones* put a premium on a risk analysis-based approach to food safety with the burden of scientific assessment being placed on the importing and regulating member.

7.3.2   *Institutional Transformation of the SPS Agreement*

After several years of retaliatory tariffs on its exports to the US and Canada, the EU brought a WTO dispute settlement complaint to a WTO panel. It argued that it complied with the SPS Agreement through Article 5.7 regarding its ban on beef from cattle raised on hormones and that the tariffs should be lifted. Article 5.7 allows a WTO member to take provisional SPS measures in case relevant scientific evidence is insufficient. It then has an obligation of conduct to seek the scientific information needed for a risk assessment. At the time the EU brought this dispute settlement complaint, the Codex Alimentarius standard with a maximum residue limit continued to be in existence and was based on a risk assessment. The US Food and Drug Administration had also risk-assessed the growth hormones and established a maximum residue limit.

The case turned on the question whether provisional measures due to scientific evidence being insufficient could be taken under Article 5.7 notwithstanding these existing risk assessments. In other words, the legal question was whether Articles 5.1 and 5.7 dealt with mutually exclusive situations. It also turned on whether the policy protection purposes of the regulator had a bearing on the legal determination of whether scientific evidence was insufficient. The panel found that the existing risk assessments on growth hormones precluded recourse to Article 5.7 (World Trade Organization 2008a, b). The panel in *Continued Suspension* also rejected the argument that the protection purposes of the regulator mattered for whether scientific evidence was insufficient.

The Appellate Body reversed the panel's finding. What the decision in the hormones saga shows is twofold: when it comes to complying with the SPS Agreement and to implementing findings, a member is not necessarily required to lift its SPS measure and allow import of a substance that is internationally considered as safe. Instead, it can seek to comply with the SPS Agreement by engaging in further scientific analysis of the measure and by casting doubt on the international scientific consensus. The same applies in regards to the protection purposes of the regulator: based on its preferences for protecting certain sub-groups of the population or protecting against certain types of exposure, the WTO member can ask more detailed data and analyses from the scientists. The EU could have, for instance, asked for data on children or cross-exposure to sex hormones through other avenues. Such evidence and data can be difficult to produce. What the EU in fact achieved in *Continued Suspension* was an affirmation of its regulatory policies for food where the precautionary principle has constitutional status and where it is also recognized that policy factors such as economic, societal or ethical factors also provide relevant information for the decision on whether or not to regulate (European Parliament and Council 2002).

Curiously, in the face of the possibility of an importing member asking for more and more specific data, a WTO member seeking to export its foodstuffs is well advised to assess them comprehensively. Through both mechanisms, the SPS Agreement stimulates the production of scientific knowledge rather than trade in foodstuffs as such. This suggests that the SPS Agreement really gives a positive impetus to a shared knowledge economy in which the production of knowledge as a non-rival good is encouraged among importing and exporting members. Through allocating a joint responsibility for the production of knowledge and the need to engage with the protection purposes of regulators in other WTO members, regulatory learning and convergence may also be facilitated.

7.4   Conclusion

What we witness today is that levels of agricultural support are ever increasing—except that such support has been shifted into the Green Box. In that sense, disciplines on domestic support have actually lessened. As we have showed in our analysis, the substantive Green Box criteria remain ambiguous and in particular do not require a demonstration that the financial support actually makes a positive impact on the production of these public goods. On the other hand, with the expiration of the peace clause of the AoA, the special privileges enjoyed by developed countries for the immunity of their agricultural subsidies policies from the Subsidies and Countervailing Measures litigation also terminates, which has brought about profound implications. A number of landmark WTO cases on agricultural subsidies, such as US-Cotton, EU-Sugar, Canada-Dairy, shed great lights on the significance of WTO dispute settlement mechanism in reshaping developed countries' policies for agricultural subsidies (Josling et al. 2006). Arguably, the constraints on export subsidies have contributed to making domestic Green Box subsidies for environmental protection all the more important. As we also show, the reforms of the Common Agricultural Policy undertaken by the EU have remained under-ambiguous in that levels of support have not been tied to levels of output of public goods or positive externalities. Nevertheless, the rule book on reporting and accounting under the Paris climate change agreement agreed upon at COP 24 may make an indirect contribution to strengthening the disciplines of the Green Box insofar as financial support measures for agriculture to combat climate change must actually be shown to make a positive contribution to climate change mitigation. The Green Box, EU CAP reform and climate change law can thus stimulate growth and competitiveness of the bioeconomy. Under the SPS Agreement, we observe a softening of the disciplines on risk assessment and a relative weakening of international standards because measures based on precautionary action under Article 5.7 were made easier. What this has encouraged is the co-production of scientific knowledge between exporting WTO members as potential complainants and importing WTO members and a stimulation of the knowledge bioeconomy.

REFERENCES

Anania, G., and M.R.P. d'Andrea. 2012. The Common Agricultural Policy After 2013. *Intereconomics* 47 (6): 316–342.

Deardorff, A. 2014. *Terms of Trade: Glossary of International Economics.* 2nd ed. Singapore: World Scientific Publishing.

Díaz-Bonilla, E., and J. Hepburn. 2016. *Export Competition Issues After Nairobi: The Recent World Trade Organization Agreements and Their Implications for Developing Countries.* Washington, DC: International Food Policy Research Institute. IFPRI Discussion Paper 01557.

European Parliament. n.d. WTO Agreement on Agriculture|EU Fact Sheets|European Parliament. http://www.europarl.europa.eu/factsheets/en/home. Accessed 23 Sept 2018.

European Parliament and Council. 2002. Regulation (EC) No 178/2002 of the European Parliament and of the Council of 28 January 2002: Laying Down the General Principles and Requirements of Food Law, Establishing the European Food Safety Authority and Laying Down Procedures in Matters of Food Safety. *Official Journal of the European Communities* 31: 1–14.

———. 2013. Decision No 529/2013/EU of the European Parliament and of the Council of 21 May 2013; on Accounting Rules on Greenhouse Gas Emissions and Removals Resulting from Activities Relating to Land Use, Land-Use Change and Forestry and on Information Concerning Actions Relating to Those Activities. *Official Journal of the European Union* 165: 80–97.

Healy, S., R. Pearce, and M. Stockbridge. 1998. *The Implications of the Uruguay Round Agreement on Agriculture for Developing Countries.* Training Materials for Agricultural Planning, 41. Rome, FAO.

Horn, H., and P.C. Mavroidis. 2007. *The American Law Institute Reporters Studies on WTO Law: The American Law Institute Reporters' Studies on WTO Case Law: Legal and Economic Analysis.* Cambridge: Cambridge University Press.

Josling, T., L. Zhao, J. Cercelen, and K. Artha. 2006. Implications of WTO Litigation for the WTO Agricultural Negotiations. IPC Issue Brief 19.

Latvia Presidency of the Council of the European Union. 2015. Submission by Latvia and the European Commission on behalf of the European Union and Its Member States.

McMahon, J. 2016. *The WTO Agreement on Agriculture: A Commentary.* Oxford: Oxford University Press.

McMahon, J.A., and M.G. Desta. 2012. *Research Handbook on the WTO Agriculture Agreement: New and Emerging Issues in International Agricultural Trade Law.* Cheltenham: Edward Elgar Publishing.

Meléndez-Ortiz, R., C. Bellmann, and J. Hepburn. 2009. *Agricultural Subsidies in the WTO Green Box: Ensuring Coherence with Sustainable Development Goals.* Cambridge: Cambridge University Press.

OECD. 2002. *Alternative Liberalization Scenarios and Their Impacts on Quota Rent and Tariff Revenues in Selected OECD Agricultural Markets.* Paris: OECD. COM/AGR/TD/WP(2002)23/FINAL.

Orden, D., D. Blandford, and T. Josling. 2001. *WTO Disciplines on Agricultural Support: Seeking a Fair Basis for Trade.* Cambridge: Cambridge University Press.

Potter, C., and K. Thomson. 2011. Agricultural Multifunctionality and Europe's New Land Debate. In *EU Policy for Agriculture, Food and Rural Areas*, ed. A. Oskam, G. Meester, and H. Silvis, 213. Wageningen: Wageningen Academic Publishers.

United Nations. 2015. Paris Agreement.

———. 2016. Report of the Conference of the Parties on its Twenty-First Session, Held in Paris from 30 November to 13 December 2015. FCCC/CP/2015/10/Add.1

World Trade Organization. 1998a. EC Measures Concerning Meat and Products (Hormones). WT/DS26/AB/R and WT/DS48/AB/R.

———. 1998b. The WTO Agreement on the Application of Sanitary and Phytosanitary Measures (SPS Agreement).

———. 2008a. *United States—Continued Suspension of Obligations in the EC-Hormones Dispute.* Geneva: World Trade Organization (WTO). WT/DS320/AB/R

———. 2008b. *Canada—Continued Suspension of Obligations in the EC-Hormones Dispute.* Geneva: World Trade Organization (WTO). WT/DS321/AB/R

———. 2019. WTO Analytical Index Agreement on Agriculture – Annex 2.

———. n.d. Glossary—A Guide to 'WTO Speak'. https://www.wto.org/english/thewto_e/glossary_e/glossary_e.htm. Accessed 23 Sept 2018.

CHAPTER 8

Future Developments of the Institutional Framework

Kai Purnhagen

8.1 INTRODUCTION

Brexit and the rise of populism in Member States has left its marks on the European integration process (Purnhagen 2020a). At the time of writing this chapter, the Heads of States in the European Union (EU) have found consensus on Ursula von der Leyen as a new President of the Commission. The difficulties in finding consensus between the various axes of interest and power (East vs. West, EP vs. Head of States, conservative vs. socialist), the fact that Brexit has been delayed so long that the UK took part in EP elections and the fact that a person who had never appeared in the election campaign and has never even been discussed during the whole procedure and all of this in the shadow of a growing anti-EU sentiment have disclosed the specifics of the current institutional structure of the EU. This cumbersome procedure could be viewed as a necessary evil to reflect a consensus-driven institution, which is defiant toward Member States interest as a strong basis of the integration project. It could also illustrate the problems of the systems that govern the EU, where coalitions, Member

K. Purnhagen (✉)
Law and Governance Group, Wageningen University,
Wageningen, Gelderland, The Netherlands
e-mail: kai.purnhagen@wur.nl

L. Dries et al. (eds.), *EU Bioeconomy Economics and Policies: Volume I*,
Palgrave Advances in Bioeconomy: Economics and Policies,
https://doi.org/10.1007/978-3-030-28634-7_8

State interest and other factors determine and eventually stall a more democratic governance procedures. Either way, the lessons learned from Brexit and the rise of populism across the EU should make clear that a reform of EU law and its institutions is warranted. This is not least the case as, if Brexit ever happens, it will have an impact on the institutional structure as the resulting differences in the weighing of votes in the Council will shift powers more toward the Member States representing the Eastern part of the EU. Several proposals for reform are on the table, ranging from a rigorous return to the internal market paradigm to a thorough establishment of a European republic, a fully fledged "United States of Europe" (European Commission 2017).

While these *les grand idées* are certainly helpful to further drive the EU integration process, there are also several more pragmatic proposals on the table. In this chapter, I will discuss three proposals that, according to my subjective view, had most impact on the discussion and may also represent the several images, as each one of them gives different reasons to the crisis of the EU[1]: the proposal of the former German judge on the German constitutional court Dieter Grimm, the proposal from the French President Emmanuel Macron and the answer to this by Annegret Kramp-Karrenbauer. Subsequently, I will evaluate the different proposals.

8.2   THE REFORM PROPOSALS

The starting point of criticism, on which the proposals for institutional reform builds upon, is the view that the EU institutions would be suffering from weak legitimacy and acceptance (European Commission 2017). However, the causes for this phenomenon are debated and are being reflected in the different reform proposals on the table.

8.2.1   The Proposal of Dieter Grimm: A New Constitution for the EU—More Democracy, More Subsidiarity

Dieter Grimm's view is very much tainted from his training as a lawyer and from his practice as a judge on the German constitutional court. According to his assessment, the EU derives its essential legitimacy from the nation states, which are institutionally represented in the Council. However, according to this view, during the course of European integration, the

[1] Many more proposals have been published, quite a number of them more elaborated. Space constrains me in elaborating more in other proposals.

European Parliament has steadily grown into a second pillar of legitimacy, as it has been freely and secretly elected by European Union citizens and has grown to achieve more and more power in the legislative process. As it had been shown in Brexit and in other debates on the future of Europe, a large bulk of criticism targets the practical work of the European Commission and the Court of Justice of the European Union (CJEU). Both institutions are not elected, but have in fact developed to become the strongest drivers of European integration in politics and in law (Schmidt 2018; Ehlermann 1992; Mancini 1989; Weiler 1993). A catalyst for this development had been the lack of a constitution at the EU level, which allowed the CJEU to fill this void with far-reaching constitutionalizing judgments (Lenaerts 2013, at 16; Purnhagen 2013, at 144–145). However, after getting into the force of the Treaty of Maastricht, the Lisbon Treaty and, in particular, the growing body of more principles-based secondary legislation, it is being argued that the constitutionaliza-tion process has come to an end and gives way more to a governing mode, paying more deference to individuals, Member State and EU institution's desires (Lenaerts 2013, at 16). Most of the proponents of this kind of critique furthermore target the Commission, which would in large parts act like a national government, but parliamentary control of the Commission would be limited (Linsenmeier 2016).

Dieter Grimm's proposal seamlessly connects to the criticism voiced above. In his book (Grimm 2016), he develops mainly three different reform proposals:

1. National law should no longer determine the rules according to which the European Parliament is elected. Rather, the European par-ties, each with a Europe-wide program, should be elected on the basis of a European electoral law. In this way, the parties should be enabled to put realistic, that is, implementable, program proposals into the vote. Such a reform does not even require a change in the treaties.
2. The European Union urgently needs to improve its capacity to act. At the same time, the principle of subsidiarity must be respected in order not to undermine national sovereignty. This means that it requires a distribution of competences along the subject matter. As in a federal order, competences must be located where they can best be dealt with.
3. Finally, the overarching constitutionalization of the Treaties must be stopped. This means that the EU needs a lean constitution.

Constitutions are not the subject of a daily political debate; they are the basis on which the political debate is conducted. In practical terms, this means that a large part of the Treaties, in particular, the Treaty on the Functioning of the European Union, should be transformed into secondary Union law.

8.2.2   The Proposal of Emmanuel Macron: A New Political Foundation of the EU of Bits and Pieces

French President Emmanuel Macron has delineated his ideas first in a speech delivered in December 2017 in Athens (Macron 2017), then in an open letter in March 2019 (Macron 2019). While, in the former, Macron has identified his view on the reasons of the crisis of the EU, in the open letter, he advanced more concrete proposals based in the rather theoretical ideas advanced in Athens.

According to Macron's view as delivered in his speech in Athens, the EU legitimacy and acceptance crisis does not have constitutional roots (as Grimm proposed), but rather political ones. In the past, politicians would have lied to their peoples regarding the impact of changes at the global level and the role the EU has to play in this. But it was not the lies in itself that had eroded trust, on the example of the Greek debt crisis, he illustrates that it was rather the price that the people had to pay who trusted their leaders and believed in these lies. What was particularly problematic was the fact that national leaders told their peoples that nation states alone can solve most of the problems and that the European Union cannot better serve to protect individual interest in its collectivity. This development has also a direct connection to the legitimacy crisis:

> "What happened a few months ago in the United Kingdom is not a whole different story: suddenly, the people of that island rose up against choices often supported by its own leaders and said "this Europe is not for me. I do not have my place here, and I no longer understand it. These rules have become absurd. Look at this Europe where I am losing my own rights, and where I am expected to make more and more effort to live less well."[2]
> That is what the British people said last year."

---

[2] Emmanuel Macron, European Union—Speech by the President of the French Republic (Athens, 7 September 2017), available at https://www.diplomatie.gouv.fr/en/french-foreign-policy/european-union/events/article/european-union-speech-by-the-president-of-the-french-republic-athens-07-09-17

In other words, it is each one's individual preference, and the EU's ability to form and defend these as collective preferences, which justifies EU's sovereignty and which legitimizes the EU. The reform proposals advanced later took up these ideas and advanced them to develop more concrete proposals for an institutional change. Macron essentially advanced six concrete proposals with regard to an institutional reform.

1. The creation of a Europe-wide social safety net program guaranteeing a minimum European wage "appropriate to each country." This program should be discussed each year.
2. Reinstalling freedom of movement within the borderless Schengen area. "No community can create a sense of belonging if it does not have bounds that it protects." To oversee EU's internal security, he called for "a common border force and a European asylum office."
3. Creation of a "European Agency for the Protection of Democracies." The Agency is responsible to protect Member State elections, in particular, from foreign influence. In addition, Macron proposed banning foreign financing of European political parties.
4. To finance halving the use of pesticides by 2025, reduction of carbon emissions status to zero by 2050 and increase food safety, Macron proposes "a European Climate Bank to finance the ecological transition, a European food safety force to improve our food controls and, to counter the lobby threat, independent scientific assessment of substances hazardous to the environment and health."
5. To reconnect Europe to its peoples, Macron foresees a conference for Europe that would allow Member States and European institutions "to engage with citizens' panels … academics, business and labour representatives, and religious and spiritual leaders" and "propose all the changes our political project needs."
6. In Macron's vision, not all Member States need to confirm with these changes. He would also accept the fact that a two-speed Europe would allow some countries to integrate further inside of the Union. This accounts, in particular, for monetary union reforms. According to Macron, a separate parliament should be established among the members of the Eurozone, which would allow a deeper integration of monetary policy at the EU level.

8.2.3   The Proposal of Annegret Kramp-Karrenbauer: More Supranationality Where It Matters

What is maybe most striking about Annegret Kramp-Karrenbauer's proposal (Kramp-Karrenbauer 2019) is its lack of a theoretical foundation, direction of where the EU should be going. It seems to be drafted solely in response to Macron's proposal and, hence, contains a rather defensive language. If at all, Kramp-Karrenbauer's vision encompassed the rejection of a European superstate. More concretely, Kramp-Karrenbauer outlines the following proposals[3]:

1. the EU should better protect its external borders
2. a Europe-wide pact and a commission for climate protection with consultation to ensure popular support
3. a permanent seat for the EU on the UN Security Council
4. a European Security Council involving the UK for foreign and security policies
5. an EU investment budget for joint research, development and technology
6. the European Parliament should focus its work in Brussels, rather than alternating with Strasbourg
7. Europe should try to shape a version of Islam that is compatible with its values—imams and teachers trained in the "tradition of enlightenment and tolerance"
8. EU officials should no longer be exempt from national income tax

8.3   ASSESSMENT

There have been many more proposals published for an institutional reform. Space constrains me to introduce them all. However, the ones presented here are the ones that, according to my subjective view, have been discussed the most. However, for each of these proposals, serious doubts can be raised as to whether they will really solve what has been identified as an institutional crisis in the EU:

---

[3] Outlined at https://www.dw.com/en/angela-merkel-successor-akk-responds-to-emmanuel-macrons-vision-for-europe/a-47840072

Dieter Grimm's proposal carries serious doubts as to whether such criticism based on insights and solutions from the area of state-nations can be transferred to supranational institutions such as the EU. Many of the criticism raised is not new and does not address the fact that the EU is a different "beast" than a state-nation. It could well be that the "shortfalls" identified are just tackled in a different way and to serve a different purpose in the EU compared to state-nations. For example, the Council acts in unity with the parliament as a "control organ" of the Commission to enforce the balance of powers. Hence looking at the relationship between parliament and Commission to identify a lack of control only is too limited. Kramp-Karrenbauer's criticism seems more like a knee-jerk reaction to the rising populism and anti-EU sentiment in Germany. It looks rather like a loose proposal of different aspects, where a connection to the EU as an institution and its underlying problems is difficult to find. Macron's assessment of the state of the Union as voiced in his Athens speech seems to be the most accurate description of the underlying problems of the EU, if one compares his assessment with the data we have on people's preference across the Union. However, the institutional changes he proposes in concreto are not really new and it is uncertain if they will be realizable at the EU level. Furthermore, Macron also lacks the provision of any evidence how these institutional reforms will combat the legitimacy and acceptance problems the EU faces.

So how to go on? In my view, the crisis of the EU is not the one of institutions but rather of the fact that, in large areas, the EU either jeopardizes EU citizen's satisfaction of preferences or fails to communicate how the EU contributes to citizen's satisfaction of preferences. Any institutional reforms will only have a marginal impact on this. Rather, a rigorous and continuous professional assessment of citizen's preferences across the Union and design of Union policy action based on such an assessment (within the boundaries of Union law) will succeed. It needs to be clear to Union citizens that the Union is better than the nation state in coordinating and pooling individual interest in the EU and defending it at an international level. Rather than appearing as a supranational regulatory state, the Union shall act more as a manager of different interests, pooling preferences and fostering solidarity among its members and existing institutions. The law plays a very important role in this, as the principle of solidarity, which has been buried in the Treaties for quite some time (Wunder 2019), shall be given a more prominent role (Purnhagen 2020b).

REFERENCES

Ehlermann, C-D. 1992. The European Communities, Its Law and Lawyers, (1992) 29 CmlRev, 218.

European Commission. 2017. White Paper on the Future of Europe, COM(2017)2025 of 1 March 2017. Available at https://ec.europa.eu/commission/sites/beta-political/files/white_paper_on_the_future_of_europe_en.pdf

Grimm, D. 2016. *Europa ja-aber welches? Zur Verfassung der europäischen Demokratie.* München: C.H. Beck.

Kramp-Karrenbauer, Annegret. 2019. Making Europe Right. *Die Welt*, March 10. Available at https://www.welt.de/politik/article190051703/Annegret-Kramp-Karrenbauer-Making-Europe-Right.html

Lenaerts, K. 2013. The Court's Outer and Inner Selves: Exploring the External and Internal Legitimacy of the European Court of Justice. In *Judging Europe's Judges*, ed. M. Adams, H. de Waele, J. Meeusen, and G. Straetmans, 15. Oxford: Hart.

Linsenmeier, K. 2016. Plädoyer für eine Reform der EU-Institutionen, August 25. Available at https://www.boell.de/de/2016/08/25/plaedoyer-fuer-eine-reform-der-eu-institutionen

Macron, E. 2017. European Union – Speech by the President of the French Republic. *Athens,* September 7. Available at https://www.diplomatie.gouv.fr/en/french-foreign-policy/european-union/events/article/european-union-speech-by-the-president-of-the-french-republic-athens-07-09-17

———. 2019. For European Renewal. *Paris*, March 4. Available at https://www.elysee.fr/emmanuel-macron/2019/03/04/for-european-renewal.en

Mancini, G. 1989. The Making of a Constitution for Europe, (1989) 26 CMLRev., pp. 595 et seq.

Purnhagen, K. 2013. *Systematization in EU Product Safety Law.* Dordrecht: Springer Science.

———. 2020a. European Integration: A Historical Overview. In *EU Bioeconomy Economics and Policies*, ed. L. Dries, W. Heijman, R. Jongeneel, and K. Purnhagen, 19–26. Cham: Palgrave.

———. 2020b. From Supranationality to Managing Diversity – A (re-)New(ed) Paradigm for the Establishment of the Internal Market? In *Internal Market 2.0*, ed. I. Govaere and S. Garben. Oxford: Hart (forthcoming).

Schmidt, S. 2018. *The European Court of Justice and the Policy Process: The Shadow of Case Law.* Oxford: Oxford University Press.

Weiler, J. 1993. Journey to an Unknown Destination. A Retroperspective and Prospective of the European Court of Justice in the Area of Political Integration. *Journal of Common Market Studies* 31: 417. et seq.

Wunder, A. 2019. The Usage of Solidarity in the Jurisdiction of the ECJ. In *The Transformation of Economic Law*, ed. L. de Almeida, M. Cantero, M. Durovic, and K.P. Purnhagen, 389–403. Oxford: Hart.

PART III

Agriculture

CHAPTER 9

Common Market Organisation

Huib Silvis and Roel Jongeneel

9.1 Introduction

9.1.1 Scope of the Common Market Organisation in Agriculture

The Common Market Organisation (CMO) is a set of rules which regulates agricultural markets in the European Union (EU). It builds on the rules for the common market in goods and services and covers specific policy tools for agricultural markets. The CMO sets out the parameters for

---

This chapter is a revision of Huib Silvis and Roald Lapperre, Chapter 8. Market, price and quota policy: from price support to safety net. In: Arie Oskam, Gerrit Meester and Huib Silvis (Eds) (2011), EU policy for Agriculture, Food and Rural Areas, Wageningen Academic Publishers.

H. Silvis
Performance and Impact Agrosectors, Wageningen Economic Research,
The Hague, The Netherlands
e-mail: huib.silvis@wur.nl

R. Jongeneel (✉)
Agricultural Economics and Rural Policy Group, Wageningen University,
Wageningen, Gelderland, The Netherlands
e-mail: roel.jongeneel@wur.nl

L. Dries et al. (eds.), *EU Bioeconomy Economics and Policies: Volume I*,
Palgrave Advances in Bioeconomy: Economics and Policies,
https://doi.org/10.1007/978-3-030-28634-7_9

intervening in agricultural markets and providing sector-specific support (e.g. for fruits and vegetables, wine, olive oil sectors, school schemes). It also includes rules on marketing of agricultural products (e.g. marketing standards, geographical indications, labelling) and the functioning of producer and interbranch organisations. Finally, it covers issues related to international trade (e.g. licenses, tariff quota management, inward and outward processing) and competition rules. The CMO's legal basis is Regulation (EU) No 1308/2013.[1]

9.1.2   Historical Background

Developing the common agricultural market made it necessary to remove trade barriers between the Member States. In this process, the existing agricultural market and price policies of the individual Member States were replaced by Common Market Organisations (CMOs). For a number of basic products, with a large agricultural area, the CMO system provided a common price floor. For many other products, market organisations were designed without such a price floor but with protection from external competition.

9.1.3   Successive Reforms

Although budgetary problems and environmental objectives played a role, the reduction of product price support was determined to a large degree by the pressure from trade partners. In the context of international trade liberalisation (The General Agreement on Tariffs and Trade [GATT]/ World Trade Organisation [WTO] negotiations), the EU's import restrictions came under pressure, and even more so its provision of export subsidies. With the MacSharry reform of 1992, this pressure led to a break with tradition in the Common Agricultural Policy (CAP), when it was decided to convert part of the market and price policy into income policy. Prices of supported agricultural products were lowered, and producers were compensated with direct payments. This action was reiterated by the reforms of Agenda 2000, the Fischler reform of 2003, the reforms of sev-

[1] https://ec.europa.eu/agriculture/markets_en

eral market organisations,[2] the so-called Health Check decisions of 2008 and the reform for the 2014–2020 period of 2013.

9.1.4   Structure of This Chapter

The direct income support policies are addressed in the next chapter. This chapter focuses on the agricultural market and price policies. Firstly, there will be a brief general overview of objectives and instruments of agricultural market and price policies (Sect. 9.2). Then, the original principles of the Common Agricultural Policy (Sect. 9.3) and the classic market organisations are described (Sect. 9.4). This is followed by an overview of the successive reforms in the main market organisations (Sect. 9.5). The reduction of the scope of classical market measures has been accompanied by a stronger emphasis in the CAP on a regulatory environment to strengthen farmers' organisational structures. In addition, a new directive has been prepared to protect farmers and small- and medium-sized businesses in the food supply chain against unfair trading practices (Sect. 9.6). The evolution of the Common Market Organisation in agriculture from price support to safety net is assessed in the final part (Sect. 9.7).

9.2   AGRICULTURAL MARKET AND PRICE POLICIES

9.2.1   Objectives

Due to their political sensitivity, food prices around the world are practically never left fully to the free market principles of supply and demand. However, government policies for these prices differ from country to country and over time (OECD 2018). Price measures and any quantity measures can be introduced to meet various objectives: (1) food security, (2) low food prices to keep wages low, (3) protection for producers and/or consumers against major price fluctuations and (4) support for the income of the farming population.

Since the 1930s, agricultural price policies in many industrialised Western countries have focused primarily on supporting farm incomes. Such policies express political wishes and reflect the economic ability of Western countries to give agriculture and the countryside a fair share in

---

[2] Mediterranean products (2004), sugar (2006), vegetables and fruit and wine (2007).

overall prosperity. As these policies are the result of compromise, conflicts and confusion among the bargaining players, they also reflect the balance of power between the various stakeholders.

9.2.2   Measures

A whole arsenal of instruments has been developed to influence the domestic price levels of agricultural products. In the EU, with its threatening surpluses of many agricultural products, these measures can broadly be divided into two categories: limiting supply and increasing demand. However, since nearly all agricultural products can be traded internationally, a domestic market policy cannot operate without trade policy instruments to control imports and exports.

Examples of supply-restricting measures are:

- direct production control measures, such as production quotas;
- temporary or permanent non-cultivation (set-aside) or extensification (lower yields or stocking rates) of agricultural land;
- taxing imports such that foreign supplies are reduced or even eliminated as no longer attractive;
- establishing import quotas.

Examples of demand-boosting measures are:

- granting subsidies on certain categories of domestic consumption;
- subsidising exports;
- compulsory use of domestically produced products;
- allowing producers to sell at a minimum price to official purchasing agencies.

An alternative to market and price policy is to influence agricultural income via direct income payments. This sort of compensation system leaves the commodity markets largely in the hands of private suppliers and purchasers. Measures at the border are then not necessary, so the domestic market may be open to the outside world.

Over time, and from product to product, the CAP has included both price and income support measures. Although price support is traditional EU policy, direct income compensation has been gaining ground since the MacSharry reform of 1992, and now accounts for the bulk of CAP expenditure.

9.2.3   Trade Distortion

The effects of the market and price policies on other countries form a sensitive issue. In the literature, direct payments are generally regarded as less trade-disruptive (distorting) than price support. It is generally acknowledged that decoupled income support may have an effect on production, but much less than price support or input support. The OECD (2018) regularly reports on the effects of the different support measures.

The largest distortion is caused by subsidies on inputs such as fertilisers, feed, water and energy, followed by market price support and output payments. Decoupled income payments based on historical entitlements have the least effect on production. Further economic analysis of these policy instruments can, for example, be found in Alston and James (2002) and Schmitz et al. (2010).

9.3   Principles of the CAP

In the discussions towards the Treaty of Rome, the original members of the EU-6 ultimately decided to include agriculture and trade in agricultural products as a separate chapter. As a result, agriculture occupied a peculiar position in the Treaty. This was not an easy decision, since earlier European initiatives to cooperate in agricultural policy matters had failed. Within the framework of the common market, a compromise was found to reconcile the divergent interests of France and Western Germany.

The separate 'Agriculture' chapter of the European Economic Community (EEC) Treaty stipulated in its first article that agriculture and trade in agricultural products should be part of the common market (Article 38 of the EEC Treaty; currently Article 32 of the EEC Treaty). The legislators foresaw that this could only be realized by developing a European substitute for the existing national agricultural market and price policies.

According to Article 39 of the Treaty of Rome, the initial objectives of the CAP were (1) to increase agricultural productivity, (2) to ensure a fair standard of living for the agricultural community, (3) to stabilize markets, (4) to assure the availability of supplies and (5) to ensure that supplies reach consumers at reasonable prices.

The core of the policy is the Great Grain Deal, which secured the agricultural interests of France—first of all grain production—in the cooperation with the more industrial-oriented West German Republic. Integrating the economies in Europe was aimed at achieving more stability and peace. Germany was all in favour of this policy, not least because it had much to gain from a large industrial market. Unlike Germany, France believed that its comparative economic strength was in agricultural production. Post-war France could therefore only agree to join the integration policies pro-vided it could expand its markets for agricultural products in Europe, in exchange as it were, for German industrial expansion (van den Noort 2011).

In the period 1958–1968, the so-called transition period, the CAP was gradually phased in. The emphasis from the start was on common market and price policy (rather than, say, 'structural' or farm development policy). This was understandable, since without such a policy it would not have been possible to create *one* large market for agricultural products, and thus to exploit the economic gains deriving from free competition and the 'law of one price', the fundamental rationale for the European Economic Community.

From the beginning, the Community's agricultural market and price policy rested on three principles:

Market unity, that is, completely free trade of agricultural products, amongst others, between the Member States. The aim was to have a large market for agricultural products, as created for industrial goods, without customs controls, commercial restrictions and anti-competitive subsidies. In order to achieve and maintain this market unity, it was necessary to introduce and stick to common price supports and compe-tition arrangements, to harmonise food safety, veterinary and phytos-anitary regulations, and (preferably) to maintain stable exchange rates amongst the national currencies.
Community preference, which implies a preference for domestic agricul-tural products above imported products. Often, variable import levies were used to buffer against world market price fluctuations.
Financial solidarity: in April 1962, the Member States decided to set up and contribute to a common budget fund, from which the CAP was financed, no matter on what product or in which Member State expen-diture was incurred.

Up to 1968, there were fixed exchange rates between the currencies of the Member States. Shortly afterwards, however, there were major exchange rate fluctuations, and the principle of market unity had to be abandoned for over 20 years. This resulted in considerable price differences of supported products between Member States; these were bridged with the help of a system of artificial 'green' exchange rates and monetary compensatory amounts (MCAs) for trade in farm products between Member States. The unity of market and price was finally restored at the start of the 'Single Market' on 1 January 1993 (Ritson and Swinbank 1997).

9.4 Classic Market Organisations

The CAP took the shape of a set of 'Common Market Organisations' (CMOs) or 'regimes' for agricultural products, that is, a collection of rules and regulations at the European level for a specific product (for example, milk) and derivative products (in this case, dairy products). The rules establish both quality requirements (definition of the products) and economic regulation (e.g. price supports). The latter consists of import and export measures at the borders, internal support measures and, where applicable, quantity restrictions such as milk quotas.

When the market and price policies were developed, account was taken of the major differences between the production and market conditions of agricultural and horticultural products, for example weather seasonality was important. An important distinction between the market organisations is whether they provide a stable internal price level or not.

9.4.1 Market Organisations with a Price Floor

Most attention was paid to a number of basic products (cereals, sugar, dairy, beef, wine and olive oil), which were selected for a 'classical' or 'heavy-duty' system of market organisation. These organisations were intended to achieve a certain price level in the market (the 'target price'), that is, the average price that the farmer should be able to get for his product. The measures required for this purpose can be divided into two categories: regulations at the EU border, on both imports and exports, and regulations for the internal market.

Import and export measures: products from third countries were not allowed to enter at the EU border below the 'threshold' price, derived from the target price. Whenever the world offer price was lower than the threshold price, a variable import levy bridged the difference. The counterparts of the import levies were subsidies for exports, the so-called export refunds, which facilitated exporting to third countries when world market

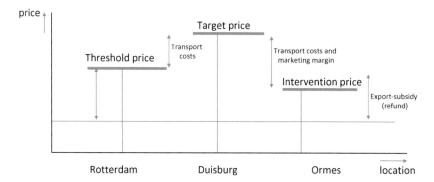

Fig. 9.1   Original price support system for cereals. (Source: Harris et al. 1983)

prices were below the internal level. The basic features of this market organisation for cereals are shown in Fig. 9.1.

Intervention and sales subsidies: alongside the external measures, the market organisations for basic products also provided measures for the internal market, giving the intervention agencies established in each Member State the opportunity to buy up products (fulfilling certain quality criteria) at a specified 'intervention' price, below which the product price was not supposed to drop. Initially, the possibility of intervention purchase was permanent for some products (butter and skimmed milk powder), and for others only during a certain period (e.g. grain) or depending on the market situation (wine, beef).

Another instrument for achieving market balance throughout the seasons was compensation payments for private storage, whereby the product was not bought up by public agencies, but remained in the possession of the company in question. Further, to prevent excessively bulky intervention stocks, sales and processing subsidies were regularly made available, for example, for the sale of skimmed milk powder for veal production or of butter to bakeries.

9.4.2   Other Market Organisations

The market organisations for products other than the basic products did not provide much price protection. As a rule, intervention purchases were not possible, for example, because the product was not easily stored. For products such as eggs, poultry meat, pork and many types of fruit and vegetables, which were less important at the start of the CAP, or whose production was less land-dependent, intervention purchases were seen as undesirable because production could easily be expanded. Moreover, price stabilisation was less necessary for some of these products because the market mechanism functioned adequately and excess stocks did not build up. The relevant CMOs therefore allowed for liberal pricing on the common market, but did provide border protection against low-priced imports from third countries, with import restrictions according to product group.

Oilseeds, and peas and beans grown for cattle fodder, formed a special case. In the 1960s, an agreement had been made in the GATT to allow the import of these products (e.g. soybeans from the USA) to take place almost free of import tariffs or customs duties. In order to guarantee a minimum price for domestic growers, premiums were granted to the EU processing industry for such products.

9.4.3   Relationship Between Market Organisations

In a certain sense, the market organisations for pork, poultry and eggs were complementary to those for grains. Support for grain prices increases feed prices for intensive livestock farming (including cattle). Without a market organisation for EU pig and poultry products, it would have been tempting to import these products from third countries, which could often produce on the basis of lower grain prices. The result would have been a greater grain surplus in the EU and a weaker position for its intensive livestock farms. It was therefore necessary to limit the import of intensive livestock products, and consequently the variable import levies on these products were formally linked to movements in cereal prices.

9.4.4   'Free' Products

For a number of products, no Common Market Organisation was established, for example, ware and seed potatoes, although the production of potato starch was supported as part of the cereals regime. Proposals for initiating a Common Market Organisation for potatoes were occasionally put on the political agenda. However, this never yielded results because of the different interests of Member States.

9.5   REFORM OF THE MARKET ORGANISATIONS

9.5.1   General Development

When imports from third countries are necessary to meet domestic demand, the system of market organisations for basic products can operate smoothly, as was the case for cereals and beef in the initial phase of the Community. In this situation, the import levies collected may be sufficient to fund the expenditures. In case, however, production grows or consumption falls in the long term, agricultural expenditure increases. When the market can no longer be 'cleared' with sales subsidies and export subsidies, market prices will fall to the intervention price level (or even below it, if high-quality criteria are used), and intervention stocks will grow. This move into the direction of unbalanced markets and rising agricultural expenditure was apparent from the outset of the CAP. This was combined with increasing pressure from third countries to integrate the EU market in the world market. In order to deal with these problems, the policy has been adapted several times. Table 9.1 gives a schematic overview of the key phases in the development of the CAP.

The classic CAP was generally regarded as one of the most protectionist farm policy regimes in the world: it protected farmers with guaranteed prices and import levies, while at the same time conferring market advantage on exporters via a system of export subsidies. Responding to widespread criticism from trading partners, the Uruguay trade round of the General Agreement on Tariffs and Trade (GATT) focused specifically on agriculture. This round not only resulted in the establishment of the World Trade Organisation (WTO) in 1995 but also in the Uruguay Round Agriculture Agreement (URAA). Under this agreement, the contracting parties agreed to reduce agricultural support and protection by establishing disciplines in the areas of market access, export subsidies and domestic support.

Market access provisions consisted of tariffication and of specific access provisions. Tariffication implied that non-tariff barriers had to be converted into tariff equivalents. The base period chosen was a period of very high protection levels, contributing to the retention of high tariffs under tariffication. To ensure that current and additional access opportunities were offered, countries had to establish tariff-rate quotas (TRQs), subject to low tariffs.

Table 9.1 Development of the EU agricultural market and price policies

Period	Characteristics
1960–1969	Establishment of different Common Market Organisations
1970–1980	In the early 1970s, sharp rises in world agricultural prices led to concerns over import dependency on protein sources. When world prices later declined, a strong agricultural income-oriented market and price policy was pursued. However, the product markets seemed to be less manageable than previously, causing major problems of surpluses and high expenditures.
1981–1992	Existing systems reached a breaking point; price reductions were introduced when production thresholds were exceeded; milk quotas came into force. Environmental problems received more attention; the EU came under huge pressure in the GATT to change the CAP.
1992–2003	Transformation—started by the MacSharry reforms of 1992 and followed by the 1999 decisions on Agenda 2000—to price reduction and farm income compensation, coupled to volume restrictions (set-aside obligation) and a more market-oriented approach
2003–2008	In the Fischler (2003/2004) and the Health Check (2008) reforms, direct payments were largely decoupled (from current production) and management guidelines (cross compliance) were introduced. Export refunds were substantially reduced and price support that survived previous reforms was phased out (dairy).
2013	The main purpose of the new CMO Regulation is to provide a safety net to agricultural markets through the use of market support tools, exceptional measures and aid schemes for certain sectors (in particular fruit and vegetables and wine), as well as to encourage producer cooperation through producer organisations and specific rules on competition, and to lay down marketing standards for certain products

Source: Own presentation

Export subsidy commitments implied a reduction of a country's volume of subsidised exports by 21% and a reduction of the value of export subsidies by 36% during the implementation period 1995–2000. Although with some exceptions, the base period had been set at 1986–1990.

Domestic support policies have been segregated into three main categories, to indicate the relative acceptability of the policies: the amber box, the blue box and the green box. Only the domestic policies that deemed to have the largest effect on production and trade, the so-called amber-box policies, were subjected to limitations. In general, these policies provide economic incentives to producers to increase current resource use or current production ('coupled' incentives). The support category that had

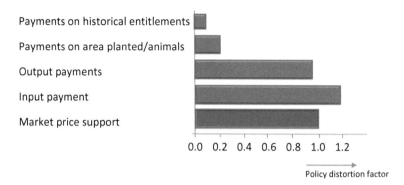

Fig. 9.2   Trade-disruptive effects of different forms of price and income support in comparison to market price support. (Source: OECD 2002)

to be reduced is quantified by the Aggregate Measure of Support (AMS), which had to be reduced by 20% from 1995 to 2000, in comparison with the base period level (1986–1988). Support measures placed in the blue box were in fact amber box payments related to supply management programmes. This box is viewed as a special exemption category to accommodate the USA and the EU. Green box policies have been considered to have the smallest effects on production and trade. Hence, these policies, which include decoupled income payments, were fully exempted from support reduction commitments.

In the early 1980s, rapidly expanding dairy expenditure was tackled by means of milk marketing quotas. The change from price support to direct payments, in particular for cereals and beef, which began in the 1990s, also caused increased budget expenditure (Fig. 9.2). The increase in decoupled payments after 2005 reflects the transition to the Single Payment Scheme.

The following paragraphs describe the specific changes in some of the most important Common Market Organisations.

9.5.2   Cereals, Oilseeds and Protein Crops

The original market organisation for cereals was threatened by the growing use in compound animal feed of competing 'cereal substitute' products, such as tapioca, cereal residues, maize gluten feed and fruit pulp (Harris et al. 1983, 354), whose imports—mainly from the USA, Latin

America and Thailand (tapioca)—increased while cereal consumption fell by 1.5% to 2% annually. When the EU became more than self-sufficient in cereals around 1980, there was a 'voluntary' agreement with Thailand to stabilise its supplies of tapioca to the EU. Subsequently, a 'guarantee threshold' was introduced for domestic EU cereal production; if production exceeded this threshold, a discount of 3% was to be applied to the next set of support prices. Later in the 1980s, a 'co-responsibility levy' was imposed. Similar guarantee threshold formulae (stabilisers) were drawn up for oilseeds and some protein crops. Decisions of 1988 also comprised voluntary regulations for setting aside grain acreage for one or five years. However, none of these various measures prevented a persistent rise in Community cereal production.

9.5.3   MacSharry Reform

This increase in production was an important argument for the MacSharry reform (named after the then European commissioner) of the EU's agricultural policy in 1992. The reform package was agreed bilaterally with the USA (Blair House agreement) and paved the way for the agriculture agreement in the GATT/WTO Uruguay Round. The package was partly concerned with restoring the market balance for agricultural products, but also with strengthening the EU's international competitive position. The finally agreed reform contained a fundamental change from price support tied to product marketing to direct income support in the form of area payments. The reform decisions for cereals boiled down to a reduction in EU prices by about 30% over a three-year period, with full compensation of the calculated decrease in gross revenue.

For larger growers of cereals, the payments were conditional on setting aside at least 15% of their area of these products. Due to the reduction in grain stocks, this set-aside percentage was decreased gradually. The reform resulted in an increase of budget expenditure for arable products by 80%— almost entirely for area payments.

The set-aside rule and area payments also applied to oilseeds and some protein crops, for which the support system had been challenged by the USA in the GATT. The oilseed agreement with the USA reached in June 1993 and ratified by GATT provides for a maximum acreage of about 5 million hectares for these crops in the EU.

9.5.4   The Agenda 2000, Fischler and Health Check Reforms

For the above arable products, the Agenda 2000 reform was much less radical than that of 1992. However, cereal prices were again reduced, this time by 15%. The compensatory payments in Agenda 2000 were limited to about 50% of the gross price reduction.

At the time of the Mid-Term Review (MTR), better known now as the Fischler reform, of June 2003, it was decided to implement complete decoupling of support with the introduction of the Single Payment Scheme. Member States did however get the opportunity to have 25% of the payments per hectare coupled to production. The intervention arrangements for cereals remained unchanged, with the exception of that for rye, which disappeared. Due to market pressures, it was decided in 2007 to lower the set-aside percentage to 0%, and set-aside was abolished in the 2008 Health Check. Import tariffs for cereals were also suspended (though re-imposed in autumn 2008).

As a consequence of these reforms, the cereal sector went over a decade from being in surplus to one for which the EU had unilaterally reduced all import protection to zero—a unique development arising from radical internal reforms *and* a dramatic rise in grain prices on the world market, caused by the rapid economic growth in Asia and the accompanying increase in demand for animal proteins. In addition, the demand for bio-fuels has risen sharply, in the face of high oil prices and strong backing from various different governments.

A concrete result of the CAP reforms is thus that the intervention price of wheat for European farmers has been cut by almost 50%. EU market prices line up with those of leading exporters.

9.5.5   Sugar

The EU is the world's leading producer of beet sugar (roughly 50% of the total). However, beet sugar represents only 20% of the world's sugar production; the other 80% is produced from sugar cane. Most of the EU's sugar beet is grown in the northern half of Europe, where the climate is more suited for growing beet. The EU also has an important refining industry that processes imported raw cane sugar.

From the outset of the sugar market organisation in the 1960s, the EU restricted its price guarantees to a certain volume of production. Each producer was entitled to the full guaranteed price only for a basic 'A quota', subject to a low 2% levy for financing the system. For an additional 'B quota', a high levy up to 39.5% was applied. Sugar produced above these quotas, the so-called C sugar, had in principle to be sold without support on the world market, and so yielded no more than the world market price, usually no more than 30 to 50% of the internal EU price. Beet producers in some Member States received a pooled price.

The sugar market organisation also provided rigorous import protection. In the context of the Lomé agreement, the EU had made preferential import agreements for sugar with the 'African, Caribbean and Pacific (ACP)' countries in Africa, the Caribbean and the Pacific. This arrangement consisted of a 1.3 million tonne duty-free import quota, for which these countries then received the high EU sugar price. This was subjected to increasing criticism from other countries and the WTO, which judged in 2004 that aspects of the sugar market organisation were contrary to its rules. In the context of the Everything But Arms (EBA) initiative, the EU had also agreed to let the least developed countries (LDCs) sell sugar on the EU market without import tariff from 2009.

So, it was decided in 2006 to reduce the official sugar price by 36%. Sugar-exporting ACP countries lost part of the price premium on their preferential sales into the EU. The estimated loss of income suffered by domestic beet growers was partially (64%) compensated with a payment decoupled from production, and intervention was limited to 600,000 tonnes per year. The second crucial element of the 2006 reform was a restructuring fund that offered to buy back the production rights of EU sugar producers. European sugar production reduced in 2009 by a third compared to 2006, with the consequence that within a short period of time the EU has been transformed from a major net exporter of sugar to a key net importer, in particular of sugar from the poorest developing countries. Along with the disappearance of export refunds for sugar in 2008 and the dismantling of the intervention mechanism into a 'safety net' since 2006, the sugar policy looks more like that for the other arable products. For the first time in a very long period, no market and price support payments for sugar were budgeted for 2010.

The sugar quota system was scrapped on 30 September 2017, after nearly 50 years. The decision to end the sugar quotas was then agreed in the 2013 reform of the Common Agricultural Policy (CAP), after the restructuring process initiated in 2006. The end of the quota system gives producers the possibility to adjust their production to real commercial opportunities. It also significantly simplifies the current policy management and administrative burden for operators, growers and traders. Various measures can be used to continue supporting the EU sugar sector to face unexpected disturbances on the market. This includes a substantial EU import tariff (outside preferential trade agreements) and the possibility to give support for private storage and crisis measures that would allow the Commission to take action in case of severe market crisis involving a sharp increase or decrease of market prices. The possibility to collectively negoti-ate value sharing terms in the contracts between EU beet producers and sugar processors is maintained after the end of the quotas. The European Commission has also improved transparency on the sugar market in antici-pation of the end of the quota system. A new Sugar Market Observatory provides short-term analysis and statistics about the sugar market, as well as analysis and outlook to help farmers and processors manage their busi-nesses more effectively.

According to EU Regulation 1307–2013, Member States (MSs) are allowed to use part of their national envelope for direct payments for cou-pled support in certain clearly defined cases. With respect to sugar beet production, 10 MSs in 2015 and 2016, and 11 in 2017, decided to apply Voluntary Coupled Support (VCS) to the sugar beet sector. The coupled payments tend to be granted in a generic way, applying to all sugar beet-producing regions within an MS rather than targeted at specific regions facing difficulty (Smit et al. 2017).

9.5.6   Dairy

The dairy market posed problems practically from the outset of the CAP, because production was rising too fast. To combat this, various measures were taken over the years, such as sales subsidies, herd conversion (to beef) and slaughter premiums, price reductions and producer co-respon-sibility levies. Milk converted to intervention stocks of butter and skimmed milk powder caused large budget costs, leading to the introduc-tion of milk quotas in 1984. This was officially intended to be a tempo-rary measure till 1988, but was extended several times. In the first instance, the total EU milk quota was equal to the 1981 supplies plus 1%, but later a substantial reduction was deemed necessary, and only at the end of the 1990s were the quotas slightly expanded again. Expenditure on the dairy regime fell steadily from the mid-1980s, with a particularly strong decline in the expenditure on storage and domestic sales in the years up to 2009.

The milk marketing quotas were allocated to individual businesses, and exceeding these quotas resulted in a high 'super' levy, initially set at 115% of the target price. The quotas were tradeable within many, but not between, Member States, some of whom still saw the quotas as an important measure for preserving milk production in economically fragile agricultural areas.

Since WTO developments indicated that export support had to be phased out and that import tariffs had to be reduced, it was decided in June 2003 to lower the intervention prices for skimmed milk powder and butter by 15% and 25%, respectively, causing the fresh milk price to also fall. Compensation of approximately 60% was paid out for this, with payments—in total about €5 billion—linked for the first few years to the quota, but since about 2007 included in the Single Payment Scheme.

Due to the support price reductions and the high prices for dairy products on the world market, price support measures such as export refunds, domestic sales measures (bakers' butter, milk powder for feed) and intervention could be dismantled. By mid-2007, there were no intervention stocks for dairy products, and after the Health Check reform of 2008, intervention against a guaranteed price was limited to relatively small amounts. Prices of dairy products fell sharply in the course of 2009, and as a result, intervention rules were changed so as to enable intervention for a longer period than originally foreseen.

Now that price support in the dairy sector has been largely replaced by decoupled direct income support, the discussion on ending milk quotas reappeared on the agenda. During the negotiations on the Health Check proposals, there was a clear majority of Member States in favour of discarding quotas by the anticipated final date of 1 April 2015. Following a 2% quota increase in 2008/09, a 'soft landing' was approached in most Member States by increasing quotas by 1% every year between 2009/10 and 2013/14.

In December 2010, the Commission proposed new legislation to regulate the dairy production chain. The legal changes provide for optional written contracts between milk producers and processors to be drawn up in advance of deliveries, which should include details of price, timing and volume of deliveries, and duration. Member States could make the use of such contracts compulsory in their territory. To rebalance bargaining power in the supply chain, dairy farmers were allowed to negotiate contracts collectively through producer organisations (see Sect. 9.6).

9.5.7   Beef

The common regime for beef encountered few problems until the 1980s, because the EU was a net importer. The situation changed with the introduction of milk quotas, which caused cattle farmers to switch to beef production. The increase in supply resulted in huge intervention stocks and exports to third countries, and thus to rising EU spending. These market problems were addressed by changes in the beef intervention policy, mainly with respect to quality requirements, purchasing periods and price levels.

In the context of the 1992 reforms, more far-reaching decisions were taken, similar to those for cereals. The intervention prices were lowered by 15% over three years, a ceiling was put in place for intervention purchases, and the 'headage' premiums for steers and suckler cows were raised. Maxima per farm and per hectare were intended to extensify beef production and to provide more opportunities for cattle farmers in areas 'disadvantaged by nature', for example, mountainous regions. As with grain, the reform of the beef policy led to an increase in the required budget, and the BSE crisis in the 1990s added the extra burden. After 2000, however, expenditure on interventions and refunds fell sharply, but spending on direct premiums rose. In 2006, most of the premiums were included in the single farm payments.

9.5.8   Single Common Market Organisation

Until 2007, the EU operated 21 separate Common Market Organisations (CMOs), each governed by its own basic Regulation. However, the Commission had been seeking to reform the CAP by moving away from the traditional approach of support measures for specific production sectors. Another significant objective was to make the functioning of the EU simpler and less bureaucratic. With its multitude of legislation covering a wide range of production sectors, the CAP was a clear target for such rationalisation. Most of the regulations followed the same structure and had numerous provisions in common, for example, rules relating to the internal market and to trade with third countries.

The Commission therefore amalgamated the provisions of the sector regulations into a single legal framework, replacing the sectoral approaches by 'horizontal' ones where possible and appropriate. Regulation 1234/2007 (Council of the EU 2007) was agreed to by EU agriculture ministers on 12 June 2007, and, after a period of phased entry into force, became fully active from 1 January 2009. Many of the decisions taken as part of the CAP Health Check in November 2008 affected the substance of this regulation, and it was formally amended by Regulation 72/2009.

The single CMO sets out the rules on intervention mechanisms (private storage aid, public storage, special measures, production quotas), specific aid schemes and trade with third countries (imports and exports). The CMO retains special clauses for different sectors. Moreover, it contains rules on state aid and competition. In principle, products covered by the CAP are subject to the basic aid and competition provisions set out in Articles 81 to 86 of the EC Treaty, except where a derogation is provided under the Regulation. The scope for such derogation is not small, as it covers 'agreements, decisions and practices' necessary for the attainment of the objectives of the CAP. In particular, normal competition law does not apply to the operations of producer organisations operating within the scope of the CAP.

In the day-to-day management of the agricultural markets for products covered by the CMO, the European Commission is assisted by the Management Committee for the Common Organisation of Agricultural Markets. This committee is attended by Member State experts on a specific commodity, depending on which issues are on the agenda for discussion.

9.5.9 Further Reforms

The core element of the reform process of the CAP has been the shift from product price support to producer income support. It has become more market-oriented and less reliant on the management of markets than before. Market instruments are used to provide market safety nets, but intervention prices are set at low levels which ensure that they are only used in times of real crisis. In terms of achieving more market orientation, the Health Check agreement of 2008 resulted in fewer and simpler market instruments. The remaining coupled payments were decoupled. The only (but important) exceptions are for the suckler cow, goat and sheep premia, where Member States may maintain coupled support. In addition, MSs were allowed to use part of their national envelope for direct payments for coupled support in certain clearly defined cases (Direct Payment Regulation (EU) 1307/2013, Art. 52–55). An example is the VCS for sugar.

The objective of past reforms to enhance the market orientation of EU agriculture is continued by adapting the policy instruments to further encourage farmers to base their production decisions on market signals. Competitiveness is addressed directly by changes to market mechanisms, particularly the removal of production constraints. All of the restrictions on production volumes for sugar, dairy and the wine sector have been ended.

Promotion campaigns about EU farm products are designed to open up new market opportunities for EU farmers and the wider food industry, as well as for helping them build their existing business. EU funding—rising from €142.5 million in 2017 to €188.5 million in 2018 and €200 million in 2020—can be used for information and promotion initiatives in EU Member States and countries outside the EU. The 2019 work programme focuses on campaigns aimed at non-EU countries with the highest potential for growth such as Canada, Japan, Mexico and Korea. Within the EU itself, the EU will co-finance campaigns designed to promote the different EU quality schemes and labels (organic, protected designation of origin [PDO], protected geographical indication [PGI], traditional speciality guaranteed [TSG], product of EU's outermost regions).

Applicable since the 1 August 2017, the school fruit, vegetables and milk scheme combines the two previous schemes (school fruit and vegetables scheme and school milk scheme). The total EU budget for the scheme is €250 million per school year, with €150 million for fruit and vegetables and €100 million for milk.

The Omnibus regulation (EU Regulation 2017/2393), endorsed on 16 October 2017, amends the financial regulation governing the implementation of the EU budget and 15 sectorial legislative acts, including agriculture. The Omnibus regulation for agriculture brought several changes in the implementation of the Common Agricultural Policy, aiming to simplify the implementation of the policy.

9.6   GOVERNANCE OF MARKETS

9.6.1   Support for Producer and Interbranch Organisations

The reduction of the scope of classical market measures in the CAP has recently been accompanied by a stronger emphasis on a regulatory environment to strengthen farmers' organisational structures. The 2013 reform of the EU's Common Market Organisation regulation enhanced governance of cooperation among producers—in particular through an emphasis on producer organisations, their associations and interbranch organisations.

Producer organisations (whether or not organised as cooperatives) contribute to strengthening the position of producers versus other downstream actors in the food supply chain by carrying out a wide array of activities (e.g. concentrating supply, improving marketing, providing assistance to their members, etc.). By working more closely with one another, producers are able to achieve economies of scales and synergies to process and market the products of their members.

Associations of producer organisations have a dual purpose: they play the same role as producer organisations and they also coordinate the activities of their member organisations.

Interbranch organisations are vertically integrated organisations which comprise producers and at least one member of the processing or trading part of the supply chain. Interbranch organisations provide a means of allowing dialogue between actors in the supply chain, and in promoting best practices and market transparency.

Under certain conditions, the rules adopted by recognised producer organisations, associations of producer organisations and Interbranch organisations can be extended to non-members. Under certain circumstances, non-members which benefit from the activities of these organisations shall pay financial contributions to the organisation.

For some of their activities, recognised producer organisations and interbranch organisations are granted derogations from the application of the Treaty's competition provisions.

In the fruit and vegetables sector, which has a tradition in policy support for producer organisations, the CMO Regulation provides for withdrawal of products by producer organisations under certain conditions (Article 33 CMO Regulation).

For the milk sector, producer organisations are allowed to carry out joint sales on behalf of their farmer members.

For three other sectors, that is, olive oil, beef and veal and certain arable crops, the Commission adopted guidelines on joint selling. The guidelines help explain to farmers in these sectors how, if certain conditions are fulfilled, they can jointly sell their products in compliance with EU competition rules.

Special supply management rules exist for protected designations of origin and geographical indications for cheese and ham, as well as for wine.

The basic principle of these derogations is that the potential negative impact of joint selling is compensated by the effects of other potentially efficiency enhancing activities not directly related to the selling of products (e.g. joint packaging, joint processing or joint procurement of inputs). This leads to an integration of the activities of producers that should generate gains in efficiencies. The combination of commercialisation-related activities with other types of activities aims at improving the resilience and competitiveness of producers, thereby reinforcing their position in the supply chain. The reinforced legal framework for producer organisations is backed by financial incentives under the second pillar.

9.6.2   Protection Against Unfair Trading Practices

To improve farmers' and small- and medium-sized businesses' position in the food supply chain, on 19 December 2018 the European Commission and Council reached a political agreement on new legislation on unfair trading practices.

Unfair trading practices (UTPs) are business-to-business practices that deviate from good commercial conduct and are contrary to good faith and fair dealing. The food supply chain is vulnerable to UTPs due to stark imbalances between small and large operators. Often farmers and small operators in the food supply chain do not have sufficient bargaining power to defend against UTPs.

Although many EU member countries already have different national rules on UTPs, in some countries there is no or only ineffective specific protection against UTPs. The new directive will, for the first time, ensure a standard level of protection across all EU countries.

The Commission and the Council have reached a political agreement on a new set of rules to improve the role of farmers in the agricultural and food supply chain by banning some of the most common unfair trading practices that they face.

9.6.3   Ten Blacklisted Unfair Trading Practices

1. Payments later than 30 days for perishable agricultural and food products
2. Payment later than 60 days for other agri-food products
3. Short-notice cancellations of perishable agri-food products

4. Unilateral contract changes by the buyer
5. Payments not related to a specific transaction
6. Risk of loss and deterioration transferred to the supplier
7. Refusal of a written confirmation of a supply agreement by the buyer, despite request by the supplier
8. Misuse of trade secrets by the buyer
9. Commercial retaliation by the buyer
10. Transferring the costs of examining customer complaints to the supplier

In addition, grey practices concern activities of promotion, marketing and advertising for which the buyer offers certain services to the supplier to better promote his product, but expects the supplier to contribute to the costs. These practices are allowed subject to clear and unambiguous agreement beforehand.

The UTP Directive aims to protect only those suppliers which due to a weak bargaining position need such protection. The Directive offers protection along the agri-food supply chain depending on the relative size of operators. It uses a 'step approach' based on turnover figures as a proxy that reflects the different bargaining powers of suppliers and buyers. The step approach protects a supplier from unfair trading practices engaged in by an economically stronger buyer—for example, a farmer with less than €2 million turnover is protected against buyers with a turnover exceeding €2 million. Smaller suppliers above €2 million and not exceeding €10 million are protected against buyers which have a turnover higher than €10 million. The protective effect covers suppliers having turnovers of up to €350 million.

Trading partners with larger bargaining power (> €350 million turnover) can often address issues in their contractual negotiations without need for regulatory intervention. If Member States wanted to provide protection for larger suppliers, they could do so under their national laws (due the minimum harmonisation approach chosen).

The relevant turnover is established according to the criteria of the Small and Medium Enterprises (SME) recommendation 2003/361/EC. This means that in order to establish the turnover of a supplier or a buyer, the turnover of the group, of which they are possibly members, will also be taken into account. A supplier who sells to a public authority can rely on the protection against unfair behaviour of the public authority regardless of turnover considerations.

The Directive on unfair trading practices in the agricultural and food supply chain is scheduled to be adopted in April 2019. Member States will transpose the Directive into national law by April 2021 and apply it six months later.

The UTP Directive forms an integral part of a wider governance agenda of the Commission to countervail occurrences of unfair and ineffective competition. Other examples are increased possibilities of producer cooperation in the Omnibus initiative that entered into force on 1 January 2018, as well as measures undertaken by the Commission to enhance market transparency. This policy agenda is following up on the proposals made in the November 2016 report of the Agricultural Markets Task Force, a high-level group initiated by Commissioner Hogan (AMTF 2016).

9.7   Assessment

From the outset of the CAP, the chosen system of protecting external borders and introducing price support measures on the internal market enabled the prices of the basic products to be kept relatively high and stable in comparison to those on the world market. This was often seen by non-EU countries as the creation of 'Fortress Europe'. In response to problems of market imbalances (the supply of supported products was increasing faster than demand), leading to increasing budgetary expenditures and problems with trade partners, the original system was adapted numerous times over the successive decades.

Policy reforms have considerably reduced the level and improved the composition of support by making it less market-distortive. The changes in price support to agriculture since the 1980s are reflected in the ratio of producer to border prices. In contrast to recent levels, the EU level was higher than the OECD average and much higher than that of the USA in the 1980s (Table 9.2).

Table 9.2   Ratio of producer to border price in EU, USA and OECD, 1986–2017

	1986–1988	1995–1997	2015–2017
EU	1.69	1.33	1.05
USA	1.12	1.06	1.03
OECD	1.48	1.30	1.10

Source: OECD (2018)

The subsequent reforms have gradually transformed the Common Market Organisation from a product price support system into a market oriented system with safety net provisions to account for the handling of extreme shocks. It should be reminded that the successful reduction of price support has very much depended on the compensation of income effects by direct payments, which is the topic of the next chapter.

REFERENCES

Alston, J., and J. James. 2002. The Incidence of Agricultural Policy. *Handbook of Agricultural Economics* 2B: 1689–1749.

AMTF. 2016. *Improving Market Outcomes, Enhancing the Position of Farmers in the Supply Chain.* Brussels: Agricultural Markets Task Force, Report November 2016.

Council of the EU. 2007. Council Regulation (EC) No 1234/2007; Establishing a Common Organisation of Agricultural Markets and on Specific Provisions for Certain Agricultural Products (Single CMO Regulation). *Official Journal of the European Union* 299 (1): 1–149.

Harris, S., A. Swinbank, and G. Wilkinson. 1983. *The Food and Farm Policies of the European Community.* Chichester: Wiley.

OECD. 2002. *Agricultural Policies in OECD Countries: A Positive Reform Agenda.* Paris: OECD.

———. 2018. *Agricultural Policy Monitoring and Evaluation 2018.* Paris. https://www.oecd-ilibrary.org/agriculture-and-food/agricultural-policy-monitoring-and-evaluation-2018_agr_pol-2018-en

Ritson, C., and A. Swinbank. 1997. Europe's Green Money. In *The Common Agricultural Policy*, ed. C. Ritson and D. Harvey. Wallingford: CAB-International.

Schmitz, A., C.B. Moss, T.G. Schmitz, H.W. Furtan, and H.C. Schmitz. 2010. Agricultural Policy, Agribusiness, and Rent-Seeking Behaviour. *University of Toronto Press* 38 (2): 291–294.

Smit, A.B., R.A. Jongeneel, H. Prins, J.H. Jager, and W.H.G.J. Hennen. 2017. *Impact of Coupled Support for Sugar Beet Growing in the EU: More Sugar Beets and Lower Sugar Beet Price.* Wageningen: Wageningen Economic Research, Report 2017-114.

van den Noort, P.C. 2011. European Integration and Agricultural Protection: An Introduction. In *International Handbook on the Economics of Integration*, ed. M.N. Jovanovic, vol. III. Chapter 9. Cheltenham: Edward Elgar.

INTERNET

http://ec.europa.eu/comm/agriculture/
http://capreform.eu/

CHAPTER 10

Direct Income Support and Cross-compliance

Roel Jongeneel

10.1 INTRODUCTION

10.1.1 Mac Sharry Reform

The Mac Sharry reforms, agreed in 1992, represented an important change in the evolution of the common agricultural practices (CAP), since it partly replaced market price support per tonne, litre, and so on with direct payments per hectare or animal. As a result of this watershed reform, income transfers to farmers became more direct and visible. The income support objective formulated in the Treaty of Rome (1957) (see Chap. 3)

This chapter is a revision of Roel Jongeneel and Hans Brand, Chapter 9. Direct income support and cross-compliance. In: Arie Oskam, Gerrit Meester and Huib Silvis (Eds) (2011), EU policy for Agriculture, Food and Rural Areas, Wageningen Academic Publishers.

R. Jongeneel (✉)
Agricultural Economics and Rural Policy Group, Wageningen University, Wageningen, Gelderland, The Netherlands
e-mail: roel.jongeneel@wur.nl

© The Author(s) 2019
L. Dries et al. (eds.), *EU Bioeconomy Economics and Policies: Volume I*,
Palgrave Advances in Bioeconomy: Economics and Policies,
https://doi.org/10.1007/978-3-030-28634-7_10

125

is still relevant: farmers should be ensured a 'fair income'.[1] Farm incomes are widely supported in the industrialized countries, with arguments to justify this support including equity concerns, market failures and rigidities which characteristically hamper adjustments in agricultural factor markets, and, last but not least, lobbying and rent-seeking by farm interest groups (see e.g. Gardner 1986; Swinnen 2008).

10.1.2   From Price Support to Direct Payments

The switch from price support to direct payments was first applied to the major crops, notably cereals. In addition, compulsory set-aside was imposed on the arable sector. Also, livestock headage payments were introduced, the total amount of which was limited to predetermined maximum eligible livestock numbers (see also Chap. 9). Later on, this type of reform was deepened and extended to other sectors (e.g. dairying and later on to fruit, vegetables, and wine). The Mac Sharry reform started at 100 per cent compensation by direct payments of calculated revenue loss associated with the abolition of price support. In later reforms the announced price declines were only partly compensated, at rates between 50 and 70 per cent.

The majority of the CAP expenditure now consists of direct payments. In order to comply with World Trade Organization (WTO) rules on agricultural support, these payments are, since the Fischler reform of 2003 and the Health Check of 2008, largely (more than 90 per cent) decoupled from production, but linked to sustainability criteria: compliance with minimum standards related to food safety, hygiene, environment, animal welfare, and land management is added as a side condition to receive these payments. Non-compliance with these standards can lead to payment reductions or exclusions.

This chapter is organized as follows. Section 10.2 elaborates on direct income support, how it is decoupled from production, and the way in which member states have implemented the payments. Section 10.3 focuses on cross-compliance and the evolution of this conditionality. Also, compliance levels and impacts on competitiveness are discussed. Section 10.4 discusses the compatibility of direct income support with the WTO criteria on

---

[1] With what is a 'fair income' never being defined, this objective remains a vague policy objective.

trade liberalization. Section 10.5 provides a brief ex post impact assessment of both the single payment scheme (SPS) and cross-compliance.

10.2   DIRECT INCOME SUPPORT AND DECOUPLING

10.2.1   *Transition to Direct Payments*

The EU's notable agricultural policy reform in switching from classical market price support to direct payments is not without precedent in the theory and practice of agricultural policymaking. Economic theory, in particular welfare economics, emphasizes the distortive nature of price support and argues that prices should reflect scarcity (or abundance). Income support should be pursued by other measures, preferably lump sum payments to beneficiaries or some other form of non-distortive direct payments. Following this logic, a succession of agricultural economists from the 1960s onwards have advocated the use of 'decoupled' compensation payments in CAP reform, for example, the van Riemsdijk (1973) proposals, and the 'bond scheme' advocated by Tangermann and Swinbank amongst others (see Swinbank and Tranter 2004). Moreover, even the CAP itself included some direct payments, notably in less-favoured areas since the 1970s.

Although direct payments to farmers increased steadily in importance after the Mac Sharry reform of 1992, they were initially not decoupled from current levels of farm production, and their combination with compulsory set-aside aimed at curbing cereal production did not guarantee neutrality with respect to impacts on production. Therefore, the direct payments were criticized as still being distortive, and for this reason the WTO considered them as part of the so-called blue box of policy measures which should be dismantled over time. With the 2003 Mid-Term Review/Fischler reform, however, an important next step in decoupling was taken (Swinnen 2008) with the introduction of the Single Farm Payment (SFP) in the EU-15 and the Single Area Payment Scheme (SAPS) in most of the new member states (NMSs). By 2006, 82 per cent of EU direct payments were decoupled from specific output or resource levels, and this share further increased to 92 per cent after the full implementation of the 2008 Health Check decisions. Although receipt of the SFPs still requires that SFP 'entitlements' are tied to the number of 'eligible hectares', EU farmers now choose their production patterns in the light of (less distorted) market price signals. Initial exceptions for areas used for vegetables, fruits, or potatoes were reduced when such land also became eligible for payment entitlements (Regulation 1182/2007).

10.2.2   Minimizing Distortionary Impacts of Support

Direct payments are aimed at having minimal or no allocative effects (see Table 10.1). Thus they can be considered as 'real' income support and come close to the 'ideal' lump sum payments of economic theory. However, there is still some debate about the extent to which 'decoupled' really means that support is completely delinked from production. Indeed, a number of effects that might directly or indirectly affect production have been discussed in the literature. *First*, direct payments influence the farmers' income levels and thus have a so-called wealth effect (Féménia et al. 2010). As a result of this, farmers may change their behaviour, for example, by reducing their labour input on the farm. *Second*, since a significant share of farmers produce at a loss (revenues do not cover full costs), direct payments contribute to allowing such firms to stay in business (Key and Roberts 2009). As such, they may slow the evolution of the structure of agricultural production. *Third*, farmers are often risk-averse. With direct payments, part of their returns now have a rather fixed and stable pattern, with a relative decline in the part depending on fluctuating prices or uncertainties associated with weather and diseases (Severini et al. 2016). This may induce farmers to go for riskier enterprises, with a positive impact on associated outputs and input use. *Fourth*, direct payments are likely to impact on land prices, in particular when these payments based on historical production entitlements are 'converted' into an amount per hectare of land (Ciaian and Swinnen 2006). The impact on land prices has been widely acknowledged, even by the proponents of decoupled payments. Changed (higher) land prices affect the distribution of benefits and costs between landowners and tenants, the relative price structure faced by farmers, their costs, income, wealth, and so on, and as such are likely to affect their behaviour. The extent to which this will be the case depends on the elasticity of land transactions with respect to its price, which is generally found to be very low. Swinnen, Ciaian, and Kancs (2008) concluded that "*[o]n average, the impact on land markets of the change to the SPS appears to be weak and did not lead to lower capitalisation than under coupled policies*", though some variation among the EU-15 study countries and regions was observed. *Fifth*, there might be a so-called liquidity effect: if farmers are constrained by lack of cash or credit, the availability of direct

Table 10.1 Direct payments and their targeting

Direct payment	Description
Obligatory direct payment measures	
Basic payment	The basic payment ensures basic income support for farmers engaged in agricultural activities. Depending on the choices made by each national authority, the basic payment accounts for between 12 per cent and 68 per cent of their national budget allocation. The basic payment is applied either as the basic payment scheme (BPS) or as a transitional simplified scheme, the single area payment scheme (SAPS).
Green payment	Member states must allocate 30 per cent of their direct payment allocation to this greening payment. It is a new addition to the already existing set of instruments of the CAP dedicated to environmental and climate measures, such as cross-compliance and voluntary rural development measures, dedicated to environmental and climate issues. Farmers receive the green direct payment if they can show that they comply with three obligatory practices: Crop diversification: At least three crops are required on farms with more than 30 ha of arable land. Furthermore, the main crop may not cover more than 75 per cent of the arable land. Maintenance of permanent pasture: A ratio of permanent grassland to agricultural land is set by member states at national or regional levels (with a 5 per cent margin of flexibility). Moreover, farmers are not allowed to plough or convert permanent grassland in designated sensitive areas. Ecological focus areas: Farmers with arable land exceeding 15 ha must ensure that at least 5 per cent of their land is an ecological focus area with a view to safeguarding and improving biodiversity on farms. Ecological focus areas may include, for example, fallow land, landscape features, afforested areas, terraces, hedges/wooded strips or nitrogen fixing crops such as clover and alfalfa which help to improve soil organic matter. Member states may allow farmers to meet one or more greening requirements through equivalent (alternative) practices, which then can replace one or several of the three established greening measures.
Young farmer payment	This payment is a top-up payment added to the basic payment, which is granted for a maximum of five years from the moment a young farmer takes over as the head of a farm holding. The payment can account for up to 2 per cent of total direct payment national allocations.

(continued)

Table 10.1 (continued)

Direct payment	Description
Optional direct payment measures	
Redistributive payment	In order to redistribute support to smaller farmers, member states may allocate up to 30 per cent of their national budget to a redistributive payment for the first eligible hectares. The number of hectares for which this payment can be allocated is limited to a threshold set by national authorities (30 ha or the average farm size in member states if the latter is more than 30 ha). The amount per hectare is the same for all farmers in the country where it is applied, and cannot exceed 65 per cent of the average payment per hectare. Ten member states have decided to opt for the redistributive payment. The amount of the top-up payment per hectare varies from country to country (in 2015, they ranged from €25 in France to €127 in Wallonia).
Payments for areas with natural constraints (ANCs)	Areas with natural constraints include typically mountain areas, but they are not limited to these. Up to 5 per cent of the national allocation for direct payments can be used for top-up payments to farmers in these ANC areas. Only two member states (Denmark and Slovenia) apply this option.
Small farmers scheme	The small farmers scheme (SFS) is a simplified direct payment scheme granting a one-off payment to farmers who choose to participate. The maximum level of the payment is decided at the national level, but in any case may not exceed €1250. The small farmers scheme includes simplified administrative procedures, and participating farmers are exempt from greening and cross-compliance sanctions and controls. The scheme is applied in 15 EU countries.
Voluntary coupled support	Member states may continue to link (or couple) a limited amount of direct payments to certain products. The aim of this type of support is to maintain the level of production in regions or in sectors undergoing difficulties and that are particularly important for economic, social, or environmental reasons. The share of direct payments that member states can dedicate to voluntary coupled support is generally limited to 8 per cent, although certain exceptions are allowed. All member states (except Germany) apply the VCS and the range of sectors covered vary greatly from one country to another.

Source: Based on European Commission (2017)

income support can induce additional on-farm investments, and thus indirectly affect output positively. This effect may be strengthened by the fiscal regimes or by differences in the interest rates for debts and savings. The liquidity effect may be particularly relevant for the new member states, where agriculture is going through a stage of transition, and credit constraints can be highly relevant.

10.2.3   Decoupled Direct Income Payments

The Single Payment Scheme (SPS)—with payments called Single Farm Payments (SFPs)—provides direct income payments to farmers in the 'old' EU-15 and in a couple of new member states. The Single Area Payment Scheme (SAPS) applied in most NMSs is based on national ceilings agreed during their accessions to the EU, and provides a uniform fixed payment per hectare of utilized agricultural area, minus areas of permanent crops and forests. Both SPS and SAPS follow the definition of decoupling as specified in Annex II of the Uruguay Round Agreement on Agriculture. Policies satisfying this criterion are so-called Green Box policies of WTO ('no or at least minimal production and trade distorting'), which are exempted from subsidy reduction requirements. According to the OECD (2006), decoupling implies that the size of the direct income payment should be fixed or, if related to an agricultural production variable, be outside the farmer's control. The size should not be determined by the volume of current production of specific agricultural products or the level of specific inputs used. In addition, the payment should be directly financed from general taxation, thereby also excluding impacts on consumption. Decoupling payments not only 'freezes' policy support to a past reference point, but also breaks the relation with several present and future policy objectives. As such, they present *relatively untargeted* expenditures.

10.2.4   The Single Payment Scheme

As regards the implementation of the Single Payment Scheme (SPS) introduced by the Midterm Review in 2003, member states had some room for discretion. The old member states were allowed to introduce the scheme between January 2005 and January 2007. The basis for SPS implementation is the establishment of a maximum amount—the 'national ceiling' or total of direct aids (and equivalent payments) paid in a historic reference period (generally 2000–2002)—which each member state can spend on direct aids. Active farmers are allotted 'entitlements' to direct payments based on their individual reference amounts of past payments. Each entitlement is calculated by dividing the reference amount by the number of eligible hectares on which payments were received in the reference years. Eligible hectares normally include all types of agricultural land except land used for permanent crops (excluding energy crops, e.g. short-rotation coppice) and forestry. Entitlements are activated annually by matching them with a corresponding number of eligible hectares. In general, transfer of entitlements is allowed, but only within member states and in some cases only within regions. Transfers without land are allowed, but farmers taking over payment entitlements can only receive payment if the number of entitlements is matched to the correct number of eligible hectares.

Member states had three options in how to determine direct payments: (1) The basic (historic) approach grants each farmer entitlements corresponding to the payments received during the reference period and the number of hectares then used. (2) The regional or flat-rate approach bases a farmer's entitlement on the calculated average payments per hectare received by farmers in a certain region (or state). The main difference from the historic approach is that the payment rates are averaged out (and thus somewhat redistributed), rather than varying between individual farmers. (3) The 'hybrid' approach allows member states to mix the two other schemes. Whereas EU-15 member states choose either option 1 or 3, most of the new member states adopted the Single Area Payment Scheme based on national ceilings agreed during the accession negotiations, and with a uniform fixed payment per hectare granted to all farmers.

10.2.5   Evolution and Targeting of Direct Payments

The direct payments are important for several reasons (see Fig. 10.1). First, they are, with an annual amount of more than €40 billion, by far the biggest expenditure item in the total EU farm budget (share is about 72 per cent). Second, direct payments benefit nearly 7 million farms throughout the EU, which is the large majority of the total farm population. Third, direct payments often represent an important share of the agricultural income of farms: on average, nearly half of farmers' income in the period 2007–2017 consisted of direct support.

After completion of the decoupling of payments with the Health Check reform of the CAP, in CAP2020 reform of 2013, a kind of retargeting of direct payments was introduced. However, the delink with production is preserved, with a minor share of so-called voluntary coupled payments being an exemption. As a result the direct payment system is transformed into a fairer (income distribution) and greener (environment, biodiversity, and climate) system of support. As from 2015, active farmers have access to compulsory schemes applicable in all EU countries, as well as to voluntary schemes if established at the national level. Table 10.1 provides a

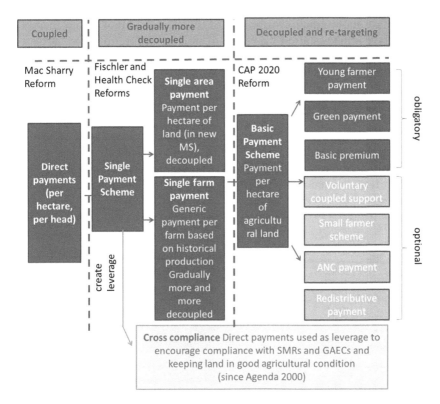

Fig. 10.1   The evolution of the direct payment scheme. (Source: Based on European Commission 2018)

short overview of the various targeted direct payments as these exist since 2015.

The 2013 CAP reform aimed also to achieve improvement in both external and internal convergences. External convergence regards a redistribution of direct payments over member states in favour of farms with lower incomes in the newer member states. The national envelopes of those member states where the average payment (in EUR per hectare) is below 90 per cent of the average are gradually increased (by one-third of the difference between their current rate and 90 per cent of the average). The national envelopes for member states receiving above average amounts are correspondingly adjusted downwards. Internal convergence is about creating a more equal distribution of direct payments within a member state, and implies shifted payments from larger, more intensive farms to smaller, more extensive farms. Member states had several options for achieving convergence. They could already apply a flat rate in 2015, or move to a flat rate in 2019, or apply partial convergence by 2019 (see Fig. 10.2). Member states applying the Single Aras Payment Scheme have already a flat rate per hectare.

Another factor contributing to internal convergence is the reduction and capping of basic payment. The reduction of payments applies only to the basic payment (and not to the total direct payments), and the obligation in terms of reduction is set at a very low level (5 per cent reduction

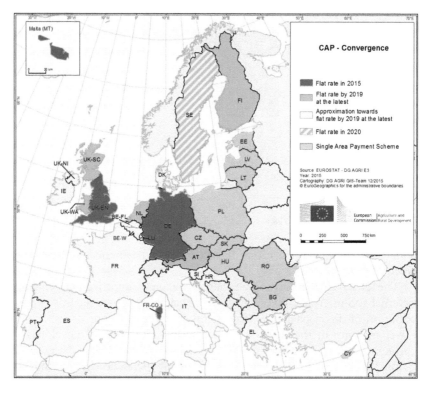

Fig. 10.2 Internal convergence arrangements of EU member states. (Source: European Commission (2018), graph based on information system for agricultural market management and monitoring (ISAMM) notifications from member states)

from €150,000 of BPS/SAPS, with the possibility to deduct salaries from the amount of basic payment before applying the reduction). Steeper reductions and capping can be implemented but are not compulsory. Member states applying the redistributive payment with more than 5 per cent of their national ceiling allocated to the scheme may decide not to apply the mechanism at all (BE-Wallonia, DE, FR, HR, LT, and RO). In general, member states have been resistant to capping and agreed only with limited capping arrangements, although the EU Commission several times proposed more ambitious schemes.

10.3   CROSS-COMPLIANCE

10.3.1   *Conditionality and Support*

Next to the decoupling of the direct payments, the Mid-Term Review of 2003 made the direct payments conditional on recipients meeting several minimal on-farm standards, with the aim of promoting a more sustainable agriculture. This concept of 'cross-compliance' originated in the United States, where it was used from the 1970s onwards. Claiming support under one commodity programme (policy regime), US farmers had to meet the rules of that programme and simultaneously certain obligations of other programmes. In this way, a linkage between programmes was introduced. The term has since been extended and used in particular to refer to linkages between agricultural and environmental policies (Baldock and Mitchell 1995; Aviron et al. 2009).

With growing pressure in the late 1980s to integrate environmental considerations into the CAP, cross-compliance became part of the EU debate on agricultural policy reforms. It is difficult to incorporate the concept into market support (which, in general, is not paid directly to individual farmers), but the 1992 Mac Sharry reform and its follow-ups increased reliance on direct payment instruments and thus the potential relevance of cross-compliance. Moreover, the greater transparency of these payments has prompted a debate on the non-market 'value added' or contributions of EU agriculture, in particular its tangible social and environmental services. Although elements of environmental cross-compliance were introduced into the CAP by the Mac Sharry reform, its impact initially remained rather limited. Member states were obliged to apply 'appropriate' environmental conditions to the management of compulsory set-aside in arable cropping. Moreover, they were allowed (but not obliged) to introduce environmental requirements for the direct payments offered as headage payments for beef cattle and sheep. Only a limited number of member states (notably the UK) implemented such schemes.

The Agenda 2000 reform of the CAP extended the application of direct payments, and cross-compliance then became a more prominent part of the agricultural policy package. The 'common rules regulation' no. 1259/1999 (Article 3) required member states to take measures to ensure that agricultural activities were compatible with environmental requirements. It gave member states several options for such measures, among which were support in return for agri-environmental commitments, the introduction of general mandatory environmental requirements, and the introduction of specific environmental requirements as a condition for direct payments.

10.3.2   Objectives of Cross-compliance

With the 2003 policy reform, cross-compliance has become compulsory. For the Commission, cross-compliance has several objectives. The first is to contribute to the development of sustainable agriculture. This is achieved through farmers respecting the rules relating to the relevant aspects of cross-compliance. The second objective is to make the CAP more compatible with the expectations of society at large. The third is to increase the awareness of farmers with respect to specific legislation regulating agriculture. There is now a growing body of opinion that agricultural payments should no longer be granted to farmers who fail to comply with basic rules in certain important areas of public policy. At the same time, cross-compliance should help to justify to society the direct payments for farmers. Over time, its scope was extended from its original environmental focus to a much wider range of public concerns, each of which was already covered by EU legislation, for example, animal welfare, food safety, and maintaining agricultural land in good agricultural and environmental condition (GAEC). Cross-compliance involves two groups of standards (see Table 10.2):

Statutory management requirements (SMRs) and
Good agricultural and environmental conditions (GAECs) of agricultural land.

Table 10.2 SMRs and GAEC standards as applicable after the 2013 CAP reform

Domain	Issue	SMR	GAEC
Environment, climate change, good agricultural condition of land	Water	Protection of waters against pollution caused by nitrates from agricultural sources	Establishment of buffer strips along water courses; Water use for irrigation is subject to authorization, compliance with authorization procedures Protection of ground water against pollution
	Soil and carbon stock		Minimum soil cover Minimum land management Maintenance of soil organic matter level through appropriate practices (including ban on burning arable stubble)
	Biodiversity	Conservation of wild birds Conservation of natural habitats and of wild flora and fauna	
	Landscape, minimum level of maintenance		Retention of landscape features, including hedges, pons, ditches, trees, field margins, terraces
Public health, animal health and plant health	Food safety	General principles and requirements of EU food law Prohibition on the use of certain substances (hormones, thyrostatics) in stock farming	
	Identification and registration (I&R) of animals	I&R of pigs I&R of bovine animals and the labelling of beef and beef products I&R of ovine and caprine animals	

(*continued*)

Table 10.2 (continued)

Domain	Issue	SMR	GAEC
	Animal diseases	Rules for prevention, control, and eradication of certain transmissible spongiform encephalopathies	
	Plant protection products	Rules concerning the placing of plant protection products on markets	
Animal welfare	Animal welfare	Minimum standards for protection of calves Minimum standards for protection of pigs Protection of animals kept for farming purposes	

Source: Based on EU Regulation 1306/2013, Annex II

10.3.3   Conditions Imposed by Cross-compliance

Farmers must comply with 13 SMRs and a number of GAEC standards, as defined, respectively, in Annex II of Regulation 1306/2013 (see Table 10.2 for a brief overview). The SMRs all derive from pre-existing EU Directives and Regulations for the EU-15, for example, the Nitrates Directive of 1991. SMR cross-compliance acts as an additional financial incentive besides the existing national systems for the enforcement of EU legislation. Farmers that are detected as non-compliant will get a penalty in the form of a reduction in the support that they get from the CAP. The payments subject to reduction include not only the direct payments (decoupled as well as coupled ones), but also most rural development payments such as area-based payments related to agri-environmental measures, areas with natural constraints (ANCs), NATURA 2000 measures, afforestation measures, forest environmental payments, agroforestry, and organic farming. The Commission Regulation sets the reduction, as a general rule, at 3 per cent of the amount granted. Member states may decide to adjust this reduction rate within the range of 1 to 5 percent, or not to reduce payments (e.g. in case the calculated fine is below a threshold value of €100). The legislation requires that applied payment reductions take account of the severity, extent, and permanence of non-compliance. Therefore, higher rates of reduction apply in case of repeated and intentional non-compliance, but these should not exceed 15 per cent. Cases of non-compliance which constitute a direct risk to public or animal health shall always lead to a reduction or even exclusion of payments. The legislation requires that applied payment reductions take account of the severity, extent, and permanence of non-compliance. Member states have to inspect annually at least 1 per cent of their farm population, where the sample selection should be risk-based; that is, farmers more likely to violate a regulation should have a higher probability of being inspected.

The GAEC framework and the obligation to preserve the national ratio of permanent pasture involved, at least in principle, new requirements. The GAEC framework focuses on four 'issues' (water, soil, carbon stock, and landscape) and involve a total of seven corresponding standards (see Table 10.2). During the CAP reforms, changes have been made with respect to the content as well as the number of cross-compliance requirement. After its introduction in the 2003 Fischler reform of the CAP, in the 2008 Health Check reform, the system was adjusted and simplified, with new measures added on water protection and management and the original (obligatory) standards being subdivided into those which are compulsory and those which are optional. With the 2013 CAP reform the number of SMR was reduced from 19 to 13.

10.3.4   Restrictions with Respect to Land Use

In addition, the rules on cross-compliance shall also include the maintenance of permanent pasture. The permanent pasture requirement was initially included in the cross-compliance package to avoid the potential conversion of permanent pasture into arable land and also the abandonment of land and associated environmental degradation. Such conversion, for which there was some threat particularly in the new member states, was supposed to have a negative environmental effect. A ban on (massive) conversion of permanent pasture into arable land should also limit possible responses of the arable crop markets. Land abandonment was also feared as a potential negative side effect of decoupling income support from production. As such, the GAEC requirements and the permanent pasture clause can be seen as a precautionary policy to prevent future problems which might otherwise occur. Because, in contrast with the pre-existing SMRs, the GAEC standards and the permanent pasture clause are new, the behavioural changes (and associated costs and benefits) induced by these standards can be attributed to the direct impacts of cross-compliance.[2] Later on, the climate benefits associated with permanent pasture preservation were mentioned as an important contribution from this cross-compliance restriction.

10.4   COMPATIBILITY WITH WORLD TRADE ORGANIZATION RULES

Under the Uruguay Round Agreement on Agriculture (URAA), all domestic support in favour of agricultural producers is subject to rules. A key objective of the WTO has been to discipline and reduce domestic support while at the same time leaving great scope for governments to design domestic agricultural policies in the face of, and in response to, the wide variety of the specific circumstances in individual countries and individual agricultural sectors. The main conceptual consideration is that there are basically two categories of domestic support—support with no, or minimal, distortive effect on trade on the one hand (often referred to as 'Green Box' measures) and trade-distorting support on the other hand (often referred to as 'Amber Box' measures). The aggregate monetary value of Amber Box measures is, with certain exceptions, subject to reduction commitments as specified in the schedule of each WTO member providing such support.[3]

10.4.1   The Green Box and Blue Provisions

The Green Box also provides for the use of direct payments to producers which are not linked to production decisions ('decoupling'). The conditions preclude any linkage between the amount of such payments, on the

---

[2] Jongeneel et al. (2008) showed, however, that a significant part of these new EU standards were already part of member state legislation and, for that reason, are not at all new for farmers.

[3] The reduction commitments are expressed in terms of a 'Total Aggregate Measurement of Support' (Total AMS), which includes all product-specific support and non-product-specific support in one single figure. WTO members with a Total AMS have to reduce base period support by 20 per cent over six years (developed country members) or 13 per cent over ten years (developing country members). In any year of the implementation period, the current total AMS value of non-exempt measures must not exceed the scheduled total AMS limit as specified in the schedule for that year. In other words, the maximum levels of such support are bound.

one hand, and production, prices or factors of production in any year after a fixed base period. In addition, no production shall be required in order to receive such payments. Additional criteria to be met depend on the type of measure concerned, which may include decoupled income support measures; income insurance and safety-net programmes; natural disaster relief; a range of structural adjustment assistance programmes; and certain payments under environmental programmes and under regional assistance programmes.

Direct payments under production limiting programmes (often referred to as 'Blue Box' measures) are exempt from commitments if such payments are made on fixed areas and yield or a fixed number of livestock. Such payments also fit into this category if they are made on 85 per cent or less of production in a defined base period. While the Green Box covers decoupled payments, in the case of the Blue Box measures, production is still required in order to receive the payments, but the actual payments do not relate directly to the current quantity of that production.

10.4.2   *Reduction Commitments*

All domestic support measures in favour of agricultural producers that do not fit into any of the above exempt categories are subject to reduction commitments. This domestic support category captures policies, such as market price support measures, direct production subsidies, or input subsidies. However, under the de minimis provisions of the Agreement, there is no requirement to reduce such trade-distorting domestic support in any year in which the aggregate value of the product-specific support does not exceed 5 per cent of the total value of production of the agricultural product in question. In addition, non-product-specific support, which is less than 5 per cent of the value of total agricultural production, is also exempt from reduction. The 5 per cent threshold applies to developed countries, whereas in the case of developing countries the de minimis ceiling is 10 per cent.

The EU's direct payments were initially classified as Blue Box support because they were considered as still being distortive, and as such they should be dismantled over time. Since the decoupling of the EU's direct payments they qualify as Green Box support, with the coupled support payment being an exemption (still Blue Box).

10.5   Assessment of Impacts of Direct Payments and Cross-Compliance

10.5.1   Farm Income Support

Farm income support is unequally distributed and poorly targeted. The main instrument used to support farm incomes is direct payments, which consume about 70 per cent of the total CAP expenditure. In 2015, in the EU28, 81 per cent of the farmers received 20 per cent of the direct payments (European Commission 2017, 2018). Thus a large group of farmers received a low amount of payments, whereas a small group received a high amount of payments. About 75 per cent of the farmers in the EU28 received less than €5000, whereas half of the beneficiaries received less than €1250 per year, and one quarter received less than €500 (EU Commission 2018). About 16,000 farmers (0.2 per cent) received a payment larger than €150,000. The share of direct payments in farm income varies considerably from about one-third for the lower income size classes to more than half of the higher income classes (EU average is about 46 per cent; EU Commission 2018). The provided income support is thus progressive: farmers with relatively higher incomes receive relatively higher payments, which contrasts with the basic need for income support principle (Terluin and Verhoog 2018). Shares of direct payments also vary over the type of farms (beef cattle and cereal, oilseed, and protein farms have the highest shares, whereas intensive livestock production [e.g. granivores such as pigs and poultry] and horticulture have relatively low shares) as well as over years (due to price volatility and varying production conditions). The inequality to a large extent reflects the inequality in farm size (measured in number of hectares per farm). Another factor contributing to the inequality is the specific criteria used by member states to allocate the direct income payments, which still diverge over member states. However, even an EU-wide uniform per hectare payment would not reduce inequality (then 86 per cent of the farmers would receive 20 per cent of the direct payment envelope; see Terluin and Verhoog (2018)).

Figure 10.3 provides an overview of the per hectare payment, and its composition in terms of targeted payments by member state in 2016. The average direct payments granted per hectare of area declared by farmers amounted to 259 €/ha in the EU, which includes the crop specific payment for cotton and the possible national 'top-ups'. This average pay-

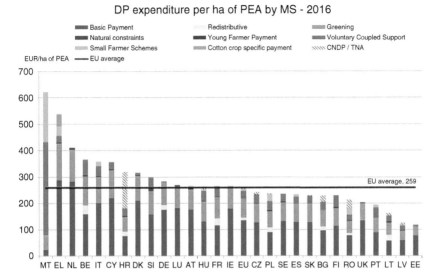

Fig. 10.3 Direct payments per potentially eligible hectare (PEA) by EU member states in 2016. (Source: European Commission 2018)

ment/ha varies from 118 EUR/ha in Estonia to 622 €/ha in Malta, reflecting to a greater or lesser extent the differences in agricultural and economic situations in the different member states.

The inequality of farm income support not only is hampering fairness, but is also a factor that negatively impacts on the preservation of a level playing field (the EU single market principle) as certain farms (larger ones) are favoured over others (small farms). To the extent that incomes of farms are supported for which there is no need for such income support, the inequality leads also to an ineffective use and a waste of scarce public resources (Erjavec et al. 2018). Moreover, it then raises land prices and is a barrier to entry for young farmers.

10.5.2   Impacts of Direct Payments

Evaluating the effectiveness of the income support provided by the CAP is, for several reasons, not easy. With the replacement of price support by direct payments, income support became more direct, and more targeted to the income policy objective. So the impact on farm income of €1 of price support will be lower than that of a €1 direct payment (transfer efficiency). The CAP also contributes to the farmers' income formation by either directly or indirectly stimulating innovation and investment and by that facilitating improvements in animal, land, and labour productivity. Productivity gains in principle improve the farmers' revenue/cost ratio and thus profitability, although depending on market characteristics (supply and demand response), a larger or smaller part of these gains might be passed on to the end users, rather than solely benefitting primary producers. The income evolution of farm households will also depend on the degree they are involved in pluriactivity and part-time farming: many farmers in the EU are engaged in off-farm activities which also contribute to their income. Farmer income evolution will, in addition, depend on the degree to which economies of scale and size can be exploited (structural change).

While noting the definitional and conceptual problems in evaluating the income support effectiveness, there is clear evidence about the contribution of direct payments to farm income. As shown in Fig. 10.4, the share of direct payments in farm income for 2019 is about one-third, while the share of direct payments (DP) in income increases with farm size.

There is evidence stating that farm incomes are not at par with the incomes of wage workers with comparable job characteristics outside agriculture. The introduction of direct payments in 1992 contributed to reduce this income 'parity gap' to about 30 per cent (Versteijlen 2008, 148), due to the inherent transfer efficiency of the direct payment instrument. However, with the EU enlargements in 2004 and 2007, the income parity gap increased to 55 per cent, despite the fact that on average more than 50 per cent of EU farmers' income can be related to these direct payments (Council 2009).[4]

---

[4] Income parity gap estimates should be interpreted carefully since there are significant measurement problems, for example, as to how and to what extent income from off-farm activities should be taken into account. Hill (1999, 352) concluded that there are negative as well as positive income disparities. Thus, income distribution might be a concern for specific cases, and targeted payments could be used as a policy instrument for income support.

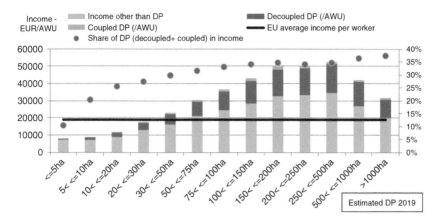

Fig. 10.4 Direct payments and their share in farm income (€/agricultural work unit) by farm size (area-based). (Source: European Commission 2018)

There are several studies (Raggi et al. 2013; Olper et al. 2014; Koester and Loy 2016) indicating that CAP payments play a positive role in retaining farmers in the sector, but that they, at the same time, slow down structural change, which may hamper the long-run viability of farms.

10.5.3 Leverage Creation and Compliance

As regards cross-compliance, not complying with the involved standards imposes a double sanction on the farmer: the reduction in CAP payments and a punishment due to transgression of a national law. Cross-compliance contributes to establish a clear baseline of basic standards that farmers should satisfy (e.g. a licence to produce). As such, it also clarifies the obligatory standards and practices farmers have to satisfy and also defines a demarcation line when farmer actions deliver services that are beyond legal standards and be potential subjects of financial compensation.

Recent data on compliance rates could not be accessed. Shortly after its introduction, in 2005, 240,898 on-farm inspections were carried out (Commission 2007), and 11.9 per cent of inspected farmers had their payments reduced. For the old member states, where the SMRs as well as the GAECs must be satisfied, this percentage was higher (16.4 per cent non-compliances) than in case of the new member states, which only were inspected with respect to the GAECs (6.1 per cent). The total value of reductions imposed was €9.84 million (or 0.03 per cent of total direct income support). Most of the deductions (68 per cent for the EU as a whole, but up to 98 per cent in some member states) then were minimal, not more than 1 per cent of the received payments. In about 14 per cent of cases, reductions of 3 per cent were imposed, while in 12 per cent of cases the deduction amounted 5 per cent. The applied penalty rates as well as the 5 per cent maximum are relatively low. This means that the reductions are likely to have a limited deterrent effect (ECA 2008). However, deterrence is not only determined from a cost/benefit calculation, also other factors, including follow up consequences of likely repeated inspections, the starting of a case under national law, and morality issues play a role (Herzfeld and Jongeneel 2011).

Most (71 per cent) of the detected non-compliances involved the identification and registration (I&R) of animals, but the Nitrates Directive and the GAECs were also subject to a significant number of non-compliances (10 and 13 per cent, respectively). With respect to the Nitrates Directive, there were legal infringement procedures against a few member states, indicating that not only at farm level, but also at member state level, compliance was sometimes not satisfactory. However, in many other cases, best estimates indicate high levels of compliance, suggesting that more intensive inspections will hardly lead to significant further improvements in degree of compliance.

In principle, standards and the degree of compliance to these standards might give rise to additional costs associated with compliance, which in turn might diminish the competitiveness of EU agriculture. The extent to which this will happen depends on many factors, including the prevailing degree of (non-)compliance and the costs of compliance. Most cross-compliance standards have the character of specifying minimum standards, which for most farms have long been integrated into current production costs. Indeed, significant numbers of farmers participate in voluntary certification schemes specifying alternative criteria that go beyond the minimum standards associated with cross-compliance.

From a review of all SMR and GAEC standards, it appeared that, in particular the Nitrates Directive, food safety requirements and animal welfare standards might give rise to non-negligible increases in production costs, at least at the individual farm level, and potentially also at the sector level (the latter depending on the number of affected farms and their share of production). While the SMRs mainly affect animal production, many of the GAEC standards mainly affect the arable sector. For the former, although the potential cost impact of the rules concerning the identification and registration of farmed livestock (i.e. ear tags, passports) is low, analysis shows that farmers faced significant problems with compliance. Anecdotal evidence suggests that cross-compliance has led to an improvement of behaviour in this area.

According to ECA (2008) and Sterly et al. (2018), the GAEC requirements with respect to buffer zones have made a positive contribution to biodiversity preservation.

REFERENCES

Aviron, S., H. Nitsch, P. Jeanneret, S. Buholzer, H. Luka, L. Pfiffner, S. Pozzi, B. Schüpbach, T. Walter, and F. Herzog. 2009. Ecological Cross Compliance Promotes Farmland Biodiversity in Switzerland. *Frontiers in Ecology and the Environment* 7 (5): 247–252. https://doi.org/10.1890/070197.

Baldock, D., and K. Mitchell. 1995. *Cross-Compliance within the Common Agricultural Policy: A Review of Options for Landscape and Nature Conservation.* London: Institute for European Environmental Policy (IEEP).

Ciaian, P., and J.F.M. Swinnen. 2006. Land Market Imperfections and Agricultural Policy impacts in the New EU Member States: A Partial Equilibrium Analysis. *American Journal of Agricultural Economics* 88: 799–815.

Council of the EU. 2009. Council Regulation (EC) No. 73/2009 of 19 January 2009; Establishing Common Rules for Direct Support Schemes for Farmers Under the Common Agricultural Policy and Establishing Certain Support Schemes for Farmers. *Official Journal of the European Union* 31 (1): 16–99.

Erjavec, E., M. Lovec, L. Juvanicic, T. Sumrada, and I. Rac. 2018. *Research for AGRI Committee – The CAP Strategic Plans Beyond 2020: Appraisal of the EC Legislative Proposals.* Brussels: European Parliament, Policy Department for Structural and Cohesion Policies.

European Commission. 2007. *Report from the Commission to the Council; On the Application of the System of Cross-Compliance.* Brussels: European Commission, COM(2007) 147 final.

———. 2017. *CAP Explained: Direct Payments for Farmers 2015–2020.* Brussels: European Commission.

———. 2018. *Direct Payments.* Brussels: DG Agriculture and Rural Development, Unit Farm Economics. https://ec.europa.eu/agriculture/sites/agriculture/files/statistics/facts-figures/direct-payments.pdf

European Court of Auditors. 2008. *Is Cross Compliance an Effective Policy?* Luxembourg: European Court of Auditors (ECA). Special Report No. 8/2008.

Féménia, F., A. Gohin, and A. Carpentier. 2010. The Decoupling of Farm Programs: Revisiting the Wealth Effect. *American Journal of Agricultural Economics* 92 (3): 836–848.

Gardner, B. 1986. Farm Commodity Programs as Income Transfers. *Cato Journal* 6 (1): 251–261.

Herzfeld, T., and R. Jongeneel. 2011. Why Do Farmers Behave as They Do? Understanding Compliance with Rural, Agricultural and Food Attribute Standards. *Land Use Policy* 29 (1): 250–260.

Hill, B. 1999. Farm Household Incomes: Perceptions and Statistics. *Journal of Rural Studies* 15 (3): 345–358.

Jongeneel, R., I. Bezlepkina, and M. Farmer, eds. 2008. *Cross-Compliance: Final Report.* The Hague: LEI, Project No. SSPE-CT-2005-006489.

Key, N., and M.J. Roberts. 2009. Non-pecuniary Benefits to Farming: Implications for Supply Response to Decoupled Payments. *American Journal of Agricultural Economics* 91 (1): 1–18.

Koester, U., and J.P. Loy. 2016. EU Agricultural Policy Reform: Evaluating the EU's New Methodology for Direct Payments. *Intereconomics* 51: 278–285.

OECD. 2006. Decoupling Agricultural Support from Production. *Policy Brief*, November. http://www.oecd.org/dataoecd/5/54/37726496.pdf

Olper, A., V. Raimondi, D. Cavicchioli, and M. Vigani. 2014. Do CAP Payments Reduce Farm Labor Migration? A Panel Data Analysis across EU Regions. *European Review of Agricultural Economics* 41 (5): 843–873.

Raggi, M., L. Sardonini, and D. Viaggi. 2013. The Effects of the Common Agricultural Policy on Exit Strategies and Land Re-Allocation. *Land Use Policy* 31 (3): 114–125.

Severini, S., A. Tantari, and G. Di Tommaso. 2016. Do CAP Direct Payments Stabilise Farm Income? Empirical Evidences from a Constant Sample of Italian Farms. *Agricultural Economics* 4: 6. https://doi.org/10.1186/s40100-016-0050-0.

Sterly, S., R. Jongeneel, H. Pabst, H. Silvis, J. Connor, D. Freshwater, M. Shobayashi, Y. Kinoshita, C. Van Kooten, and A. Zorn. 2018. *Research for AGRI Committee - A Comparative Analysis of Global Agricultural Policies: Lessons for the Future CAP.* Brussels: European Parliament, Policy Department for Structural and Cohesion Policies.

Swinbank, A., and R. Tranter. 2004. *A Bond Scheme for the Common Agricultural Policy Reform.* Wallingford: CABI Publishing.

Swinnen, J. 2008. *The Perfect Storm: The Political Economy of the Fischler Reforms of the Common Agricultural Policy.* Brussels: CEPS, 181. http://papers.ssrn.com/sol3/papers.cfm?abstract_id=1333090

Swinnen, J., P. Ciaian, and d'A. Kancs. 2008. *Study on the Functioning of Land Markets in the EU Member States Under the Influence of Measures Applied Under the Common Agricultural Policy.* Brussels: Centre for European Policy Studies (CEPS), Final report to European Commission.

Terluin, I., and D. Verhoog. 2018. *Verdeling van de toeslagen van de eerste pijler van het GLB over landbouwbedrijven in de EU.* Wageningen: WUR, Report 2018-039.

van Riemsdijk, J.F. 1973. A System of Direct Compensation Payments to Farmers as a Means of Reconciling Short-Run to Long-Run Interests. *European Review of Agricultural Economics* 1 (2): 161–189.

Versteijlen, H. 2008. Toekomst van de directe inkomenssteun. In *EU-beleid voor landbouw, voedsel en groen; Van politiek naar praktijk*, ed. H. Silvis, A. Oskam, and G. Meester. Wageningen: Wageningen Academic Publishers.

WEBSITES

Direct Payments explained:
http://ec.europa.eu/agriculture/markets/sfp/index_en.htm
Cross compliance explained:
https://ec.europa.eu/agriculture/direct-support/cross-compliance_en

CHAPTER 11

Animal Health Policy

Coen van Wagenberg, Willy Baltussen, and Roel Jongeneel

11.1 INTRODUCTION

Infectious diseases of livestock cause loss of production in the animals they affect. The severity of disease, and therefore the degree of economic loss, varies with the nature of the infectious agent and with its interaction with the host. If left uncontrolled, those diseases which are highly infectious spread rapidly and those which cause high levels of mortality or debility in affected livestock can have a severe impact on a country's economy. Examples of such diseases are foot and mouth disease (FMD), African

This chapter is a revision of Fred Landeg, Nick Coulson and Monique Mourits, Chapter 11. Animal health policy. In: Arie Oskam, Gerrit Meester and Huib Silvis (Eds) (2011), EU policy for Agriculture, Food and Rural Areas, Wageningen Academic Publishers.

C. van Wagenberg • W. Baltussen
Consumer and Chain Unit, Wageningen Economic Research,
The Hague, The Netherlands
e-mail: coen.vanwagenberg@wur.nl; willy.baltussen@wur.nl

R. Jongeneel (✉)
Agricultural Economics and Rural Policy Group, Wageningen University,
Wageningen, Gelderland, The Netherlands
e-mail: roel.jongeneel@wur.nl

L. Dries et al. (eds.), *EU Bioeconomy Economics and Policies: Volume I*,
Palgrave Advances in Bioeconomy: Economics and Policies,
https://doi.org/10.1007/978-3-030-28634-7_11

swine fever (ASF) and avian influenza (AI). More insidious diseases such as bovine tuberculosis and brucellosis cause chronic production losses. Those infectious diseases of animals which can also cause disease in human beings (zoonoses) may have very significant public health implications, for example, salmonellosis (food poisoning) or bovine spongiform encephalopathy (BSE).

In order to control animal diseases and limit their impacts, science has to inform an understanding of infectious agents, how they survive in the environment, their mechanisms of infection, how they produce disease and how they spread. Animal diseases may be spread directly by contact between animals. They may also be spread indirectly on the clothing and footwear of people, vehicles, equipment and feedstuffs which have been contaminated with an infectious agent. Diseases may also be spread by animal products such as meat, meat products, milk, milk products, semen, ova and embryos, which have been either derived from infected animals or contaminated by the infectious agent. Controls are therefore aimed at cutting off these mechanisms of transmission. However, some diseases present particular control problems; for example, FMD may be transmitted through the wind over distances more than 200 kilometres and AI may spread via migratory birds. Other diseases may be transmitted by insect vectors, for example, bluetongue. Some diseases have spillover from wildlife hosts into domestic animals, for example, classical swine fever (CSF) and ASF, where wild boar may provide a reservoir of infection.

From the middle of the nineteenth century, as the understanding of the nature of infectious animal disease and its impact on the economy or on public health grew, so too did efforts to control it, mainly in developed countries. Diseases of concern which were highly infectious or insidious in nature could not be controlled without government intervention, whose objective was to achieve the highest health status of country freedom from disease, eradicating it where possible. Once a control programme was started or disease-free status had been established, prevention of disease introduction became a key policy driver through the imposition of import controls on animals and their products. Animal health controls could therefore act as a barrier to trade.

In the context of the Single European Market and intra-EU trade, there needed to be harmonisation of animal health legislation and standards to facilitate the free movement of livestock and their products which are safe for both consumers and livestock. However, when the European Economic Community (EEC) was established in 1958, the animal health status of each of the founding member states, and of those countries of Western Europe that were eventually to form the enlarged EU, varied greatly, as did their approach to control. Initially, member states used their national animal health legislation and controls to guarantee trade in healthy live animals and their products. This required bilateral negotiation where the importing country set the trade requirements. It was therefore possible, under political influence, for veterinary authorities to operate a certain degree of protectionism.

11.2   THE EU FRAMEWORK FOR ANIMAL HEALTH

The diseases that the EU needed to focus on to harmonise the internal market in animals and animal products were essentially those diseases listed by the World Organisation for Animal Health (OIE). The OIE is an intergovernmental organisation set up in 1924 to combat animal diseases on a global basis. It has 182 members (mid-2019), including all EU member states. The OIE develops standards relating to rules that member countries can use to protect themselves from the introduction of diseases and pathogens, without setting up unjustified trade barriers. The OIE originally classified animal diseases into two lists:

OIE List A was defined as those transmissible diseases that have the potential for very serious and rapid spread, irrespective of national borders, that are of serious socio-economic or public health consequence, and that are of major importance in the international trade of animals and animal products;
OIE List B was defined as those transmissible diseases that are considered to be of socio-economic and/or public health importance within countries and that are significant in the international trade of animals and animal products.

These lists still provide excellent working definitions of the rationale for EU intervention, and are reflected to this day in the EU approach to disease control for trade purposes. The OIE standards are recognised by the World Trade Organization (WTO) as reference international sanitary rules for trade under the Agreement on the Application of Sanitary and Phytosanitary Measures (SPS Agreement) (see Chap. 4). In 2004, in order to be in line with the terminology of the SPS Agreement, the OIE moved to a single list by classifying diseases as specific hazards and giving all listed diseases the same degree of importance in international trade. In 2019 this list now includes 117 animal diseases, infections and infestations.

As soon as a disease is suspected, the EU requires control measures to be taken against major epidemic diseases or exotic diseases, that is, those diseases not normally present in the EU. These are essentially the former OIE List A diseases (see Table 11.1). In the case of an outbreak of any of these diseases, the animals on the infected holding are killed and their carcasses destroyed. Animals which are believed to have been exposed to infection may also be culled in order to prevent the spread of disease. Emergency vaccination may be used as an adjunct to control, but prophylactic vaccination is not permitted for many of them, since it may hide the presence of disease. The objective of control is to achieve the highest OIE health status of 'Country freedom from disease without vaccination'. For vector-borne diseases such as bluetongue, vaccination is the only effective control once the virus is established in the insect vector.

In the case of an outbreak of exotic disease, the concept of 'regionalisation' is important with respect to intra-EU trade. This means limiting the application of measures to control the disease to a specific area where the disease is known to exist, without applying restrictions on the movement of animals and animal products in the rest of the country. Regionalisation and the application of proportionate risk-based controls should minimise the effects of outbreaks of animal disease on the wider rural economy, where tourism and recreational activities play an important role.

The EU has compulsory eradication and monitoring programmes for diseases already in the Union such as brucellosis and tuberculosis (original OIE List B diseases), which are subject to national control programmes; these may be co-financed by the EU (see below).

Table 11.1   Original OIE List A diseases

Foot and mouth disease	Vesicular stomatitis
Swine vesicular disease	Rinderpest
Peste des petits ruminants	Contagious bovine pleuropneumonia
Lumpy skin disease	Rift Valley fever
African horse sickness	Sheep pox and goat pox
Classical swine fever	African swine fever
Bluetongue	Highly pathogenic avian influenza
Newcastle disease	

Source: OIE, https://www.oie.int/animal-health-in-the-world/the-world-animal-health-information-system/old-classification-of-diseases-notifiable-to-the-oie-list-a/

11.2.1   EU Decision-Making in Animal Health

The general framework for EU decision-making has been set out in Chap. 5, and is essentially the same for animal health policy and legislation. It is worth noting, however, that the EU legislation on animal health was usually adopted by the Council under Article 37 TEU (consultation procedure). This allowed a more rapid response to an emergency disease situation. However, if food safety or human health is concerned, the European Parliament also played already a primary role in the adoption of legislation under Article 152 TEU (co-decision procedure). The Lisbon Treaty, brought into force on 1 December 2009, extends co-decision to all areas of animal health and welfare legislation. Since 2014, the regulatory committee for animal health and welfare is the Standing Committee on the Plants, Animals, Food and Feed (SCoPAFF).

11.2.2   Third-Country Imports

Controls over the importation of live animals and their products are essential to safeguard the EU's consumers and its animal health status, and there is a large block of legislation covering import requirements. As there is free movement of goods once they enter the EU, this legislation is harmonised. Third countries must be approved and listed for the particular commodity. As a general rule, the EU is compliant with the OIE standards with respect to importations from third countries. Veterinary certification is required and, at a practical level, animals and their products from third countries may only enter the EU at approved border inspection posts (BIPs) where documentary and physical checks take place.

11.2.3   Intra-EU Trade

Rules for intra-EU trade of live animals require that an animal health certificate accompanies each consignment of animals, which is moved between member states or from a member state to a third country (Regulation (EU) 2016/429, Section 7). Operators have to notify each movement of live animals to the national competent authority (CA) in the member state of origin of the movement. Before the movement takes place, they have to enter data about the animals, itinerary and transport vehicle into the electronic data system Trade Control and Expert System (TRACES). The CA checks the provided notification data, an official veterinarian performs checks at the origin of the consignment prior to its departure to verify that animal health and welfare requirements are met, issues a health certificate in case requirements are met and/or performs non-discriminatory checks of the consignment at destination. The obligations vary depending on the species of animals or their products and the context of the movement. For example, the veterinary check at the location of origin is mandatory for animals moved for slaughter, but not needed in the case of day-old chicks. The costs of these activities related to the animal health check for animals for slaughter and day-old chicks were estimated between €13 million and €33 million per year (IBF et al. 2017). These costs are mainly made for pigs and poultry for slaughter and in the Netherlands and Germany, because the majority of consignments in the EU are for these animal species and originate in these member states.

11.2.4   EU Finance for Animal Health

The provisions for the management of the food chain expenditure under the Multiannual Financial Framework (MFF) 2014–2020 are laid down in Regulation (EU) No 652/2014. It covers the spending for animal health measures, plant health measures and official control activities, and establishes a common financial framework (CFF) for those areas. The CFF Regulation aims at modernising, simplifying and rationalising the previous financial and legal framework, adapting it to the requirements of the MFF 2014–2020. The CFF was designed as a part of the 'Smarter Rules for Safer Food Chain Package', which also included proposals for an EU Animal Health Law (AHL), an EU Plant Health Law, the regime for production and making available on the market of plant reproductive material and the rules which govern official controls.

At the moment of writing this chapter (May 2019) the Animal Health Law[1] (AHL) and Plant Health Law sectorial proposals have been adopted (for details on the plant health part, see Chap. 12). The general objective of the CFF is to contribute to a high level of health for humans, animals and plants along the food chain and in related areas, by preventing and eradicating diseases and pests and by ensuring a high level of protection

---

[1] Regulation (EU) 2016/429 of the European Parliament and of the Council of 9 March 2016 on transmissible animal diseases and amending and repealing certain acts in the area of animal health ('Animal Health Law') (Official Journal of the European Union, L 84, 31 March 2016).

for consumers and the environment, while enhancing the competitiveness of the Union food and feed industry and favouring the creation of jobs. To achieve this objective, the CFF has a maximum total budget of almost €1.9 billion over seven years. It is mainly designed to support member states through grants that are co-funding certain measures in the field of animal health, plant health and official controls.

The CFF's four specific objectives correspond to each of the four policy areas referred to in the general objective: human health, animal health, plant health and official controls. They are accompanied by performance indicators for measuring the progress. Priorities for veterinary and phytosanitary programmes are laid down in Annex III to the Regulation itself, and provide the orientations for the above-mentioned programmes, to be further developed and updated annually (or multiannually) in the context of the specific work programmes. Annual or multiannual work programmes are also established for all measures covered by the CFF, except emergency measures and unexpected event.

The CFF co-funds measures related to:

veterinary eradication, control and surveillance programmes implemented by the member states, which are aimed to progressively eliminate animal diseases and to implement disease control measures: the EU financial contribution for veterinary programmes represent by far the largest amount of expenditure under the EU food safety budget;

veterinary and phytosanitary emergency measures, which are aimed to timely cope with emergency situations related to both animal health and plant health;

European reference laboratories activities, which are aimed to ensure high-quality, uniform testing in the EU and to support Commission activities on risk management and risk assessment in the area of laboratory analysis;

Better Training for Safer Food initiative, which is a training initiative addressing national authority staff involved in official controls in the areas of food and feed law, animal health and welfare and plant health rules;

coordinated control plans, which are organised on an ad hoc basis, in particular with a view of establishing the prevalence of hazards in feed, food or animals.

In addition to the pre-existing measures, the CFF also co-funds phyto-sanitary survey programmes concerning the presence of pests in the Union territory, which involves surveillance measures preventing the introduction into the EU or the spread within the EU of harmful organisms considered to be the most dangerous or not known to occur in the Union territory. Table 11.2 provides an indicative overview of the allocation of the CFF budgets.

The provisions for emergency measures against 25 listed diseases of animals and fish are similar, save that 60% of costs are paid in the case of FMD but only 50% in the case of other diseases. The emergency measures funded by the CFF are for diseases that are required to be controlled by the destruction of affected animals, and include compensation paid to owners of animals killed for control purposes; costs of slaughter and disposal of carcases; costs of destroying contaminated animal products, feed and equipment; and costs of cleansing and disinfection. Payment from the CFF is subject to strict conditions of full compliance with EU animal health legislation and accurate accounting. Member states are seldom reimbursed fully for the claims they make. However, depending on the size of disease outbreaks in any year, the costs can be substantial. Table 11.3 shows the levels of payments from the CFF by disease for recent years. Bovine tuberculosis, rabies and salmonella are the diseases having the highest expenditure shares, together representing about two-third of the total annual expenditure on fighting of diseases.

The CFF also co-finances member states which claim for national schemes for the monitoring and eradication of certain diseases. Allocations are divided into three categories (I–III), where Category I, which attracts

Table 11.2   Forecast of annual budgets of CFF for the period 2014–2020

Year	2014	2015	2016	2017	2018	2019	2020
Eradication programmes and other veterinary measures	180.0	178.5	177.0	175.0	171.5	171.5	171.0
Plant health survey and seeds	5.0	10.0	14.0	19.0	25.0	28.5	30.5
Controls	45.7	47.4	50.4	53.6	57.5	60.0	62.2
Animal health and plant health emergency measures	20.0	20.0	20.0	20.0	20.0	20.0	20.0
Support/administrative measures	2.7	2.7	2.7	2.7	2.7	2.7	2.7
Total	253.4	258.6	264.1	270.3	276.7	282.7	286.4

Source: EU Commission, DG SANTE, Unit D4—Food safety programme, emergency funding, 2017

Table 11.3 Comparative table of CFF by disease (in 1000 euro)

Disease	2015	2016	2017	Average share (%)
Classical swine fever	2324	2553	1967	1.51
Avian influenza	2111	2065	2048	1.37
Bluetongue	6281	6730	7997	4.63
Transmissible spongiform encephalopathies	14,155	11,797	9329	7.79
Sheep and goat brucellosis	11,798	12,228	9383	7.36
Bovine brucellosis	10,901	10,312	9556	6.79
African swine fever	2663	7572	9638	4.36
Salmonella	15,972	19,956	18,954	12.08
Rabies	16,777	21,376	24,955	13.90
Bovine tuberculosis	64,024	61,934	55,962	40.13
Total	147,317	156,523	149,789	100.00

Source: EU Commission, DG SANTE, Unit D4—Food safety programme, emergency funding, 2017 and 2018

over 96% of the available funding, is for animal diseases which have a significant impact on public health, including transmissible spongiform encephalopathies such as BSE. Category II includes some of the original OIE List A diseases, and Category III some diseases originally on OIE List B. In 2017 the CFF allocated approximately €150 million to these schemes.

The CFF also makes contributions—of approximately €2.5 million each year—to the funding of designated community reference laboratories (CRLs), recognised as centres of excellence in member states for the diagnosis of specific animal diseases in the EU and the provision of expert advice.

11.3   EU ANIMAL HEALTH LEGISLATION

At the end of 2004, the European Commission launched a root-and-branch independent review of the EU animal health policy. The review covered what had been achieved in the past, how well it had been achieved and how policy should develop in the future. There were a number of drivers for a review. Much of the existing policy had been developed in a piecemeal fashion between 1988 and 1995 when there were only 12 member states. Legislation had been made in haste, usually in response to a disease crisis. New and emerging diseases such as severe acute respiratory syndrome (SARS), and Hendra and Nipah viruses had arisen which were zoonotic and which had originated from wildlife reservoirs. There was concern over the global spread of a strain of avian influenza (H5N1) which was zoonotic and killed over 50% of those human beings unfortunate enough to become infected. With globalisation of trade, the volume of trade in animal products within the EU and with third-country trading partners had increased substantially.

During the preceding decade, the EU had suffered large and very costly epidemics of disease: classical swine fever (CSF), foot and mouth disease (FMD) and highly pathogenic avian influenza (HPAI). In the face of these large outbreaks, there was growing public concern as to whether killing of large numbers of animals in order to control disease was the right approach. This concern was greatest in a sector of the EU which had grown with increasing affluence and which kept livestock not for commercial reasons but as a hobby. Hobby keepers often place an emotional value on their livestock beyond any commercial value, which was the basis of compensation in any disease eradication programme. Also, the institutional framework of the EU had changed, and there had been significant advances in the science and technology needed to inform animal health policy. Once the review had been completed, there was an extensive stakeholder consultation following which the Commission published a Communication: 'A new Animal Health Strategy for the European Union (2007–2013) where Prevention is better than cure' (European Commission 2007), otherwise known as the EU Animal Health Strategy 2007–2013.

A European Court of Auditors (2004) special report on the eradication, control and monitoring programmes to contain animal diseases, concluded that the animal disease programmes adequately contained animal diseases, and that the Commission's approach is supported by good technical advice, risk analysis and a mechanism for prioritising resources (ECA 2016). A noted drawback is that it is difficult to evaluate the cost-effectiveness (CE) of programmes due to the lack of available models and standardised for such an analysis. For veterinary programmes, unit costs and ceilings are used as a financial compensation system. These contribute to a lower administrative burden for DG SANTE as well as for member states. Although it takes a long time to identify and agree unit costs and ceilings, once established they create clarity and transparency in funding. To date, unit costs and ceilings have not been used for other spending areas within the CFF, but might well be considered. An observation made by the ECA is that the exchange of epidemiological information and the ready access to historic results could be better supported by relevant information systems.

11.3.1   EU Animal Health Strategy 2007–2013 'Prevention Is Better Than Cure'

The Strategy was a six-year work programme with four high-level goals:

To ensure a high level of public health and food safety by minimising the incidence of animal diseases, food-borne diseases and biotoxins, and chemical risks to humans

To promote animal health by preventing/reducing the incidence of animal diseases and in this way support the rural economy

To improve economic growth/cohesion/competitiveness by assuring free circulation of goods and animal movements proportionate to the risk of spreading disease and to the welfare of transported animals

To promote farming practices and animal welfare which prevent threats related to animal health and minimise environmental impacts in support of the EU Sustainable Development Strategy

The work programme was set out in the Action Plan for the implementation of the EU Animal Health Strategy (European Commission 2008). It was divided into four pillars of work:

Prioritisation of EU intervention
The EU animal health framework
Prevention, surveillance and preparedness
Science, innovation and research

These points (also called the four pillars) are briefly described below.

11.3.2   Prioritisation of EU Intervention

Pillar 1 of the strategy promises the use of risk assessment and risk management to identify threats relevant to the four high-level goals of the Strategy, to determine the level of acceptable risk to the EU and, since resources are limited, to prioritise the actions to be taken. Cost-benefit analysis and an assessment of likely effectiveness of any proposed action will be used to prioritise and determine any interventions. Decisions will be based on sound science. History has shown that there will always be new and emerging animal diseases. Where a new threat has been identified but there is scientific uncertainty about the likelihood of it occurring, the precautionary principle will be applied,; that is, proportionate and provisional measures will be adopted to ensure a high level of health protection pending further scientific information. While a sensible ideal, it will be interesting to see how the politicians in member states are prepared to apply the precautionary principle in the face of a new threat to public health from a disease of animal origin, which causes severe disease or death in human beings. In the face of uncertainty, politicians have tended to overreact, and behaviour towards animal health-related risks varies between member states.

11.3.3   A Modern EU Animal Health Framework

There are a number of strands to pillar 2 of the strategy. For good reason, EU animal health policy has historically evolved in a piecemeal fashion. The plan was to have a single horizontal legal framework which will define and integrate common principles and requirements of existing legislation including import controls, intra-EU trade, animal disease control, animal nutrition and animal welfare (see below how this has been achieved via the Animal Health Law). The plan is to simplify existing legislation and replace it by the new framework and convergence with international standards (OIE/Codex standards).

Developing efficient cost and responsibility sharing schemes is a further strand of pillar 2. Based on past experiences, it was felt that if livestock keepers contributed to the costs of an outbreak, they would take more responsibility with respect to prevention by practising good biosecurity. The costs of EU disease control in the enlarged EU and potential future costs of epidemics was an important driver in any cost and responsibility sharing initiative. The practical difficulties of implementing an EU-wide cost and responsibility sharing initiative should not be underestimated. There is a diverse range of views amongst member states, from some that have already a levy system in place, to others that require private insurance to top-up compensation, and yet others that believe that, as livestock keepers suffer consequential loss, this should be their only contribution to cost sharing.

11.3.4   Threat Prevention, Surveillance and Crisis Prevention

Pillar 3 of the strategy covers supporting on-farm biosecurity measures, which are the other side of the cost and responsibility sharing coin. The outcome will be the issuance of EU guidance and possible funding of infrastructure to support on-farm biosecurity.

However, as the costs of operating biosecurity measures becomes greater due to the increasing risk of disease introduction, there will be mounting pressure to become more proactive and to cooperate with third countries to stop new diseases at their source, and ultimately to achieve freedom from introduced animal diseases through building in resistance and resilience. New science (pillar 4) with advances in detection, monitoring and modelling of biosecurity threats will be an important feature of this inevitable evolution of biosecurity systems.

Pillar 3 also covers identification and tracing (essential for disease control), traceability of food for human consumption, better border biosecurity, and surveillance and crisis preparedness. Part of the identification of animals is the identification and registration of animals at farm level, which is also supported by the Common Agricultural Policy (CAP) via its cross-compliance mechanism. Veterinary surveillance is an essential component of any animal health strategy. In the case of epidemic diseases such as FMD, early detection is key to rapid implementation of control measures and to limiting the eventual size of an epidemic. In the case of insidious diseases such as salmonellosis, tuberculosis and brucellosis, a programme of laboratory testing is required to detect disease. Surveillance can be costly and hence the strategy requires prioritisation as in pillar 1. The need for each member state to have detailed contingency plans to deal with incursions of animal disease, tested through regular exercises, was a lesson learnt from the FMD crisis of 2001.

11.3.5   Science, Innovation and Research

Pillar 4 has the objective of stimulating and coordinating risk analysis, science, innovation and research contributing to a high level of public health and to the competitiveness of EU animal health business. Innovative developments may well provide alternative approaches to disease control within the EU and remove the need to control some diseases by mass killing of affected animals.

One of the key outputs of the Animal Health Strategy 2007–2013 'Prevention is better than cure' is the Animal Health Law which was introduced in 2016.

11.3.6   EU Animal Health Law (Regulation (EU) 2016/429)

The European Parliament and the Council adopted Regulation (EU) 2016/429 on transmissible animal diseases ('Animal Health Law') in

March 2016. The AHL will apply in all EU member states from 21 April 2021. The Animal Health Law is part of a package of measures proposed by the Commission in May 2013 to strengthen the enforcement of health and safety standards for the whole agri-food chain. This Regulation is about animal diseases that are transmissible to animals or humans. It provides for principles and rules for the prevention and control of such animal diseases in kept animals (i.e. animals under human control) and wild animals and animal products. It covers both terrestrial and aquatic animals. More precisely, these rules consist of requirements for disease prevention and preparedness; disease awareness; biosecurity; traceability of animals and where necessary products thereof; intra-EU movements and entry into the EU of animals and animal products; surveillance; disease control and eradication; and emergency measures.

Overall, the single, comprehensive Animal Health Law will support the EU livestock sector in its quest towards competitiveness and safe and smooth EU market of animals and of their products, leading to growth and jobs in this important sector:

The huge number of legal acts are streamlined into a single law

Simpler and clearer rules enable authorities and those having to follow the rules to focus on key priorities: preventing and eradicating disease

Responsibilities are clarified for farmers, vets and others dealing with animals

The new rules allow greater use of new technologies for animal health activities—surveillance of pathogens, electronic identification and registration of animals

Better early detection and control of animal diseases, including emerging diseases linked to climate change, will help to reduce the occurrence and effects of animal epidemics

There will be more flexibility to adjust rules to local circumstances, and to emerging issues such as climate and social change

It sets out a better legal basis for monitoring animal pathogens resistant to antimicrobial agents supplementing existing rules and two other proposals currently being negotiated in the European Parliament and Council, on veterinary medicines and on medicated feed

Several delegated and implementing acts have been adopted by the Commission until April 2019 to make the new rules applicable.

11.4   ECONOMIC ASSESSMENT OF ANIMAL HEALTH PROGRAMMES

As discussed above in the EU's Animal Health Strategy, a reference to economic aspects is made in pillars 1 (cost sharing) and 2 (cost-effectiveness). Cost-effectiveness (CE) analysis is a tool to relate outputs or impacts of an intervention to its costs. CE analyses have been widely applied in the human health domain, but are less frequent in the animal health field (Martins and Rushton 2014).

CE analyses are mostly done *ex ante*, to help set priorities for the funding of health care and food safety programmes or evaluate different alternative strategies. The essence is that for each intervention, the costs associated with that strategy can be compared with an alternative strategy aimed at contributing to the same objective. In this regard, the full set of interventions, measures or programmes covered by the common financial framework associated with Regulation (EU) 652/2014, as well as the objective of the evaluation, are important. An *ex post* evaluation can be done to evaluate the effect of a strategy.

From a CE perspective the objective of such an evaluation could be still formulated in different ways. For example:

to get an indication of the added value of the EU contribution
to compare additions to intervention strategies
to compare approaches between different MSs (e.g. in case study analyses)
to get an insight into the effectiveness of allocation of budget amongst different alternatives within or between EU policy areas

In case an intervention results in improved outputs or impact (effect), but at the same time the costs increase, the incremental cost approach to CE is useful and incremental CE ratios for various interventions or programmes can be ranked to set funding priorities.

11.4.1   Cost-Effectiveness Ratio

Cost-effectiveness (CE) analysis is a tool to relate outputs or impacts of an intervention to its costs. Its basic form is:

$$CE = \frac{\text{cost of intervention}}{\text{effectiveness of intervention}}$$

CE ratios can be presented as an average ratio (see expression above), but also as an incremental cost-effectiveness ratio where different intervention alternatives are compared. The basic structure of an incremental CE ratio (iCE) is:

$$iCE = \frac{\text{cost of intervention A} - \text{cost of intervention B}}{\text{effect of intervention A} - \text{effect of intervention B}}$$

See, for example, Detsky and Nagly (1990) for a worked-out example.

11.4.2   Steps in a Cost-Effectiveness Analysis

CE analysis involves a number of steps (Martins and Rushton 2014), which are briefly described here (see Fig. 11.1 for a schematic overview).

Firstly, CE analysis always requires a perspective or viewpoint from which the analysis is pursued. Roughly speaking, the two options are here the programme option and the societal option.

The next step regards the identification of the problem and the link with the intervention. The identification step may, for example, be based on the intervention logic of the CFF Regulation. In the proposed CE analysis, appropriate levels of analysis will have to be chosen, which allow for a meaningful use of the CE indicators.

The third step, which is closely connected with the previous one, involves the determination of a conceptual model, which further describes the mechanisms that play a role in the defined problem domain, and outlines the full range of events arising from the intervention. To do this often, a decision tree approach is chosen (Pettiti 2000). This is the step which provides insight into the linkage between inputs (efforts, costs) and outputs (results, impacts). Having clarity on this, the next steps are to further identify and estimate the costs and the outputs.

As regards the costs (representing the numerator part of the CE ratio), this first includes an estimate of the costs of all the goods, services and other resources that are consumed in the provision of the analysed intervention. Second, costs can also arise because of side effects and present and future consequences associated with the analysed policy intervention

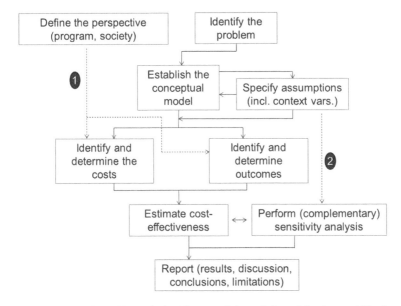

Fig. 11.1 Steps in a CE analysis. (Source: Adapted from Martins and Rushton 2014)

(e.g. indirect and aftermath costs related to a disease outbreak that has been successfully addressed by an emergency intervention policy measure) (Siegel et al. 1996). In the health literature it is a usual practice to focus on the direct costs of the intervention or policy measure analysed. Often guidelines are used, which clearly establish the categories of costs that should be considered as direct costs. They include categories like costs of tests, medicines, labour costs arising from intervention-related activities, such as surveillance and monitoring efforts, disease eradication actions (e.g. slaughtering of animals).

In order to estimate the effectiveness of the intervention (representing the denominator part of the CE ratio), a vast range of measures is used in the literature, which reflects the diversity of effects associated with the typical kind of policy intervention measures in this domain. Effectiveness estimate measures include premature deaths averted, change in life expectancy, improvement in the years of potential life gained (YLGs), quality of life years (QALYs), disability-adjusted life years (DALYs) (Brazier et al. 2007; Boardman et al. 2014), reductions in the number of disease cases, prevalence, risk on disease outbreak (e.g. due to a prevention programme) and so on. Effectiveness can be estimated by measuring the results of an intervention, as well as by measuring the impact of an intervention. Measurement of the full impact might be often difficult (e.g. how to measure the impact of an improved health status on the gains this created with respect to a country's trade position, such as being less vulnerable to an export ban). The estimation of effect may require the use of an epidemiological model tailored to the policy intervention or project environment that is analysed (e.g. Bergevoet et al. 2009). The difficulties with respect to impact assessment does not preclude the use of CE indicators, since reliable output indicators will be usually available (Brent 2003).

Having the information from steps (4) and (5), the CE ratio can be calculated as presented before (by putting the appropriate numbers in the denominator and the numerator of the CE ratio expression). As has been denoted, CE analysis always implies that a number of assumptions have to be made, which will influence the outcome of the CE indicator. Sensitivity analysis may be used to analyse how sensitive the CE indicator is with respect to specific assumptions that are made and by that provide the analyst and client insight into a reliable range of the CE indicator.

The final step concerns the proper reporting of the analysis and outcomes, which presents the CE results, how they are affected by the different components underlying them, the assumptions they are based on, and the limitations inherent to the analysis (e.g. the potential role of context or confounding variables).

11.4.3   Complexities in Animal Health Programme Assessments

The CE results are sensitive to the time horizon of the analysis. For that reason, it is important to cover the appropriate (or entire) time on which the analysed intervention has its impact (Brent 2003; Cohen and Reynolds 2008). Similar to the standard approach in cost/benefit analysis, when costs are spread over time, these should be properly discounted to allow for a proper aggregation (net present value-calculation).[2] As an example,

---

[2] Note that while costs are expressed in monetary units and easily can be aggregated, effects are measured in their own (physical) non-monetary units. However, this does not preclude the discounting of the effects when they occur at different moments over time. Moreover, an argument could be made to use consistent discount rates when discounting costs and effect rather than treating both differently.

in case of an emergency (disease outbreak), it is likely that costs associated with an emergency payment measure not only concern outbreak period, but that also payments are made in later periods. Costs and effects of interventions need to be carefully related to each other, and then proper aggregation of costs and effects need to be accounted for, including discounting (Brent 2003, chapter 6). To establish this linkage in the literature frequently epidemiological-economic models are used, which not only enable the linkage of costs to final impacts, but also allow to account for the role of control or context variables.

For the evaluation of health policy measures or projects, as for any other kind of project, not only the objectives (see Fig. 11.1) but also the baseline and other alternatives have to be identified. The baseline or benchmark choice co-depends on the scope of the evaluation. In case the alternative of having the current or evaluated policy would be discontinuing the policy or have no policy intervention at all, the without intervention measure or project alternative is an obvious candidate to use as a benchmark. For each (other) alternative, then the incremental costs and effects relative to this benchmark are identified and determined. The benchmark choice is an important issue, and it should be realistic.

Most CE analyses described in the literature are so-called ex ante studies. The CE technique is helpful in evaluating different alternatives or strategies. As was mentioned before, most of the time the analysis is supported by epidemiological models that simulate expected effects given a specific strategy. Sensitivity analyses in such evaluations should also indicate when an alternative strategy should be preferred. In the *ex post* monitoring, the main focus could then be to monitor whether key indicators are reaching tipping points so alternative strategies need to be considered. A complicating factor in ex post CE analysis is that the control or context variables are no longer constant (in contrast with ex ante CE analysis using modelling tools in which these variables are controlled), but are changing at the same time as the intervention efforts are made (and maybe in different directions for different member states). As such, this likely affects the linkage between the intervention and the final impact, and for a sound CE analysis the impact of the change in context variables on the programme performance need to be corrected for. The reason why in the literature ex post evaluations are relatively scarce is probably because of the many complexities involved and because CE analysis is especially interesting when comparing different alternatives. Once a strategy is chosen for implementation (as is the case in an ex post situation) comparison with (hypothetical) alternatives (that could have been chosen) is often of less interest.

It should be mentioned that at this moment there are already two approaches followed by DG SANTE to guarantee objective-oriented policy measures and preserve resource efficiency. First, the set of operational indicators that has been developed has a clear link with the (specific) objectives as they are defined in Regulation (EU) No 652/2014, and which thus allow to monitor performance in this regard. Though improvements might be possible, this is an important input for the impact evaluation of the policy. Second, DG SANTE uses an extensive so-called fee-grid approach, which defines eligible unit cost levels or imposes maximum limits to unit costs for different (disease-specific) eligible cost categories. These per unit cost indicators are simple cost/output indicators which have clear limitations, but are nevertheless second best instruments to monitor efficiency with respect to resource use.

11.5   CONCLUSIONS

The EU's animal health policy helps to protect more than 500 million consumers in the EU and facilitates the functioning of agri-food supply chains. The competitive position of this sector is supported by the EU's high food safety standards, which contribute to a global perception of high-quality European products.

The European Court of Auditors (2004) concluded that the animal disease programmes adequately contained animal diseases, and that the Commission's approach is supported by good technical advice, risk analysis and a mechanism for prioritising resources. Serious animal health diseases have been brought under control or have been eradicated, allowing the production of safe, wholesome food within the EU. Notable successes of the policy are the decreases in cases of BSE in cattle, salmonella in poultry and rabies in wildlife. However, the EU continues to remain under the threat of exotic animal diseases and will continue to do so as new animal diseases emerge. As an example, the eradication of ASF, bovine brucellosis and tuberculosis and ovine and caprine brucellosis are posing continuing challenges in some member states.

The CFF contributes to achieving and supporting EU added value. Member states benefit from the prioritised and targeted implementation of EU co-funded activities, especially for emergency, eradication, control and monitoring measures for animal diseases and plant pest throughout the Union. The financial solidarity that the CFF provides enables member states to take required actions according to their interests. Otherwise these may have been beyond the (financial) capacity of an individual member state. Moreover, the CFF enables harmonised and robust controls, which satisfy an important need with respect to an effective food safety policy.

In the last half century, the EU has come a long way towards achieving a fully harmonised legal framework for the importation and trade of live animals and animal products. With the new Animal Health Law, which was adopted in 2016, the EU has made a single, comprehensive animal health regulation to further strengthen the enforcement of health standards for the whole agri-food chain. Until April 2019, delegated and implementing acts have been adopted by the Commission to make the new rules applicable. This comprehensive Animal Health Law also aims to support the EU livestock sector in its quest towards competitiveness and safe and smooth EU market of animals and of their products.

REFERENCES

Bergevoet, R.H., G. van Schaik, J. Veling, G.B. Backus, and P. Franken. 2009. Economic and Epidemiological Evaluation of Salmonella Control in Dutch Dairy Herds. *Preventive Veterinary Medicine* 89 (1–2): 1–7.

Boardman, A.E., D.H. Greenberg, A.R. Vining, and D.L. Weimer. 2014. *Cost-Benefit Analysis: Concepts and Practice*. 4th ed. Upper Saddle River: Pearson Education.

Brazier, J., J. Ratcliffe, A. Tsuchiya, and J. Salomon. 2007. *Measuring an Valuing Health Benefits for Economic Evaluation*. New York: Oxford University Press.

Brent, R.J. 2003. *Cost-Benefit Analysis and Health Care Evaluations*. Cheltenham: Edward Elgar.

Cohen, D.J., and M.R. Reynolds. 2008. Interpreting the Results of Cost-Effectiveness Studies. *Journal of the American College of Cardiology* 52 (25): 2119–2126.

Court of Auditors. 2004. Special Report No 8/2004. Official Journal of the European Union. Special Report. OJ 2005/C 54/01.

Detsky, A.S., and I.G. Nagly. 1990. A Clinician's Guide to Cost-Effectiveness Analysis. *Annals of Internal Medicine* 113: 147–154.

ECA. 2016. *Eradication, Control and Monitoring Programmes to Contain Animal Diseases (Special Report)*. Luxembourg: European Union.

European Commission. 2007. *A New Animal Health Strategy for the European Union (2007–2013) Where Prevention Is Better Than Cure*. Brussels: European

Commission, Communication COM 539 (2007). http://ec.europa.eu/food/animal/diseases/strategy/animal_health_strategy_en.pdf

———. 2008. *Action Plan for the Implementation of the EU Animal Health Strategy*. Brussels: European Commission, Communication COM 545 (2008), Brussels. http://www.eubusiness.com/topics/agri/animal-health-guide.03/

IBF International Consulting, WUR, VetEffecT, and European Commission. 2017. *Study on intra-European Union (intra-EU) Animal Health Certification of Certain Live Animals*. Publications Office of the European Union, Luxembourg, ISBN 978-92-79-73525-7, https://doi.org/10.2875/809481.

Martins, S.B., and J. Rushton. 2014. Cost-Effectiveness Analysis: Adding Value to Assessment of Animal Health, Welfare and Production. *Revue scientifique et technique-Office international des épizooties* 33 (3): 1–18.

Pettiti, D.B. 2000. *Meta-Analysis, Decision-Analysis, and Cost-Effectiveness Analysis – Methods for Quantitative Synthesis in Medicine*. 2nd ed. New York: Oxford University Press. (Monographs in Epidemiology and Biostatistics No. 31).

Siegel, J.E., M.C. Weinstein, L.B. Russell, and M.R. Gold. 1996. Recommendations for Reporting Cost-Effectiveness Analyses. *JAMA* 276 (16): 1339–1341. https://doi.org/10.1001/jama.1996.03540160061034.

CHAPTER 12

Plant Health and Plant Protection Policies

Huib Silvis, Johan Bremmer, and Roel Jongeneel

12.1 Introduction

Protection of plant health involves a complex of preventive and curative measures. Preventive measures involve the breeding of varieties with resistance against plant pests and diseases, the controlled production of pest-free seeds and planting material, and the application of production methods such as crop rotation. With increasing trade, transport and movement of plants (including seeds and plant products), and also human travel around the world, the risk of introduction and spread of pests into new areas has increased. To reduce the impact of existing pests, an integrated

H. Silvis
Performance and Impact Agrosectors, Wageningen Economic Research,
The Hague, The Netherlands
e-mail: huib.silvis@wur.nl

J. Bremmer
Innovation- and Risk Management and Information Governance Unit,
Wageningen Economic Research, The Hague, The Netherlands
e-mail: johan.bremmer@wur.nl

R. Jongeneel (✉)
Agricultural Economics and Rural Policy Group, Wageningen University,
Wageningen, Gelderland, The Netherlands
e-mail: roel.jongeneel@wur.nl

© The Author(s) 2019   173
L. Dries et al. (eds.), *EU Bioeconomy Economics and Policies: Volume I*,
Palgrave Advances in Bioeconomy: Economics and Policies,
https://doi.org/10.1007/978-3-030-28634-7_12

pest management approach is increasingly conducted, of which the use of plant protection products (PPPs) is one element. Over time, many PPPs have been used in preventive applications to protect plants in advance of pest infestation and in curative applications to reduce pest population levels.

Present EU plant health legislation supervises the sale and use of PPPs and sets standards to monitor and control pesticide residues. It also ensures quality conditions for sale of seeds and propagating material within the EU, and covers the intellectual property rights granted to plant varieties, as well as the conservation and use of genetic resources. Concerning exotic plant pests, legislation aims at protection against the introduction of exotic pests and invasive plants into the EU and against their spread within the EU. The term 'plant health policy', or phytosanitary policy, has become particularly associated with these legislative measures designed to minimize the impact of exotic pests.

In this chapter the EU plant health policy is positioned within the international framework on plant health legislation as defined by the WTO agreement on Sanitary and Phytosanitary Measures (WTO-SPS) and the International Plant Protection Convention (IPPC). First, the need for legislative measures against plant pests is discussed, followed by a description of the international standards on these measures. Subsequently, some notable features of the EU policy on exotic diseases are described, followed by a brief outline of the EU policy on the use of PPPs.

12.2   Plant Pests and Diseases

In European agriculture, examples reflecting the socio-economic relevance of plant pests and diseases may best be highlighted by the case of potatoes. Historically, the potato blight fungus showed the enormous impact pathogens can have, by being responsible for the Irish potato famine in the 1840s. More recently, the potato ring rot and potato brown rot bacterial pathogens are serious ongoing concerns for European potato production (CABI/EPPO 1997). A current example is *Xylella fastidiosa*, causing high mortality of olive trees in Italy and damaging both the landscape and the olive production.

Not only diseases affecting cultivated plants but also diseases affecting plants in natural ecosystems can have a significant social and, potentially, economic impact. An historical example is the epidemics of Dutch elm disease in Europe during the twentieth century (Brasier and Buck 2001).

12.2.1   *Transboundary Plant Pests and Diseases*

Transboundary plant pests and diseases affect food crops, causing significant losses to farmers and threatening food security. The spread of transboundary plant pests and diseases has increased dramatically in recent years. Globalization, trade and climate change, as well as reduced resilience in production systems due to decades of agricultural intensification, have all played a part. Transboundary plant pests and diseases can easily spread to several countries and reach epidemic proportions. Outbreaks and upsurges can cause huge losses to crops and pastures, threatening the livelihoods of vulnerable farmers and the food and nutrition security of millions at a time. Locusts, armyworm, fruit flies, banana diseases, cassava diseases and wheat rusts are among the most destructive transboundary plant pests and diseases. Plant pests and diseases spread in three principal ways: trade or other human-migrated movement; environmental forces—weather and windborne; insect or other vector-borne pathogens.

In principle, decisions regarding prevention and control of native pests are made at the farm level by the individual farmer, using a variety of crop protection methods. This may include the use of PPPs, although the use of pesticides itself is subject to a range of legislation (see paragraph 12.5). However, the introduction of an exotic pest poses a serious threat to the production of a large area, because it is not effectively prevented by individual producers. This may be due to lack of knowledge, effective measures and sometimes incentives serving other interests. In these cases, governmentally regulated interventions on prevention and control are needed.

This is particularly important for pests affecting natural ecosystems, since large parts of these areas are not managed by private producers. The rate of introduction and spread of exotic pests has increased steadily over the last century (Waage et al. 2005) mainly as a result of expanding globalization of trade in plant material. Once established, these organisms are generally impossible to eradicate, difficult to control, and may cause high additional yield losses. Governments may take responsibility for protecting their territory against the introduction and spread of these exotic pests by using a variety of legislative and regulatory (phytosanitary) measures. The right and need of countries to impose these measures to protect plant health are internationally recognized by the WTO agreement on Sanitary and Phytosanitary Measures (WTO-SPS) and the International Plant Protection Convention (IPPC). These international agreements are necessary to ensure that the applied measures are used only for the protection of plant health and not as unjustified barriers to trade.

12.3   THE INTERNATIONAL FRAMEWORK ON PLANT HEALTH POLICY

To prevent the introduction and spread of plant pests and diseases and to promote appropriate measures for their control, the WTO-SPS agreement requires a scientific underpinning for trade-restricting measures based on international standards, guidelines and recommendations (see Chap. 7). The International Plant Protection Convention (IPPC) is the only international body for setting and implementing International Standards for Phytosanitary Measures (ISPMs), being one of the 'Three Sisters' of the WTO Sanitary and Phytosanitary Measures (SPS) Agreement, along with the Codex Alimentarius Commission and the World Organization for Animal Health (OIE).

12.3.1   The International Plant Protection Convention (IPPC)

The IPPC is an international plant health agreement which aims at protecting the world's plant resources from the spread and introduction of pests. The Convention has been deposited with the Director-General of the Food and Agriculture Organization of the United Nations (FAO) since its initial adoption by the Conference of FAO in 1951. The IPPC's main governing body is the Commission on Phytosanitary Measures (CPM). It meets annually to review global plant protection needs, review and adopt ISPMs and set the annual IPPC work programme. In 2018, it had 183 contracting parties. The IPPC has several mechanisms for fostering cooperation among contracting parties. These include developing ISPMs, fostering information exchange, developing capacity and providing legal and policy guidelines (IPPC 2019).

IPPC Annual report 2018, http://www.fao.org/documents/card/en/c/CA3783EN

The ISPM procedure of the IPPC aims to develop a series of largely interlinked standards. The majority of those adopted in the early years consist of 'horizontal' standards providing general guidance for the development and operation of plant health procedures. Within this framework, 'vertical' pest or commodity-specific standards are being developed to give precise guidance for dealing with particular situations (Ebbels 2003).

Principles of Plant Quarantine as Related to International Trade (ISPM no. 1) is a very important horizontal standard. It facilitates the development of other standards and guides governments in reducing or eliminating unjustifiable phytosanitary measures. Its purpose is to support the IPPC and to ensure coherence with the WTO-SPS (Ebbels 2003). More specialized horizontal standards include aspects of risk analysis (ISPM nos. 2 and 11), surveillance and eradication (ISPM nos. 6 and 9), the establishment of pest-free areas (ISPM no. 4), export certification and phytosanitary certificates (ISPM nos. 7 and 12), pest reporting (ISPM no. 17) and non-compliance notification (ISPM no. 13). Taken together, these horizontal standards provide guidance and the approach that national plant protection authorities should adopt in dispensing their obligations under the IPPC.

The development of 'vertical' standards defining specific instructions regarding the measures necessary to deal with particular pests, individual techniques or technologies, or specific commodities is of more recent date.

The total package of standards serves not only as a model for developing measures, but also as a reference point for evaluating or challenging measures. By using standards for designing and implementing phytosanitary systems, countries reduce the level of analytical resources needed, can expect to withstand the scrutiny of trading partners and meet their obligations under the IPPC and the WTO-SPS (Schrader and Unger 2003; Chapter 4).

To promote interregional cooperation, the IPPC includes provisions for the establishment of Regional Plant Protection Organizations (RPPOs), which act at an intergovernmental level without any legal force, although their advisory powers can be strong. Currently there are nine RPPOs, among which is the European and Mediterranean Plant Protection Organization (EPPO).

12.3.2   *The European and Mediterranean Plant Protection Organization*

The EPPO is an intergovernmental organization responsible for cooperation in plant health within the Euro-Mediterranean region. Founded in 1951 by 15 European countries, EPPO now has 52 members. Its objectives are to protect plants by developing international strategies against the introduction and spread of pests which are a threat to agriculture, forestry and the environment, and by promoting safe and effective pest control methods. Following the terms of the International Plant Protection Convention (IPPC), EPPO is a Regional Plant Protection Organization and thus participates in global discussions on plant health. EPPO is a standard-setting organization which has produced a large number of standards in the areas of plant protection products and plant quarantine. These standards constitute recommendations that are addressed to the National Plant Protection Organizations of EPPO member countries. Finally, EPPO promotes the exchange of information between its member countries by maintaining information services and databases on plant pests and by organizing conferences and workshops.

https://www.eppo.int/ABOUT_EPPO/about_eppo

12.4   PLANT HEALTH POLICY WITHIN THE EU

The EU plant health policy was established by Council Directive 2000/29/ EC. The main objective of this directive is to protect plants and plant products against the introduction and spread of pests within the EU. To this end, it regulates the trade of plants and plant products and other materials within the EU as well as imports from the rest of the world in accordance with the international plant health standards and obligations as defined by the IPPC.

In October 2016, the European Parliament and the Council adopted Regulation (EU) 2016/2031 on protective measures against plant pests (Plant Health Law). On 13 December 2016, the Regulation entered into force and will be applicable from 14 December 2019. These rules constitute the EU Plant Health Regime, which has been in place since 1977 and was fully reviewed by the European Commission in May 2013. The new rules aim to modernize the Plant Health Regime, enhancing more effective measures for the protection of the Union's territory and its plants. They also aim to ensure safe trade, as well as to mitigate the impacts of climate change on the health of the crops and forests.

12.4.1   Regulated Plants

From 14 December 2019, all plants (including living parts of plants) will need to be accompanied by a phytosanitary certificate to enter into the EU, unless they are listed in Commission Implementing Regulation (EU) 2018/2019 as exempted from this general requirement (not requiring to be accompanied by a phytosanitary certificate). Currently, the list of plants exempted from the obligation to carry a phytosanitary certificate from 14

December 2019 are the following fruits: pineapples, coconuts, durians, bananas and dates.

12.4.2   *Intra-EU Trade*

EU plant health rules cover the movement and trade within the EU of certain plants, plant products and other objects which are potential carriers of harmful organisms. The movement between and within member states of certain plants, plant products and other objects which are potential carriers of harmful organisms of relevance for the entire EU (Annex V Council Directive 2000/29/EC) must be accompanied by a plant passport. The aim of this document is to give assurance of adequate plant health status and to permit the origin of the traded materials to be traced (viz. identification and registration system). The proper issue of plant passports is the responsibility of the member state in which the traded material has been produced or into which it is imported from a third country. Plant passports are issued by the responsible official plant protection service (normally National Plant Protection Organizations [NPPOs]), or by producers or traders authorized to do so. A specific code on the plant passports allows the identification of the official plant protection services responsible for the control of the producers and traders in the region. In addition, it contains a unique registration number for the producer or trader, and indicates the country of origin if the plants have been imported from a third country. All producers and traders of regulated plants and plant products have to be registered by the responsible official service and have to be visited and inspected regularly.

12.4.3   *Trade in Plants and Plant Products from Non-EU Countries*

The Plant Health Law increases the prevention against the introduction of new pests via imports from third countries. The introduction into the EU territory of high risk plants will be provisionally prohibited from 14 December 2019 until a full risk assessment has been carried out.

12.4.4   *Control Measures*

Member states that discover the presence of a listed plant pest within their territory are obliged to notify the Commission and other member states and to take measures to eradicate, or, if this is not possible, to prevent the spread of the pest concerned. This action is compulsory, whether the regulated pest has been found as an outbreak on a crop or found on material received in trade with another member state.

12.4.5   *EU Notification System for Plant Health Interceptions: European Union Notification System for Plant Health Interceptions (EUROPHYT)*

EUROPHYT (European Union Notification System for Plant Health Interceptions) describes a notification and rapid alert system dealing with interceptions for plant health reasons of consignments of plants and plant products imported into the EU or being traded within the EU itself. EUROPHYT is established and run by the Directorate- General for Health and Consumers of the European Commission. EUROPHYT provides support for the implementation of preventative measures by ensuring that the data on risks to plant health from trade in plants and plant products is up to date and accurate. EUROPHYT is a web-based network and database. It connects plant health authorities of the EU member states and Switzerland, the European Food Safety Authority and the Directorate-General for Health and Food Safety of the European Commission.

Where a member state considers that there is an imminent danger of introduction or spread of a non-listed plant pest, it should notify the Commission of the measures it would like to see taken and may temporarily take additional emergency measures. The Commission has an obligation to examine such an emerging situation as soon as possible. As defined by international trade rules, any control measure taken against the introduction and spread of new pests must be justified by a science-based pest risk analysis. Upon request by the Commission, the Scientific Panel on Plant Health of the European Food Safety Authority (EFSA 2019) evaluates pest risk analyses produced by EU member states or third parties (non-EU countries) in order to provide the required scientific advice. EU control measures may be adopted if risk analyses at EU level reveal that further measures against the non-listed pest are necessary.

The costs of measures may be compensated by the EU to a maximum of 50% of eligible expenditure (i.e. costs incurred by an NPPO), the remainder being borne by the affected member state. The costs of remedial measures and crop destruction are paid by the owner of the infected crop. This is in contrast to the EU financing of animal health, where the value of private property destroyed for the public good (viz. the control of a contagious disease) is at least partly compensated by EU and member state (see Chap. 11). Other than animal diseases, plant diseases do not threaten human health. Therefore, needs with respect to plant health have a more economic (protecting production and trade) and environmental (protecting nature and landscape) background than needs with respect to animal health.

As for animal health, provisions for the management of expenditure relating to plant health and plant reproductive material are laid down in Regulation (EU) No 652/2014 (the Common Financial Framework (CFF) Regulation). One of the objectives is to contribute to the timely detection of pests and their eradication where those pests have entered the Union. The specific objectives for plant health are the coverage of the Union territory by surveys for pests, in particular for pests not known to occur in the Union territory and pests considered to be most dangerous for the Union territory, and the time and success rate for the eradication of those pests. To compensate for the costs incurred by member states in the spending areas covered by the CFF Regulation, generally a grant system is used. The CFF Regulation describes the eligible measures which may benefit from a Union contribution as well as the eligible costs and applicable rates. It establishes priorities for appropriate focusing of financial support for phytosanitary programmes.

12.5   PLANT PROTECTION PRODUCTS

Registration of pesticides and their formulations by government agencies began after World War II and was given a serious further impetus by the publication of Rachel Carson's alarming book *Silent Spring* (1962). *Silent Spring* focused on the use of insecticides such as DDT (dichlorodiphenyl-trichloroethane), but at the same time initiated much wider attention on the use of pesticides. In the EU, this resulted in Regulation 91/414 for strengthening and harmonizing PPP standards within the member states.

The use of PPPs (pesticides/biocides) is still substantial in the EU and has not declined over the past decade. Moreover, average figures hide very high application levels at particular places and/or for intensive growing of plants. Even more important is the reduction and renewal of active ingredients, which may cause harm to humans and ecosystems. This is an ongoing process under Regulation 91/414/EEC and its successor Regulation (EC) 1107/2009, applicable as of 14 June 2011. Based on these regulations, all active ingredients in PPPs need to be assessed regularly to be listed in Annex I (Directive 91/414/EEC) as approved ingredients. Individual member states can only authorize plant protection products whose active ingredients are included in this list. Harmonization of the assessment process to consider the safety of active ingredients within the EU is of crucial importance. However, such a harmonization should also incorporate the effects of differences in, for example, climatic conditions (pesticide residues are more harmful in a cold than in a warm climate) and local circumstances (near rivers and canals, or in nature preservation areas).

12.5.1   Plant Protection Products Application Management System

The Plant Protection Products Application Management System (PPPAMS) was developed by the European Commission to enable industry users to create applications for PPPs and submit these to EU countries for evaluation. EU countries then manage these applications within the system, concluding with authorization of the PPP or refusal of the application. The system is designed to support EU countries in fulfilling their legal obligations under Regulation (EC) No 1107/2009, notably Article 57(1) and (2).

12.5.2   The Case of Neonicotoids

The use of neonicotoids is an interesting case. In 2013 the European Commission placed restrictions on the use of pesticide products containing the active substances clothianidin, thiamethoxam and imidacloprid. This followed an assessment by EFSA which showed that the substances posed risks to bee health. Member state governments may override the restrictions and issue emergency authorizations in cases where there is evidence that the threat from particular plant pests cannot be contained by other means. Several member states have repeatedly granted such authorizations since 2013. EFSA has examined the scientific basis for emergency authorizations of neonicotinoid pesticides which were granted in seven EU member states in 2017. EFSA's reports evaluate on a country-by-country basis whether other pesticides could have been substituted for the neonicotinoid products and assess the availability of non-insecticidal alternatives. In 2017, EFSA developed a methodology for evaluating requests to use insecticides when there is a serious danger to plant health. The European Commission subsequently asked EFSA to use the methodology to assess the exceptional uses of neonicotinoid pesticides authorized in 2017 by Bulgaria, Estonia, Finland, Hungary, Latvia, Lithuania and

Romania. The reports consider only the justification for issuing the emergency authorizations. The methodology does not cover measures taken by member states to mitigate the risk to bees and the environment from neonicotinoid-based pesticides. In May 2018, following endorsement by member states, the European Commission further restricted the use of neonicotinoids on the basis of a new risk assessment from EFSA (2018).

12.5.3   Sustainable Use of Pesticides

The use of pesticides is addressed by Directive 2009/128/EC. This aims to achieve a sustainable use of pesticides in the EU by reducing the risks and impacts of pesticide use on human health and the environment and by promoting the use of integrated pest management (IPM) and alternative approaches or techniques, such as non-chemical alternatives to pesticides. EU countries have drawn up National Action Plans to implement the range of actions set out in the Directive. The main actions relate to training of users, advisors and distributors of pesticides, inspection of pesticide application equipment, the prohibition of aerial spraying, limitation of pesticide use in sensitive areas and information and awareness raising about pesticide risks. EU countries must also promote integrated pest management (IPM), for which general principles are laid down in Annex III of the Directive. According to a report on the implementation of the Directive, all member states had adopted national action plans (NAPs), in many cases with significant delays, and with a huge diversity in their completeness and coverage. IPM is a cornerstone of the Directive, but compliance with the principles of IPM at individual grower level is not being systematically checked by member states. Furthermore, member states have not yet set clear criteria in order to ensure that the general principles of IPM are implemented by all professional users (DG Health and Food Safety 2017).

12.5.4   Regulatory Fitness and Performance Evaluation

In November 2016 the Commission published a roadmap on the Regulatory Fitness and Performance (REFIT)[1] evaluation of the EU leg-

---

[1] REFIT (Regulatory Fitness and Performance) is a rolling programme to keep the entire stock of EU legislation under review and ensure that it is 'fit for purpose'; that regulatory burdens are minimized and that all simplification options are identified and applied.

islation on plant protection products and pesticides residues. This road-map is the first step in the evaluation process and outlines the purpose, content and scope of the evaluation. Do the regulations meet the needs of citizens, businesses and public institutions in an efficient manner? The Commission approves active substances, that is, the agent used to achieve the protective effect, for the use in PPPs. In order to protect consumers, the Commission also sets maximum residue levels (MRLs) for pesticides, that is, the highest levels of pesticide residues that are legally tolerated in or on food or feed, including imported products. The evaluation aims to perform an evidence-based assessment of the implementation of the PPP and MRL regulations and address synergies, gaps, inefficiencies and administrative burdens. The evaluation process is constituted of different steps. The evaluation is foreseen to be finalized in 2019.

12.6   Concluding Remarks

Phytosanitary risk management serves plant production and ecosystems by preventing introduction of invasive organisms harmful for plant health. Ecosystems can be disturbed and plant production can be affected by quality and production losses. Since infestation with a few organisms can be sufficient for causing a disaster, to reduce the phytosanitary risk as much as possible, a zero-tolerance policy is applied. This serves sustainable crop protection in the country at risk, since plants do not have to be treated by crop protection products against harmful organisms that are absent.

However, global trade in plants and plant products is the major pathway for introduction of invasive organisms. In order to prevent the introduction of harmful organisms, they have to be controlled in the country of origin. Because of the zero-tolerance policy, application of biocontrol methods is in many cases not sufficient. The basic principle of biocontrol methods is the application of biocontrol agents reducing the population of harmful organisms below economic injury levels and reaching population levels in which harmful organisms and biocontrol agents are balanced. By consequence, both harmful organisms and biocontrol agent can be present on products for export destination.

An additional complication is the absence of an international level playing field in registration of biocontrol agents. A biocontrol agent registered in a country can be considered as a harmful organism in a neighbouring country. In some cases, effective treatments without using pesticides can be applied to eradicate harmful organisms (e.g. cold treatments against insects). However, this cannot be applied on all products and is not effective for all harmful organisms. In such cases application of pesticides is necessary to safeguard export.

The objective to prevent plants and plant products being infested with harmful organisms conflicts with the objective of making crop protection more sustainable. Especially developing countries investing in development of export markets suffer from this tension.

The focus of this chapter has been on plant health (including invasive species), ignoring the opportunities for applying new technologies or more sustainable production methods. In particular, the interaction between new plant varieties and production methods and the use of plant protection methods is an interesting area for future developments, with Genetically Modified Organism (GMOs) as one of the leading technologies. As will be shown in Chapter 26, the present GMO policy of the EU allows an asynchronous approval process between member states. In general, EU policy on GMO approval is rather restrained, which could be a threat to its international competitiveness, considering the higher level of GMO acceptance in non-EU countries.

REFERENCES

Brasier, C.M., and K.W. Buck. 2001. Rapid Evolutionary Changes in a Globally Invading Fungal Pathogen (Dutch Elm Disease). *Biological Invasions* 3: 223–233.

CABI/EPPO. 1997. *Quarantine Pests for Europe*. 2nd ed. Wallingford: CAB International.

Carson, R. 1962. *Silent Spring*, 378. Boston: Houghton Mifflin.

DG Health and Safety. 2017. *Overview Report; Sustainable Use of Pesticides*. Brussels: European Commission, DG(SANTE) 2017-6291.

Ebbels, D.L. 2003. *Principles of Plant Health and Quarantine*, 302. Wallingford: CABI.

EFSA. 2018. Neonicotinoids: EFSA Evaluates Emergency Uses. Last Modified June 21, 2018. http://www.efsa.europa.eu/en/press/news/180621

———. 2019. European Food Safety Authority. Official Website Available at www.efsa.europa.eu/

IPPC. 2019. International Phytosanitary Portal (IPP). The Official Website for the International Plant Protection Convention. Available at https://www.ippc.int

Schrader, G., and J.G. Unger. 2003. Plant Quarantine as a Measure Against Invasive Alien Species: The Framework of the International Plant Protection

Convention and the Plant Health Regulations of the European Union. *Biological Invasions* 5: 357–364.

Waage, J.K., R.W. Fraser, J.D. Mumford, D.C. Cook, and A. Wilby. 2005. *A New Agenda for Biosecurity*, 198. London: Horizon Scanning Programme, Department for Environment.

WEBSITES

http://ec.europa.eu/food/plant/index_en.htm
http://www.efsa.europa.eu/
http://www.eppo.org/
https://www.ippc.int/
https://ec.europa.eu/info/departments/health-and-food-safety_en

CHAPTER 13

Environment and Agriculture

Huib Silvis, Roel Jongeneel, and Vincent Linderhof

13.1 Introduction

European society is concerned about pollution of water and atmosphere, degradation of landscape and loss of biodiversity, all of which are classic examples of negative externalities. Protecting, preserving of natural areas

---

This chapter is a revision of Floor Brouwer and Huib Silvis, Chapter 20. Rural areas and the environment. In: Arie Oskam, Gerrit Meester and Huib Silvis (Eds) (2011), EU policy for Agriculture, Food and Rural Areas, Wageningen Academic Publishers.

H. Silvis
Performance and Impact Agrosectors, Wageningen Economic Research,
The Hague, The Netherlands
e-mail: huib.silvis@wur.nl

R. Jongeneel (✉)
Agricultural Economics and Rural Policy Group, Wageningen University,
Wageningen, Gelderland, The Netherlands
e-mail: roel.jongeneel@wur.nl

V. Linderhof
Green Economy and Landuse Unit, Wageningen Economic Research,
The Hague, The Netherlands
e-mail: vincent.linderhof@wur.nl

187

L. Dries et al. (eds.), *EU Bioeconomy Economics and Policies: Volume I*,
Palgrave Advances in Bioeconomy: Economics and Policies,
https://doi.org/10.1007/978-3-030-28634-7_13

and reducing these negative externalities therefore necessitate public policy. The EU has some of the world's highest environmental standards, developed over decades, to address a wide range of issues. Today, the main priorities are combating climate change, preserving biodiversity, reducing health problems from pollution and using natural resources more efficiently and responsibly. All of these issues are relevant in rural areas. This chapter focuses on environmental policy with special attention for the effects on agriculture.

The main function of agriculture is the production of food and other primary goods, including biomass for energy production (energy crops, crop residues, manure processing). However, farming also influences, positively and negatively, ecological processes related to water and soil quality, carbon storage, waste absorption and flood management, as well as the management of valuable habitats and landscapes. As a commercial activity, agriculture is aimed principally at production, which, relying on the availability and exploitation of natural resources, creates environmental pressures. Technological developments have contributed to an intensification of agriculture in the past decades. The original CAP measures contributed to this intensification, with price support favouring increasing use of fertilisers and pesticides, which resulted in pollution (and in some areas excessive use) of water and soils and damage to certain important ecosystems. Landscape change has been another environmental development of agricultural development.

To enhance the ecological sustainability of farming, two policy frameworks of the EU play an important role: environmental policy and the CAP.

Societal pressures to reduce environmental pollution led to the First Environmental Action Programme of the European Community in 1972. This formed the start of tackling environmental problems at a European level. In the beginning, the focus was on pollution from industrial sources, but gradually the interest in agriculture increased. At the end of the 1980s, reduction of water pollution by nitrates and pesticides was the major issue, and since then environmental policy has become increasingly important for agriculture. The Single European Act of 1986 recognised environmental protection as one of the building blocks of EU policy. European environment policy until 2020 is guided by the Seventh Environment Action Programme (EAP).

In the present CAP three priority areas have been identified for action:

- biodiversity and the preservation and development of 'natural' farming and forestry systems, and traditional agricultural landscapes;
- water management and use;
- dealing with climate change.

Farmers are encouraged by the CAP to continue playing a positive role in the maintenance of the countryside and the environment:

- enhancing compliance with environmental laws by sanctioning the non-respect for these laws by farmers through a reduction in support payments from the CAP (first pillar);
- targeting aid at rural development and climate measures promoting environmentally sustainable farming practices, like agri-environment schemes (second pillar).

While the environmental dimensions of the CAP mainly provide positive elements for environmental quality, EU environmental policy is characterised by restrictive measures. Before dealing with these measures, the chapter first addresses the theoretical background of environmental policy.

13.2   THEORETICAL BACKGROUND

In the course of economic development, elements of the environment—soil, water, air, nature and landscape—are altered in ways that are regarded as either harmful or beneficial. Unfortunately, the negative effects tend to prevail: in terms of the Regulatory Indicators for Sustainable Energy (RISE) report (Buckwell **2009**; Jongeneel et al. **2016**), market development provides too many environmental bads and too few environmental goods. Nevertheless, for centuries, farming went on without being subject to targeted environmental measures.

Typically, the spatial nature of environmental concerns in agriculture is important, and appropriate policy responses require a careful assessment of both the bio-physical causalities and the economic and institutional contexts. Desirable environmental outcomes of farming tend to disappear when the land management systems that historically helped to create them become subject to structural and technological change. Environmentally favourable features such as hedgerows, pastures, fallow land and extensive grazing lose their economic meaning for agricultural production. And, while landscape amenities, cultural heritage and biodiversity values formerly existed as unpaid by-products of farming, their preservation started to imply costs. This gave rise to policy responses, with farmers being paid for a range of activities undertaken in the interest of society, including landscape maintenance, enhancement of biodiversity and the conservation of nature.

As regards the negative influences on the environment, societal concerns with respect to increasing environmental pressures generated by agriculture has led to constraints on farming activities. These restrictions usually have come in the form of mandatory standards, either on the environmental qualities to be preserved or as required agricultural practices.

In order to achieve an agreed environmental target, providers should be encouraged to comply with society's demands. In effect, this requires changing the allocation of resources to an outcome different from what would be achieved if farmers and other suppliers followed only market signals where the public goods and services are not captured. As changing the allocation inevitably involves (opportunity) costs, there is the need to answer the question of who bears those costs: the farmer or the taxpayer?

Economic theory provides an orthodox answer to this question by referring to the setting of property rights. These rights determine who receives an income from employing factors of production (land and capital) for the provision of certain goods and services. The establishment and attribution of property rights result in stipulations concerning what someone may or may not do with a certain physical entity.

The 'polluter pays' principle (PPP) states that the polluter and not the government or society at large should bear the cost of reducing unacceptable levels of pollutant discharge. A few notable exceptions include the development of new pollution control technologies, pollution control infrastructures constructed in conjunction with regional development and control infrastructures targeting existing industries, areas or installations that would face severe difficulties because of environmental policies. The PPP principle is justified both on efficiency and on ethical and fairness grounds (Grossman 2007). The PPP was formulated in the early 1970s at the time when strict environmental regulations were first being implemented by member states of the Organization for Economic Cooperation and Development (OECD).

The PPP is one of several important environmental principles and acknowledged as the key principle underlying the EU's Environmental Action Programmes.[1] In an agricultural context, the PPP stipulates that farmers should bear the costs of avoiding or repairing any environmental harm resulting as a side effect of their agricultural activities. This principle can be translated into concrete policy terms by setting mandatory standards, enforced by some penalty on those who fail to achieve the required standard. Thus, the PPP conveys one strict message: payments should not be made for any action arising from the need to comply with certain pollution control standards.

To define the minimum standards of pollution control on the one hand and the provision of a public benefit on the other hand is a matter of political decision-making. Pollution is defined as releasing undesirable substances into environmental media. In terms of bio-physical interaction, the environmental quality of water, soil and air is unavoidably in an antagonistic relationship to farming activities. Real-world policy is based on defining mandatory legal standards which can be argued to reflect societal acceptance with respect to allowed externality levels. Up to these standards, abstaining from pollution is an obligation. Improving environmental quality beyond mandatory standards is, however, often considered as desirable. In the absence of an obligation, improving the state of the environment beyond mandatory requirements is considered as a service, even when it comes to public goods related to the quality of water, soil and air. Evidently, as those improvements are not free of costs, they are attainable only if these costs are covered by payments. Thus it is necessary to put the 'polluter pays' principle into a context where the 'reference level' is addressed.

The reference level (Fig. 13.1) is the dividing line between the level of responsibility which farmers are expected to take towards the environment at their own expense and those services and management practices which farmers would be willing to provide in return for remuneration (OECD 1998). Generally therefore, it is said that the PPP applies up to the reference level, and the 'provider gets' principle (PGP) applies above the refer-

---

[1] The 'polluter pays' principle is set out in the Treaty on the Functioning of the European Union [3] and Directive 2004/35/EC of the European Parliament and of the Council of 21 April 2004 on environmental liability with regard to the prevention and remedying of environmental damage is based on this principle. The directive entered into force on 30 April 2004; member states were allowed three years to transpose the directive into their domestic law, and by July 2010 all member states had completed this.

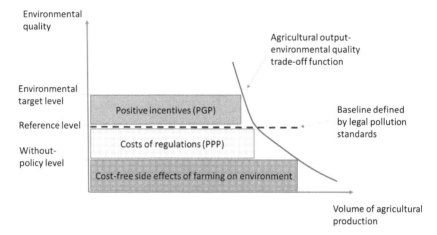

Fig. 13.1 Provision of environmental benefits versus avoiding harmful effects. (Source: Authors)

ence level as farmers will generally need compensation to provide green services beyond the legal standard level. An increase in the environmental standard level is likely to have a constraining impact on the volume of production, although this may differ depending on whether a PPP (tax) or PGP (subsidy) incentive is used.

In the environmental economics literature, there has been a discussion to what extent the PPP and PGP can lead to equivalent results. There is a well-known equivalence result between a tax on production and a subsidy on abatement, although the distributional impacts of both arrangements are quite different (Perman et al. 2011). But do policymakers have the option to use the stick (PPP) or the carrot (PGP) in stimulating environmentally friendly ways of agricultural production? In general the PGP is less efficient since the associated subsidies tend to stimulate production even though the environmental emission per unit of output may be reduced. Taxing negative externalities has a similar impact on the emission intensity per unit of output, but, in addition, favours a reduction in output as the cost of producing it increases due to the tax (e.g. Baumol and Oates 1988). There is, however, an interesting special case: when a subsidy is given which is decoupled from the production level, but linked to an environmental-friendly way of production, such a payment can be more efficient than an ordinary subsidy. Eventually, as it could support a way of production which is less land-intensive, such a payment could also be associated with a factual reduction in output.[2]

Determining the reference level is difficult, since the environment is multidimensional, interactive and dynamic. According to Buckwell (2009), the determination of reference levels has invariably been based on scientific consideration of what is desirable for the long-term health of the environment, tempered by a political process in which interest groups have a chance to express a view, that is, a mixture of scientific determination and social decision. Business interests scrutinise the costs of compliance, and often tend to argue for less ambitious standards, while environmentalists generally want the highest possible standards with little regard to economic costs. In practice, regulatory impact assessments are now routinely required as part of the process of setting reference levels. However, these are not a determining consideration, but a check that issues of benefits and costs have been thought about.

In the EU, the reference levels consist of the full range of mandatory legislation, including cross-compliance requirements (see the Chap. 10 on direct income support). Environmental concerns are thus reflected in the principles guiding the design of measures within the CAP. Farmers have to comply with mandatory requirements (defined in environmental policies) at their own cost, while agri-environmental commitments going beyond this baseline are remunerated through CAP measures.

13.3   WATER AND AIR POLLUTION

Environmental policies of the EU are mainly based on directives that have to be transposed in national rules and regulations (Table 13.1). The Nitrates Directive and the Water Framework Directive both address diffuse water pollution.

---

[2] Such type of payments come close to the lump sum payments, which according to standard economic theory can be used to support Pareto efficient equilibria. Within the context of agricultural policy, decoupled direct payments with environmental conditionalities associated to these (e.g. cross-compliance) are an operational example of such a payment. The EU's cross-compliance regime is a special case, as the compliance regards adherence to existing, whereas cross-compliance in the classical sense refers to voluntary action done in addition to the normal practice (Cardwell 2017). As argued by Perman et al. (2011), even a (decoupled) lump sum payment may affect the industry's profitability, which indirectly contributes to an expansion of the industry in the long run.

Table 13.1   Some major EU directives for water and air

Entry into force	Directive	Document number
1991	Nitrates Directive	91/676/EEC
1996	Integrated pollution prevention and control	2008/1/EC
2000	Water Framework Directive	2000/60/EC
2001	National Emission Ceilings	2001/81/EC
2003	Greenhouse gas emission allowance trading	2003/87/EC
2007	Assessment and management of flood risks	2007/60/EC
2010	Industrial Emissions Directive	2010/75/EU
2016	New National Emissions Ceilings (NEC) Directive	2016/2284/EU

Source: Own presentation

13.3.1   Nitrates Directive

Water pollution by nitrate is causing problems in all member states. The sources of nitrate pollution are diffuse (multiple discharges which are difficult to locate), and the main polluters—that is, farms—are sensitive to anything which affects their economic viability. The 1980s saw a progressive worsening of the situation (nitrate concentrations in water rose by an average of around 1 mg/l per year) owing to the growth of intensive farming of livestock (chickens, pigs) in areas that were already saturated and of intensive crop-growing involving the use of chemical weed killers and over-fertilisation.

Under the 1991 Nitrate Directive, member states must identify, on their territory:

surface waters and groundwater affected or liable to be affected by pollution, in accordance with the procedure and criteria set out in the Directive (in particular when nitrate concentrations in groundwater or surface waters exceed 50 mg/l);
vulnerable zones which contribute to pollution.

Member states must establish codes of good agricultural practice to be implemented by farmers on a voluntary basis and establish and implement action programmes for vulnerable zones. These must include measures set out in the codes of good practice, as well as measures:

to limit the application of any nitrogenous fertilisers to the soil and
to set limits for the spreading of livestock manure.

The Directive authorises member states to take additional measures or to reinforce their action programmes in order to achieve the objectives of the Directive. Member states must monitor water quality, applying standardised reference methods to measure the nitrogen-compound content. They must also report regularly to the Commission on the implementation of the Directive.

13.3.2   *Water Framework Directive*

The EU established a Community framework for water protection and management in 2000. The Framework Directive provides, among other things, for the identification of European waters and their quality characteristics, on the basis of individual river basin districts, and the adoption of management plans and programmes of measures appropriate for each body of water. In 2008, member states presented their draft river basin management plans, to be finalised and implemented On 22 December 2009.

By means of this Framework Directive, the EU provides for the management of inland surface waters, groundwater, transitional waters and coastal waters in order to prevent and reduce pollution, promote sustainable water use, protect the aquatic environment, improve the status of aquatic ecosystems and mitigate the effects of floods and droughts.

Member states completed an analysis of the characteristics of each river basin district, a review of the impact of human activity on water and an economic analysis of water use, and compiled a register of areas requiring special protection. All bodies of water used for the abstraction of water intended for human consumption providing more than ten cubic metres a day on average or serving more than 50 persons must be identified.

For each river basin district, a river basin management plan and a cost-effective programme of measures were produced, taking account of the results of the analyses and studies carried out. The measures provided for in the management plan seek to:

prevent deterioration, enhance and restore bodies of surface water, achieve good chemical and ecological status of such water and reduce pollution from discharges and emissions of hazardous substances;

protect, enhance and restore all bodies of groundwater, prevent the pollution and deterioration of groundwater and ensure a balance between groundwater abstraction and replenishment;

preserve protected areas.
The first generation of river basin management plans was published in 2009, and it is reconsidered after six years.

The member states were to encourage the active involvement of all interested parties in the implementation of this Directive, in particular as regards the river basin management plans. From 2010, member states must ensure that water pricing policies provide adequate incentives for users to use water resources efficiently, that is, the 'polluter pays' principle, and that the various economic sectors contribute to the recovery of the costs of water services, including those relating to the environment and resources.

13.3.3   National Emission Ceilings for Certain Atmospheric Pollutants

The EU has set national emission ceilings (NECs) for acidifying and eutrophying pollutants, and for ozone precursors in order to provide fuller protection for the environment and human health. In agriculture, ammonia is the most important source of acidification. The deposition of acidifying pollutants (SO_2, NO_X and NH_3) onto vegetation, surface waters, soils, buildings and monuments reduces the alkalinity of lakes and rivers and has serious effects on biological life.

Nitrogen supply to the soil is critical for plant nutrition. However, plants vary in their need for nitrogen. The deposition of nitrogen compounds (NO_X and NH_3) from the atmosphere leads to changes in terrestrial and water ecosystems, thereby altering vegetation and biodiversity. Acidification, tropospheric ozone and eutrophication of soils are transboundary phenomena.

The National Emission Ceilings Directive sets national emission reduction commitments for member states and the EU for five important air pollutants: nitrogen oxides (NOx), non-methane volatile organic compounds (NMVOCs), sulphur dioxide (SO_2), ammonia (NH_3) and fine particulate matter (PM2.5). These pollutants contribute to poor air quality, leading to significant negative impacts on human health and the environment.

A new National Emissions Ceilings (NEC) Directive (2016/2284/ EU) entered into force on 31 December 2016. Replacing the earlier legislation (Directive 2001/81/EC), the new NEC Directive sets 2020 and 2030 emission reduction commitments for five main air pollutants. It also ensures that the emission ceilings for 2010 set in the earlier directive remain applicable for member states until the end of 2019.[3]

13.3.4   Industrial Emissions Directive

The Industrial Emissions Directive (IED) is the main EU instrument regulating pollutant emissions from industrial installations. The IED was adopted on 24 November 2010. Industrial production processes account for a considerable share of the overall pollution in Europe due to their emissions of air pollutants, discharges of waste water and the generation of waste.

The IED is based on a Commission proposal recasting seven previously existing directives (including in particular the Integrated pollution prevention and control (IPPC) Directive) following an extensive review of the policy. The IED entered into force on 6 January 2011 and had to be transposed by member states by 7 January 2013. The IED aims to achieve a high level of protection of human health and the environment taken as a whole by reducing harmful industrial emissions across the EU, in particular through better application of best available techniques (BAT). Around 50,000 installations undertaking the industrial activities listed in Annex I of the IED are required to operate in accordance with a permit (granted by the authorities in the member states). This permit should contain conditions set in accordance with the principles and provisions of the IED.

The IED is based on several pillars, in particular (1) an integrated approach, (2) use of best available techniques, (3) flexibility, (4) inspections and (5) public participation.

The IED is relevant for intensive rearing of poultry or pigs:

(a) with more than 40,000 places for poultry;
(b) with more than 2000 places for fattening pigs (over 30 kg); or
(c) with more than 750 places for sows.

---

[3] https://www.eea.europa.eu/themes/air/national-emission-ceilings/national-emission-ceilings-directive

13.4   SOIL DEGRADATION

Soil is generally defined as the top layer of the earth's crust. It is a dynamic system which performs many functions and is vital to human activities and to the survival of ecosystems. As soil formation and regeneration is an extremely slow process, soil is considered a non-renewable resource. The main degradation processes to which EU soils are subject are erosion, decline in organic matter, contamination, salinisation, compaction, decline in biodiversity, sealing, floods and landslides.

Soil degradation is a serious problem in Europe, driven or exacerbated by human activity such as inadequate agricultural and forestry practices, industrial activities, tourism, urban and industrial sprawl and construction works. Sealing of soil surfaces due to an increased urbanisation and new infrastructures is the main cause of soil degradation in the most industrialised and populated countries of western and northern Europe. Soil loss by erosion is the main cause of soil degradation in the Mediterranean region. Soil deterioration by contamination is an important issue in central, western and northern Europe.

The impacts include loss of soil fertility, carbon and biodiversity, lower water-retention capacity, disruption of gas and nutrient cycles, and reduced degradation of contaminants. Soil degradation has a direct impact on water and air quality, biodiversity and climate change. It can also impair the health of European citizens and threaten food and feed safety.

Soil has not, to date, been subject to a specific protection policy at the EU level. Instead, provisions for soil protection are spread across many areas, either under environmental protection or other policy areas such as agriculture and rural development. According to the European Commission, these provisions do not ensure a sufficient level of soil protection, since their objectives and scope differ widely. Coordinated action at the European level is demanded, given that the state of soil influences other environmental and food safety aspects governed at the EU level, and given the risks of distortions of the internal market linked to remedying polluted sites, the potential for cross-border impacts and the international dimension of the problem.

The soil strategy (EC 2006) was one of the seven thematic strategies under the Sixth Environmental Action Programme. It was based on a comprehensive study and widespread consultation of the general public and stakeholders. In the strategy, the Commission proposed a framework and common objectives to prevent soil degradation, to preserve soil functions and to restore degraded soils. The strategy put forward measures to protect soil and to preserve its capacity to perform its functions in environmental, economic, social and cultural terms. It also included setting up a legislative framework for the protection and sustainable use of soil, integrating soil protection into national and EU policies, improving knowledge in this area and increasing public awareness. A key component of the strategy was the proposal for a directive enabling ember states to adopt measures tailored to their local needs and providing for measures to identify problems, prevent soil degradation and restore polluted or degraded soils.

The measures included in the Directive proposal included obligatory identification by member states, on the basis of criteria set out in the proposal, of areas at risk of erosion, organic matter decline, compaction, salinisation and landslides, or where the degradation process is already underway. Member states should set objectives and adopt programmes of measures to reduce these risks and to address the effects they have. They should also take steps to limit soil sealing, notably by rehabilitating brownfield sites and, where sealing is necessary, to mitigate its effects. The proposal also provided for member states taking appropriate measures to prevent soil contamination by dangerous substances. Member states and EU institutions should integrate soil concerns into sectoral policies that have a significant impact on soil, especially agriculture, regional development, transport and research.

In trying to handle land-use issues at the EU level, the Commission encountered constitutional difficulties. Its structure reflects the allocation of EU competencies under the EU Treaty—competencies that specifically exclude land-use planning. Regulatory powers over land use are divided into local, regional, national and EU responsibilities. The rejection by the Council of the Soils Directive illustrates how institutional demands can override policy goals—no one disputes that soils issues need to be tackled, but there was disagreement over whether soils are an EU or a member state competency. The proposed Soil Directive was rejected by the Council in 2007 and the adjusted Soil Directive was withdrawn by the Commission in 2014.

However, the Seventh Environment Action Programme (next section) recognises that soil degradation is a serious challenge. It provides that by 2020 land is managed sustainably in the Union, soil is adequately protected and the remediation of contaminated sites is well underway. It also commits the EU and its member states to increasing efforts to reduce soil erosion and increase soil organic matter and to remediate contaminated sites.

13.5   ENVIRONMENT ACTION PROGRAMME

European environment policy until 2020 is guided by the Seventh Environment Action Programme (EAP). This programme is called 'Living well, within the limits of our planet' (European Union 2014). The programme entered into force in January 2014. The EU and its member states support environmental policies as a key condition for healthy living and for creating a competitive, resource-efficient economy in Europe. Member states and the EU institutions are equally responsible for implementing the programme.

In order to give more long-term direction, the EAP sets out a vision beyond 2020, of where it wants the Union to be by 2050: 'In 2050, we live well, within the planet's ecological limits. Our prosperity and healthy environment stem from an innovative, circular economy where nothing is wasted and where natural resources are managed sustainably, and biodiversity is protected, valued and restored in ways that enhance our society's resilience. Our low-carbon growth has long been decoupled from resource use, setting the pace for a safe and sustainable global society'.

The programme identifies nine policy objectives: three thematic priorities, four enabling priorities and two horizontal objectives.

13.5.1   Three Thematic Priorities

13.5.1.1 Natural Capital
The first objective is to protect, conserve and enhance the Union's natural capital:

Biodiversity that provides goods and services we rely on, from fertile soil and productive land and seas to fresh water and clean air

Vital services such as pollination of plants, natural protection against flooding and the regulation of our climate

The EAP commits the EU and its member states to speed up the implementation of existing strategies, fill gaps where legislation does not yet exist and improve existing legislation, including the 2020 Biodiversity Strategy and the Blueprint to Safeguard Europe's Water Resources.

13.5.1.2 Resource-Efficient Economy

The second objective is to turn the Union into a resource-efficient, green and competitive low-carbon economy. The EAP requires:

full delivery of the climate and energy package to achieve the 20-20-20 targets and agreement on the next steps for climate policy beyond 2020[4];

significant improvements to the environmental performance of products over their life cycle;

reductions in the environmental impact of consumption, including cutting food waste and using biomass in a sustainable way.

There is a special focus on turning waste into a resource and to move towards more efficient use of our water resources.

13.5.1.3 Health and Environment

The third objective is to safeguard the Union's citizens from environment-related pressures and risks to health and well-being. Challenges include human health and well-being, such as air and water pollution, excessive noise and chemicals. Making Europe sufficiently resilient to challenges posed by new and emerging risks, including the impacts of climate change.

In the EAP, all parties have agreed to:

update air quality and noise legislation;

improve implementation of legislation relating to drinking and bathing water;

tackle hazardous chemicals, including nanomaterials, chemicals that interfere with the endocrine system and chemicals in combination;

come up with strategy for a non-toxic environment.

---

[4] The original renewable energy directive (2009/28/EC) establishes an overall policy for the production and promotion of energy from renewable sources in the EU. It requires the EU to fulfil at least 20% of its total energy needs with renewables by 2020. In December 2018, the revised renewable energy directive 2018/2001/EU entered into force, as part of the clean energy for all Europeans package, helping the EU to meet its emissions reduction commitments under the Paris Agreement. The new directive establishes a new binding renewable energy target for the EU for 2030 of at least 32%, with a clause for a possible upwards revision by 2023 (see Chap. 14 of Volume I).

13.5.2   Four So-Called Enablers

These four priority objectives should help Europe deliver on these goals:

- better implementation of legislation
- better information by improving the knowledge base
- more and wiser investment for environment and climate policy
- full integration of environmental requirements and considerations into other policies

13.5.3   Two Additional Horizontal Priority Objectives

The EAP is completed by two horizontal objectives. They concern making the Union's cities more sustainable and to help the Union address international environmental and climate challenges more effectively. For the latter, the EAP urges the EU and the member states to:

- engage more effectively in working with international partners towards the adoption of Sustainable Development Goals as a follow-up to the Rio+20 conference;
- work to reduce impacts on the environment beyond EU borders.

13.6   ASSESSMENT

Environmental problems have been on the political agenda of European countries since the 1960s, when environmental policies were almost exclusively developed at the level of member states. However, environmental aspects have received more and more attention in the CAP, especially after the 1992 Mac Sharry reform. This has been developed through the agri-environmental measures, since 1999, within the Rural Development Policy (second pillar). With cross-compliance in the Single Payment Scheme, environmental objectives have also gained a clear position in the price and income policies (first pillar) of the CAP.

With its Seventh Environmental Action Programme, the EU is striving for an environmental policy that is coherent with its other policies.

An overview of the EU's progress towards its environmental policy objectives is given by the European Environment Agency (EEA) 'Environmental Indicator Report 2018'. The objectives are relevant to the achievement of the Seventh Environment Action Programme (EAP) three key priority objectives: natural capital; resource-efficient, low-carbon economy; and people's health and well-being. The annual report draws on 29 indicators—updated with latest data—to provide an outlook on meeting each of the objectives by 2020. According to the report, many indicators show positive past trends but meeting relevant targets by 2020 remains a challenge.

The report confirmed the overall results of the 2016 and 2017 assessments by key Seventh EAP priority objectives:

The EU's natural capital is not yet being protected, maintained and enhanced in line with the ambitions of the Seventh EAP. The 2020 outlook remains bleak overall for the selected set of objectives related to this priority objective.

The EU is on track to meet climate and renewable energy-related targets, although it is uncertain whether it will meet its energy efficiency target. There have been resource efficiency improvements. However, waste generation increased recently and a reduction in the environmental impact of production and consumption is uncertain for the housing sector and unlikely for the food and mobility sectors.

There have been substantial reductions in emissions of air and water pollutants in recent decades. However, there are still key concerns over air quality and noise pollution in urban areas, and chronic exposure of the population to mixtures of chemicals.

Overall progress per thematic priority objective shows positive and negative trends and outlooks across the board and a gloomy outlook for natural capital. The prospects of meeting some of the selected objectives within the priority objectives have deteriorated from one year to the next. The 2017 scoreboard amended downwards the 2020 prospects for meeting the objectives that corresponded to land take and ammonia emissions indicators. The changes in these two 2020 outlooks have been retained in the 2018 scoreboard. The latest data show that ammonia emissions, arising mainly from agricultural production, have continued to increase. Also, although there are no more recent land take (i.e. land lost to artificial surfaces such as buildings and roads) data in the report, there are still no policies in sight promoting the necessary reductions in the rate of land take to remain on track to meeting the related 2020 objective.

According to the report, the low economic activity level in the EU following the 2008 financial crisis contributed to several of the positive past trends shown in the scoreboard. However, the EU's relatively high economic growth in recent years has contributed to the recent deceleration in progress observed for several of the examined indicators (EEA 2018).

The Nitrate Directive and the Water Framework Directive both address diffuse water pollution. The precise consequences of the latter for the agricultural sector across the EU may depend considerably on the way it is implemented and the level of contamination in water at the outset. Animal production will be affected in both cases because of the importance of manure and slurry as pollutants. Also important for agriculture is the Emission Ceilings Directive, which, amongst others, refers to ammonia emissions. For large intensive pig and poultry farms, the IED is also relevant.

The presence of a regulation or legislation does not mean that a problem is solved. This only holds if standards are set at the right level, and the regulations and legislation are backed by properly designed monitoring and enforcement regimes. Enforcement of environmental legislation is difficult and demands serious efforts by the enterprises in agriculture, as well as the authorities. However, along with restrictions on the exploitation of resources, public attention to the environment and sustainability also provides opportunities for agriculture, and the relation between ecology and agriculture may gradually improve.

REFERENCES

Baumol, W.J., and W.E. Oates. 1988. *The Theory of Environmental Policy.* 2nd ed. Cambridge: Cambridge University Press.

Buckwell, A., ed. 2009. *RISE Task Force on; Public Goods from Private Land.* Brussels: Rural Investment Support for Europe (RISE).

Cardwell, M. 2017. The Polluter Pays Principle in European Community and Its Impact on United Kingdom Farmers. *Oklahoma Law Review* 59 (1): 89–113.

EEA. 2018. *Environmental Indicator Report 2018; In Support to the Monitoring of the Seventh Environment Action Programme.* Copenhagen: European Environment Agency, EEA Report No 19/2018.

European Commission. 2006. *Thematic Strategy for Soil Protection.* Brussels: Commission Communication, COM(2006) 231 Final.

European Union. 2014. *General Union Environment Action Programme to 2020; Living Well, Within the Limits of Our Planet.* Brussels: Directorate-General for Environment.

Grossman, M.R. 2007. Agriculture and the Polluter Pays Principle. *Electronic Journal of Comparative Law* 11 (3): 1–66.

Jongeneel, R., N.B.P. Polman, and G.C. van Kooten. 2016. *How Important Are Agricultural Externalities? A Framework for Analysis and Application to Dutch*

Agriculture. Victoria, Canada: Resource Economics & Policy Analysis Research Group, Department of Economics. University of Victoria.

Organization for Economic Cooperation and Development (OECD). 1998. *Agriculture and the Environment: Issues and Policies.* Paris: Organization for Economic Cooperation and Development (OECD).

Perman, R., M. Yue, J. McGilvray, M.S. Common, and D. Maddison. 2011. *Natural Resource and Environmental Economics.* 4th ed. Harlow: Pearson.

INTERNET

http://ec.europa.eu/comm/agriculture/
http://ec.europa.eu/environment/action-programme/
http://ec.europa.eu/environment/agriculture/index.htm
https://www.eea.europa.eu/
www.risefoundation.eu

CHAPTER 14

Assessment of the Common Agricultural Policy After 2020

Roel Jongeneel, Emil Erjavec, Tomás García Azcárate, and Huib Silvis

This chapter is based on a study by the authors for the European Parliament with the aim to assess the proposals for the CAP after 2020. See Erjavic et al. (2018), García Azcárate (2018) and Jongeneel and Silvis (2018).

R. Jongeneel (✉)
Agricultural Economics and Rural Policy Group, Wageningen University, Wageningen, Gelderland, The Netherlands
e-mail: roel.jongeneel@wur.nl

E. Erjavec
Agricultural Policy and Economics Department, University of Ljubljana, Ljubljana, Slovenia
e-mail: emil.erjavec@bf.uni-lj.si

T. García Azcárate
Institute of Economics, Geography and Demography, Spanish National Research Council, Madrid, Spain
e-mail: tomas.gazcarate@cchs.csic.es

H. Silvis
Performance and Impact Agrosectors, Wageningen Economic Research, The Hague, The Netherlands
e-mail: huib.silvis@wur.nl

© The Author(s) 2019   207
L. Dries et al. (eds.), *EU Bioeconomy Economics and Policies: Volume I*,
Palgrave Advances in Bioeconomy: Economics and Policies,
https://doi.org/10.1007/978-3-030-28634-7_14

14.1   Challenges

Although the characteristics of the agricultural sector vary widely between member states, the main challenges are broadly the same: lagging farm incomes, increasing resource constraints (land and water) and environmental concerns (including climate), and changing consumer food preferences. In order to meet these challenges, economic viability and resource use efficiency of the sector require continuing attention. However, with respect to the EU, there are a number of specific challenges. Existing policy has a weak intervention logic and is poorly targeted, which leads to requests for Common Agricultural Policy (CAP) tailoring.

Several studies have assessed the main challenges with respect to the EU's agriculture and food sector (e.g. Pe'er et al. 2017; European Court of Auditors 2018). Using the three main objectives of the current CAP (viable farms, sustainable management of natural resources (environment) and territorial balance) as a reference, the following main challenges can be identified:

14.1.1   Viable Farms

Farm income support is unequally distributed and poorly targeted. The main instrument used to support farm incomes is direct payments, which consume about 70% of the total CAP expenditure. In 2015, in the EU28 81% of the farmers received 20% of the direct payments (European Commission 2018a, b). Thus a large group of farmers receives a low amount of payments, whereas a small group receives a high amount of payments.

The share of direct payments in farm income varies considerably from about one-third for the lower-income classes to more than half of the higher-income classes (EU average is about 46%; EU Commission 2018b). The provided income support is thus progressive: farmers with relatively high incomes receive relatively high payments, which contrasts with the basic need for income-support principle (Terluin and Verhoog 2018).

To the extent that incomes of farms are supported for which there is less need for such income support, the inequality leads also to an ineffective use and a waste of scarce public resources. Moreover, it then raises land prices, and as such direct payments can be argued to create a barrier to entry for young farmers.

EU agriculture is frequently confronted with volatile prices, natural disasters, pests and diseases. The policy reforms leading to an increase in market orientation have not only created opportunities for EU agriculture to benefit from global markets, but also made the sector more vulnerable to international shocks and market disturbances. Price variability, which tends to outweigh yield variability, is an important factor contributing to the risks faced by farmers. The comparison of the periods 1997–2006 and 2007–2016 indicates that price variability increased for key arable products (cereals, oilseeds, potatoes), dairy products and beef (cows and bulls). Every year, at least 20% of farmers lose more than 30% of their income compared with the average of the last three years (EU Commission 2018b). However, in spite of the increasing need, in 2017, only 12 member states included one or more instruments of the risk management toolkit in their rural development programmes (RDPs), with the Italian, French and Romanian programmes accounting for a large proportion of total programmed public expenditures (Chartier et al. 2016).

14.1.2   Natural Resources

As regards the environment, for a long time the CAP has had a classical productivist orientation (Thompson 2017) and has led to high intensities of production in many sectors (e.g. livestock, which is in some regions very dependent on cheap imports of feed), thereby disturbing the agroecology and imposing an increasing pressure on the environment. Agriculture is a major source of nitrogen losses, with the current nitrogen loss estimated to be 6.5–8 million tonnes per year, which represents about 80% of reactive nitrogen emissions from all sources to the EU environment (Westhoek et al. 2015). These nitrogen losses take place mainly in the form of ammonia to the air, of nitrate to ground and surface waters and of nitrous oxide, a powerful greenhouse gas. Around 81–87% of the total emissions related to EU agriculture of ammonia, nitrate and nitrous oxide are related to livestock production (emissions related to feed production being included).

The nitrogen surplus on EU farmland (averaging 50 kg nitrogen/ha) has a negative impact on water quality. Since 1993, levels of nitrates have decreased in rivers, but not in groundwater. Nitrate concentrations are still high in some areas, leading to pollution in many lakes and rivers, mainly in regions with intensive agriculture (European Court of Auditors 2018).

Ammonia is an important air pollutant, with farming generating almost 95% of ammonia emissions in Europe. While emissions have decreased by 23% since 1990, they started to increase again in 2012 (ECA).

About 45% of mineral soils in the EU have low or very low organic carbon content (0–2%) and 45% have a medium content (2–6%). Soil trends are difficult to establish due to data gaps, but declining levels of organic carbon content contribute to declining soil fertility and can create risks of desertification.

As regards the climate, greenhouse gas emissions from agriculture accounted for 11% of EU emissions in 2015. These emissions decreased by 20% between 1990 and 2013, but started to rise again in 2014. Moreover, net removals from land use, land use change and forestry offset around 7% of all EU greenhouse gas emissions in 2015.

Whereas there are several measures deployed which are targeted to bio-diversity and landscape, they are criticised for their limited effectiveness. According to the European Court of Auditors (2018), the conservation status of agricultural habitats was favourable in 11% of cases in the period 2007–2012, compared to less than 5% in the period 2001–2006. However, since 1990, populations of common farmland birds have decreased by 30% and of those of grassland butterflies by almost 50%.

14.1.3   *Territorial Balance*

In 2015, 119 million European citizens, representing almost a quarter of the EU population, were at risk of poverty and social exclusion. The average poverty rate is slightly higher in rural areas, with very contrasting situations across the Union as some countries display a huge poverty gap between rural and urban areas. Rural poverty, which appears to be less documented than urban poverty, is linked to the specific disadvantages of rural areas. These include an unfavourable demographic situation, a weaker labour market, limited access to education and also remoteness and rural isolation. The latter is associated with a lack of basic services such as healthcare and social services, and with increased costs for inhabitants on account of travel distances. These factors are considered to be the main drivers of rural poverty (EP Think tank 2017).

In terms of agriculture, it is argued that there is an investment gap which hinders restructuring, modernisation, diversification, uptake of new technologies, use of big data etc., thereby impacting on environmental sustainability, competitiveness and resilience. These bottlenecks also influence the ability to fully explore the potential of new rural value chains like clean energy, emerging bio-economy and the circular economy both in terms of growth and jobs and environmental sustainability (e.g. reduction of food waste). There are also consequences in terms of generational renewal in agriculture and more widely in terms of youth drain. Only 5.6% of all European farms are run by farmers younger than 35. Access to land, reflecting both land transfers and farm succession constraints, together with access to credit, are often cited as the two main constraints for young farmers and other new entrants (EU Commission 2018b).

14.2   The Proposed CAP Reform

14.2.1   *Future of Food and Farming*

In November 2017 the European Commission published the communication "The Future of food and farming" (European Commission 2017), which outlines the ideas of the European Commission on the future of the CAP. The general and specific objectives for the CAP after 2020 have been laid down in legislative proposals later in May 2018 (European Commission 2018a). The overarching declared principles are to make the CAP smarter, modern and sustainable, while simplifying its implementation and improving delivery on EU objectives. Key aspects of the proposals are the introduction of Strategic Plans, as well as the evidence-based approach and the stronger environmental focus.

14.2.2   *Objectives*

The general objectives of the future CAP according to the European Commission are:

To foster a smart, resilient and diversified agricultural sector ensuring food security
To bolster environmental care and climate action and to contribute to the environmental and climate objectives of the EU
To strengthen the socio-economic fabric of rural areas

These general objectives are further detailed into specific objectives, as these are presented in Fig. 14.1. When comparing these objectives with the current CAP, there is a near complete overlap, despite some rewording.

The CAP objectives will be complemented by the cross-cutting objective of modernising the sector by fostering and sharing of knowledge, innovation and digitalisation in agriculture and rural areas. Both the first pillar, agricultural income and market support, and the second pillar, rural development, contain instruments that aim to contribute to these general objectives.

Fig. 14.1 The nine CAP-specific objectives proposed for the new CAP. (Source: European Commission 2018a, b)

14.2.3   Path Dependency in Direct Payment (Aids) Schemes

Path dependency is the main characteristic of the approach where in terms of measures no paradigmatic change is proposed. Not targeted farm income orientation is still the main characteristic with more manoeuvre for MS to select the types of direct payments. To ensure stability and predictability, income support will remain an essential part of the CAP. Part of this, basic payments will continue to be based on the farm's size in hectares. However, the future CAP wants to prioritise small and medium-sized farms and encourage young farmers to join the profession. This is why the Commission proposes a higher level of support per hectare for small and medium-sized farms, proposes a capping of payments (with a limit on direct payments at €100,000 per farm), with a view to ensure a fairer distribution of payments. It also proposes a minimum of 2% of direct support payments allocated to each EU country to be set aside for young farmers, complemented by financial support under rural development and measures facilitating access to land and land transfers.

14.2.4   A New Green Architecture

In addition to the direct financial support, the new CAP claims to have a higher ambition on environmental and climate action (Matthews 2018b). The legislative proposals on the new CAP contain a new architecture for greening, which covers both pillars and consists of three components (i) enhanced conditionality; (ii) eco-scheme; and (iii) agri-environment, climate scheme and other management commitments (see Table 14.1 for a comparative overview).

Extended conditionality is the new word used for cross-compliance. The cross-compliance conditions are extended with respect to the current situation in that which are now the greening requirements (with the Green

Table 14.1 Comparison of Pillar I eco-schemes and Pillar II payments for environment, climate and other management commitments

Schemes for the climate and the environment—eco-schemes (Art 28)	Environment, climate and other management commitments (Art 65)
Funded by Pillar I (annually, not co-funded)	Funded by Pillar II (multiannually, co-funded)
Payments to genuine farmers	Payments to farmers and other beneficiaries
Payment per ha eligible to direct payment	Payment per ha (not necessarily eligible to direct payments)/animal
Annual (or possibly multiannual) and non-contractual commitments	Multiannual (5–7 years or more) and contractual commitments
Calculation of the premiums: compensation for cost incurred/income foregone, or incentive payment:	Calculation of the premiums: compensation for cost incurred/income foregone
top-up of basic income support (amount to be fixed and justified by MS)	
Baseline = conditionality + national legislation + area management	
Payments may support collective and result-based approaches	
Possibility for MS to combine both:	
eco-scheme set as "entry-level scheme" condition for Pillar II payment for management commitment	
or possibility to set a two-tier scheme: e.g. use Pillar II management commitments to support cost of conversion into organic farming and the eco-scheme to maintain in organic farming	

Source: Based on EU Commission (2018a, b)

payment as a compensation) are proposed to be all included in the new cross-compliance.

Mandatory requirements following from the proposed "enhanced conditionality" include preserving carbon-rich soils through protection of wetlands and peatlands, obligatory nutrient management tool to improve water quality, reduce ammonia and nitrous oxide levels, and crop rotation instead of crop diversification. According to the proposal, farmers will have to comply with 16 statutory management requirements that relate to existing legislation with respect to climate and environment, public, animal and plant health and animal welfare. In addition, they have to follow ten standards for good agricultural and environmental condition of the land.

Farmers will have the possibility to contribute further and be rewarded for going beyond mandatory requirements. According to the proposal, EU countries will develop voluntary eco-schemes (offering at least one is obligatory) to support and incentivise farmers to observe agricultural practices beneficial for the climate and the environment (adoption by farmers is voluntary).

According to the proposal, the payments made for eco-scheme measures should take the form of an annual payment per eligible hectare, and they shall be granted as either payments additional "top up" to the basic income support, or as payments compensating beneficiaries for all or part of the additional costs incurred and income foregone as a result of the defined commitments. This allows member states to create a profit margin for farmers when participating in eco-schemes and could induce a wider spread adoption than in the case of agri-environmental and climate action schemes under Pillar II of the CAP (see Article 65). As such, eco-schemes can be a vehicle to, relative to Agri-Evironment and Climate Scheme (AECS), get a larger share of the farmers involved in pursuing lighter measures that are beneficent for the climate and environment.

14.2.5   Change of Policy Strategy

The European Commission proposes a flexible system, aimed to simplify and modernise the CAP. The emphasis is shifted from compliance and rules towards results and performance. Following the subsidiarity principle, member states get a more important role as they have to make national strategic plans, in which they set out how they intend to meet the nine EU-wide objectives using CAP instruments while responding to the specific needs of their farmers and rural communities.

14.3   Direct Payments and Rural Development Policy

14.3.1   Still Poor Targeting of Income Support

In the proposed CAP beyond 2020, direct payments will remain the core part of the interventions (measured in terms of budget spending) of the CAP in all member states. In terms of the type of interventions offered under the direct payments heading (first pillar of the CAP), probably the most notable change as compared to the current CAP is the new eco-schemes provision, which is part of the revised green architecture. The EU's income support to farmers is suffering from inequalities in distribution of support, a lack of targeting and a lack of use of need-oriented criteria. The new CAP is likely to only address this problem to a limited extent, since the basic mechanism (hectare-based payments) is not changed (Jongeneel and Silvis 2018).

As regards the (voluntary) coupled income support, which is now labelled as "coupled income support for sustainability" this should be used in a targeted (or discriminatory) way rather than in a generic way, whereas otherwise it will distort the level playing field and go against the principle of the EU single market. The new proposal does not guarantee an improvement with respect to the current implementation practices.

The obligatory reduction of direct payments (capping) proposed by the EU Commission is, even in its proposed form, not likely to be very effective due to mandatory side condition to deduct the salaries of paid workers and imputed labour costs of unpaid labour (Matthews 2019). In the past, member states have often only adopted a rather weakened form of the capping schemes proposed by the Commission. Also with respect to this proposal, there seem to be already serious reservations by member states, which could easily lead to a further watering down of the Commission's capping proposal (Petit 2019).

14.3.2   Greening via Enhanced Conditionality and Performance Schemes

The proposed new green architecture of the CAP implies a redefinition of the baseline, as this is comprised by the enhanced conditionality (Matthews 2018a). Grosso modo, the proposed new baseline includes the current baseline plus the current greening requirements (Jongeneel and Silvis 2018).

Member states have discretionary power to tailor the baseline to local conditions and preferences. On the one hand, this may tailor the baseline level better to local circumstances, but it may also lead to a divergence of baseline levels, as member states may make different decisions (e.g. with respect to the share of non-productive areas).

The enhanced conditionality contributes to establishing a baseline with respect to climate, environment, biodiversity and health, which goes beyond the current level. The extended greening requirements apply to all holdings receiving direct payments. Eco-schemes that are obligatory for member states and voluntary for farmers create possibilities to reward farmers for actions improving climate and the environment, which go beyond the baseline as established by the enhanced conditionality. Arguments are provided to further enlarge their potential and coverage.

As eco-scheme measures have to be complementary or additional to the baseline, both are related. The eco-scheme measures should also be different from those provided under the agri-environmental and climate action schemes of the second pillar of the CAP. As they are part of the first pillar of the CAP no co-financing by MS is needed. The eco-schemes allow member states to develop innovative schemes supporting climate and environment objectives, which go beyond mere flat rate payments (see Table 14.1) and allow for smart combinations of eco-schemes with AECSs.

As it has been emphasised by the Commission, the new CAP foresees an improved delivery model, including the strengthening of performance-based measures. Some member states have experience with such systems (e.g. Entry-Level Scheme of the UK) or are considering its potential (see the Public Goods Bonus scheme as this has been developed and proposed by the Deutscher Verband für Landschaftspflege (DVL 2017); also the Netherlands is considering a point-system type of approach). An important requirement of such performance-based schemes is to have reliable, simple and robust indicators (Dupraz and Guyomard 2019).

Such schemes would well fit in the philosophy of the new CAP (e.g. from compliance to performance or action to results; public funding for public goods principle) and have attractive properties (addressing the entrepreneurial rather than administrative qualities of farmers; rewarding farmers' current efforts as well as offering farmers incentives to extend their environmental services to new areas of their farms; allowing farmers to offer an efficient mix of actions, or to "specialise" in the provision of specific public goods; offering flexibility to include a wide range of environmental services, including nutrient balancing and abstaining from artificial fertiliser use; and tailoring to regional conditions affecting agriculture, biodiversity and landscape). The proposal on the new CAP is vague in this respect, but should more explicitly stimulate performance or point-system approaches of eco-scheme implementations by member states, including "hybrid" schemes which involve simultaneously the public and private sectors (Jongeneel and Silvis 2018).

14.4   NATIONAL CAP STRATEGIC PLANNING

14.4.1   Strategic Planning

The proposed EC Regulation (COM (2018) 392) introduces comprehensive strategic planning at the MS level as one of the key new elements of the future CAP. The new delivery model may be seen as a step in the right direction, as this is the foundation of modern public policy governance. There will be also greater acceptance of the legitimacy of these policies.

The proposal draws on two precedents: the national strategy covering both CAP pillars foreseen in the fruit and vegetable regulation since 2006 and the model of strategic planning of rural development policy.

The CAP Strategic plans will presumably draw on analyses of strengths, weaknesses, opportunities and threats (SWOT) and elaborations of needs in accordance with individual specific CAP goals (see above). In this regard, forming the environmental and climate objectives will have to take into account the relevant sectoral legislation, and special attention will be given to risk management. All needs addressed by the CAP Strategic plan will have to be described in detail, prioritised and their choice justified on the basis of the latest available and most reliable data. In the next step, the intervention logic will have to be determined for each specific goal. This means setting target values and benchmarks for all common and specific indicators and choosing and justifying the choice of instruments from the offered set based on sound intervention logic. The contribution of existing mechanisms will have to be considered (impact assessment of interventions so far), and comprehensiveness and conformity with goals in environmental and climate legislation will have to be demonstrated.

A review of the environmental and climate architecture of the strategic plan will have to be enclosed, as well as a review of interventions pertaining to the specific goal of generational renewal and facilitation of business development.

The mandatory elements of the CAP Strategic plans will contain overview tables with goals, measures and funding, a chapter on governance and coordination, a section on the Agricultural Knowledge and Innovation Systems (AKIS) and digitalisation strategy, and enclosed will be the entire SWOT analysis, ex ante evaluation and description of the process and results of public consultation with stakeholders.

Strategic plans will be assessed by the Commission based on the completeness, the consistency, legal coherence, effectiveness and potential impacts of the proposals.

A concurrent review of the implementation of the CAP's strategic plans will be carried out using annual reports in which MS will describe their progress through a system of output (referring to the implementation and use of finance) and outcome (referring to immediate result produced via application of a measure) indicators to be agreed at the Union level. In case of a more than 25% deviation from the respective milestone for the reporting year in question, the Commission may request the MS to draw up an action plan with corrective measures and the expected timeframe for their implementation.

Comparing the expected dynamics and quality of monitoring with existing rural development programmes, the proposed approach is more strategic and more result-oriented, demanding quick action and corrective measures in case of non-compliance.

14.4.2   *Assessment of the Proposed Strategic Planning*

The proposal gives some prospects for simplification, but essentially the governance system is not changed and contains all the shortcomings of the previous arrangements. The key question should therefore be how the proposed Strategic plans will be applied in the real world and whether it will bring about a more effective policy.

One of the key critics (Erjavec et al. 2018) is that the necessary accountability mechanism for strategic planning is weak. Limited accountability and ability to establish efficient intervention logic are serious gaps of the new delivery model. The current legal proposal does not frame the proposed CAP-specific objectives in a result-oriented manner. Three objectives relevant to the environment and their relating indicators are not directly linked to existing environmental legislation. The current proposals are also not clear on the method of quantifying the baseline situation. The study also questions the proposed exemption of background documents and analyses envisaged in the annexes of national strategic plans from the evaluation process.

Erjavec et al. (2018) mentioned that objectives should be quantified at the EU level and if associated legislation and objectives exist in other EU policies, these should be incorporated into the quantified definition of objectives in the CAP legal proposals. The legislative proposal requires a better demarcation of common EU and national objectives.

In principle, commonly defined should be those objectives that add value when implemented on a common scale, while the objectives where the principle of subsidiarity is more salient should remain at the national level.

The current system in designing measures is restrictive: Member states can only choose measures and adapt them. Moreover, some measures are compulsory in order to prevent renationalisation of policies and to achieve societal goals.

The process of strategic planning is left to the capacities and ingenuity of the member states, without guarantees that the performance at the EU level will be measurable as the national priorities emerge from SWOT analysis and may not necessarily reflect the EU-level priorities.

There are limited compelling incentives for member states to make efforts for better policies. The procedure related to the approval of the strategic plan is practically the only mechanism in the EC's power for ensuring targeted and ambitious strategic planning. Therefore, it is of importance the Commission is empowered to make a proper qualitative assessment of the strategic plans (Erjavec et al. 2018).

CAP strategic plans should contain a satisfactory and balanced level of consultation between stakeholders and involvement of other public authorities, and that the Commission is well equipped to assess the plan within a reasonable period's length. The adoption procedure should be more formalised, with the stakeholders' opinions at the national level taken into account. This can improve the quality of the design and the legitimacy of the document.

As the approval by the Commission of the strategic plan will be the most important decision that the Commission will adopt, the current proposal represents a massive weakening of the institutional control capacity of the European parliament in the way the CAP is implemented. Therefore, the question remains of how to associate the European Parliament to this new decision process.

14.4.3   Risks of Strategic Planning at Member States Level

Striking a right balance between flexibility, subsidiarity, a level playing field at the EU level and policy control is a very complex task. Given that CAP funds have historically been based on a "measure by measure" approach, member states have little experience in programming various CAP instruments in an integrated way.

Developing planning and implementation capacities will be a major challenge for all member states, especially for small ones and those acceding EU after 2004. Empowering member states with greater subsidiarity may result in substantial administrative burden at the MS level.

For the member states with regional or federal legal organisation, the complexity of the internal negotiation of the contribution of each region to the achievement of the national and EU objectives should not be underestimated and could delay the real implementation of the new CAP.

Within chapter V of the proposed regulation (European Commission 2018b), the section on simplification is empty and left completely to MSs, which means that the Commission is leaving this at their discretion. The risks derive also from the varying capacity of actors in different member states. Flexibility may also be associated with risks of a departure from the pursuit of common goals at the EU level.

Therefore, the CAP proposals need to be accompanied by safeguards at the EU and MS levels, in particular by ensuring the effective engagement with civil society in both contributing to the design and monitoring the progress of strategic plans.

Without serious investment in personnel, processes, analytical support and inclusive preparation of Strategic plans, there may be considerable differences in policy implementation between individual member states. This could conceivably cause falling standards and negative trends in individual MS, which would in turn result in further weakening of the common policy.

14.4.4   Final Comments

The period 2021–2027 is a period of learning, in which the quality of data sources must be significantly increased, with systematic monitoring of the measures and their effects.

Both member states and EU bodies (JRC, EEA, Eurostat) have a role to play here. They see the utmost importance of strengthening the data sources related to needs analyses, and in particular, it is necessary to thoroughly reflect the appropriate data that will be employed as indicators for identifying and monitoring objectives. European Commission and member states need to be required to provide reputable and independent scientific and technical evidence to support their choices. This will require establishment of a common platform with an open access to all strategic plans, progress and evaluation reports.

14.5   COMMON MARKET ORGANISATION

14.5.1   *Marketing Standards and Rules on Farmers' Cooperation Are Unchanged*

As stated by the Commission in its presentation of the legislative proposals of June 2018, "the Common Market Organisation and its instruments remain largely unchanged". The safety net continues to be composed of public intervention and private storage aid, on the one hand, and exceptional measures, on the other. Marketing standards and rules on farmers' cooperation are unchanged. Nevertheless, the Commission underlines a "few important points for more effectiveness and simplification":

The integration of sectoral interventions in the CAP plan regulation (for fruit and vegetables, wine, olive oil, hops and apiculture)

The extension of the possibility to initiate sectorial interventions to other agricultural sectors

Amendments to rules on geographical indications to make them more attractive and easier to manage

The adjustment of allocations following the multiannual financial framework (MFF) proposal

The deletion of a number of obsolete provisions

On the main issues related to the single common market organisation (CMO), the Commission has followed the Resolution of the European Parliament of 30 May 2018 on the future of food and farming (mentioned later on as "the Resolution"). The maintaining of the specific sectoral intervention has been also largely welcomed by the different stakeholders.

The European rules on producer organisations, their associations and the interbranch organisations deserve special attention. The first version of regulation 1308/2013 ended into a ceremony of the confusion. The same wording "producer organisation" was used in the same regulation with two significantly different meanings. The Omnibus regulation and the recent ruling of the European Court of Justice on the so-called endive case, represent important and positive steps in reducing the confusion and legal uncertainties.

14.5.2   Safety Net Provision

In the proposal for the future CAP, the current safety net system is continued. It is often argued that the current level of the European reference thresholds is "unrealistic" and does not contribute enough to achieve their safety net role. This argument has been, implicitly at least, partially accepted by the Commission when it increased withdrawal prices for many fruits and vegetables from 30% to 40% of the average EU market price over the last five years for free distribution (so-called charity withdrawals) and from 20% to 30% for withdrawals destined for other purposes (such as compost, animal feed, distillation).

In an increasingly market-oriented and open economy, such as the current European one, intervention prices cannot be related to production costs for, amongst others, two reasons. Firstly, there is no objective or unique "EU production cost" as such but rather a large range of production costs depending, for instance, on agronomic, climatic, farm and investments management, land prices, labour costs, national taxation systems and monetary factors. Secondly, too high intervention prices would stimulate EU imports of competitive products and discourage exports. Even more, they could stimulate increased production in third countries which could be exported to the EU.

Market orientation of the European agricultural sector and industry is one of the major achievements of the different waves of CAP reform. This is why EU agri-food trade surplus is at record levels (EC 2018a). This does not mean that, on a case-by-case basis, intervention (or withdrawal) prices could not be revisited. In some cases, they could be increased but in others, it could be the opposite. For instance, Jongeneel and Silvis (2018) concluded recently that "the intervention price level as it is currently defined for Skimmed Milk Powder (SMP) may need reconsideration and be in need to be lowered".

14.5.3   Preventive Market Measures

Mahé and Bureau (2016) concluded that "the economics of market measures shows that they have the power to prevent or mitigate deep price disturbances, but when coming late they do not address properly the waste of productive and budget resources. Preventive policies look attractive at first glance, but their implementation raise political and institutional issues".

Internal Commission rules and their corresponding Comitology make it practically impossible for the Commission to implement preventive measures despite the fact that these are more efficient and effective. Once the Directorate-General for Agriculture and Rural Development (DG AGRI) market unit is convinced that a potential problem is going to happen in a market, a time-consuming internal decision-making and consultation process starts (García Azcárate 2018).

After that, an official Interservice consultation is launched and a proposal is presented to, and voted by, the management committee if it is a Commission Regulation and approved by the Commission if it is a European Parliament and Council Regulation. Mahé and Bureau (2016) rightly assess "that the possibility, for all the three political institutions to interfere into details such as changing prices or volumes of intervention is not the best framework for good policy making". They propose for that reason "an independent Administrative Authority for market measures".

14.5.4   Crisis Management

Crisis management in the EU operates on a set of instruments and practices that are flexible enough to address a wide variety of needs arising from unforeseen extreme events. These tools can be found mainly in regulatory provisions for exceptional market support measures, market withdrawal, non-harvesting and green harvesting, as well as public interventions, private storage aid and incentives to supply reduction. The existing EU-level crisis management instruments are effective in addressing stakeholders' needs to cope with crises (Ecorys-WUR 2019). They provide the necessary liquidity support to affected producers and reduce the need for ad hoc public aid. In addition, risk management tools constitute the first line of defence during a crisis, although the slow uptake of insurance, mutual funds and income stabilisation tools across the sector is identified as a potential gap in available crisis management responses.

In a context of increased globalisation and with a market-oriented policy, some crisis management instruments, such as public and private intervention, may have become less efficient. Derived from a long CAP history, measures related to supply and demand management are still one of the central parts of the crisis response strategy. In an open environment integrated with global markets, recourse to these measures may come at an increasingly high cost: crisis management by the EU indirectly benefits third country competitors, particularly for products where the EU is highly competitive on world markets. This may provide an argument for more international coordination with respect to market stabilisation (e.g. of the EU with key competitive suppliers) although feasibility might be a difficult issue. So far the current system and its funding have functioned reasonably well.

In the Commission's proposal for a new CAP, a new agricultural reserve is proposed to be established under the European Agricultural Guarantee Fund. The amount of this reserve will be at least €400 million at the beginning of each financial year (including expenditure on public intervention and private storage), which compares to the current crisis reserve of €500 million. Unused crisis reserve amounts can roll over to the next year to constitute the new reserves. The new proposal aims at reducing the disincentive of not using the crisis reserve in case of a crisis (starting from 2020). With more and more budget constraints limiting the flexibility of reallocating CAP funds, it is not sure whether the newly proposed reserve approach will guarantee a well-functioning system in the future (lack of funding cannot be excluded).

14.5.5   *Level Playing Field Needs Careful Attention*

The interventions made available under Title III of the legal proposal for the future CAP offer member states a wide range of opportunities, the number and flexibility of which have been increased relative to those in the current CAP.

However, this runs the risk of increasing the differences in regulatory requirements and (compensating) support between member states. Level playing field concerns can be identified for at least three types of interventions: (1) the enhanced conditionality (potential differences in requirements over member states, combined with differences in basic income support for sustainability); (2) the payments for eco-schemes which can overcompensate the costs of efforts made; and (3) coupled income support. Also the sectoral interventions include aspects at the discretion of member states that can potentially distort the level playing field.

In order to avoid this, member states should be requested to motivate their choices and safeguards should be considered. In addition, the question remains if the Commission will be institutionally and politically strong enough to impose the common interest to any national "creative" measures which would disturb the single market, even if it comes from a big member states.

14.5.6   Rural Development Policy for Coping with Market Failure

The main change in the rural development policy is the new delivery model (from compliance to performance). With respect to its core principles and its coverage, it remains basically unchanged. The agri-environment, climate and other management commitments have a wide coverage (comprising measures contributing to all nine specific objectives of the CAP), with a special focus on environment and climate (obligatory).

Natural or other area-specific constraints and area-specific disadvantages resulting from certain mandatory requirements interventions contribute to fairness to farmers and are crucial policy interventions in an EU with very heterogeneous production and regulatory conditions.

The investment intervention possibilities in the proposed RDP plays a crucial role in helping agriculture to address its many challenges and facilitating the transition to a more sustainable agriculture while ensuring its long-term viability. When properly implemented, it should primarily address market failure (non-productive investments) and restore assets after crises. Its importance justifies introducing a minimum spending share requirement.

Investments and Young farmer support need a careful specification in order to ensure a level playing field and compatibility with WTO requirements. Risk management needs to be embedded in a broad approach (including awareness raising, farmer advice, accounting for interactions between various policy measures and private sector provisions) in order to contribute to a consistent, tailored and effective policy in which the proposed policy foresees.

Cooperation and knowledge- and information-sharing interventions, when properly combined with other interventions, play a key role in an effective innovation and farm modernisation strategy. The support and extension of the coverage of farm advisory services and its contribution to the improvement of agriculture's sustainability are to be welcomed.

14.6   Concluding Remarks

There seems to be a wide consensus about the general policy objectives the CAP should pursue. Also the set of policy instruments that are proposed in the new CAP is not fundamentally different from the current CAP. Most significant are the proposed changes in the delivery model for the first pillar of the CAP, which should be more performance based and better be able to take into account the specifics of the member states.

The conceptual design of CAP Strategic planning at member state level is based on the theoretical concepts of policy cycle and evidence-based policy-making (EBPM). In real-world situations characterised by incomplete information and often conflicting policy goals, it is difficult for these two concepts to be fully realised. There are several reasons why decision-makers are not always able, or willing, to take evidence into account.

With respect to the policy, measures proposed under the new CAP as well as those with respect to the rural development policy remain largely unchanged. The most significant changes are with respect to the first pillar of the CAP, as a new green architecture is proposed (including eco-schemes as a new measure) and cross-compliance is extended into an enhanced conditionality including the current greening requirement now as standard baseline obligations.

The proposed legislation claims to be more ambitious with respect to improving the sustainability of EU agriculture, but there is still debate and uncertainty whether such a desired increased "value for money" will be finally realised (Dupraz and Guyomard 2019). The last discussion paper from the Presidency of the Council on CAP strategic plan, at the time this text was written (May 2019) clearly shows that the member states are moving in the direction of reducing the proposed ambition, limiting the commitments, increasing the flexibilities and decreasing the reporting obligations.

The increased implementation options at the member state level run the risk of distorting the level playing field in case of diverging ambition target levels between member states. In the Commission proposal, it was a potential risk. If the final result of the negotiation is close to what is today on the table of the Council, it could become a reality.

Also the measures of the CMO remain largely unchanged, although a new element is that member states will have the possibility (if they considerate necessary) to design operational programmes (otherwise called sectoral interventions) for other sectors than those that are already included in the existing regulation (fruit and vegetables, apiculture, wine, hops and olives).

REFERENCES

Chartier, O., Cronin, E., Jongeneel, R., Hart, K., Zondag, M-J. and Bocci, M., eds. (2016). *Mapping and Analysis of the Implementation of the CAP; Final Report*. Brussels: European Commission. https://ec.europa.eu/agriculture/sites/agriculture/files/external-studies/2016/mapping-analysis-implementation-cap/fullrep_en.pdf

Dupraz, P., and H. Guyomard. 2019. Environment and Climate in the Common Agricultural Policy. *EuroChoices* 18 (1): 18–25.

DVL. 2017. *Gemeinwohlprämie –Umweltleistungen der Landwirtschaft einen Preis geben; Konzept für eine zukunftsfähige Honorierung wirksamer Biodiversitäts-, Klima-, und Wasserschutz-leistungen in der Gemeinsamen EU-Agrarpolitik (GAP)*. Ansbach: Deutscher Verband für Landschaftspflege (DVL).

Ecorys-WUR. 2019. *Improving Crisis Prevention and Management Criteria and Strategies in the Agricultural Sector; Final Report*. Brussels: European Commission, DG-Agri.

EP Think tank. 2017. Rural Poverty in the European Union. Last Modified March 13. http://www.europarl.europa.eu/thinktank/en/document.html?reference=EPRS_BRI(2017)599333

Erjavec, E., M. Lovec, L. Juvančič, T. Šumrada, and I. Rac. 2018. *Research for AGRI Committee – The CAP Strategic Plans Beyond 2020: Assessing the Architecture and Governance Issues in Order to Achieve the EU-Wide Objectives*. Brussels: European Parliament, Policy Department for Structural and Cohesion Policies.

European Commission. 2017. *Report on the Distribution of Direct Payments to Agricultural Producers (Financial Year 2016)*. Brussells: European Commission.

———. 2018a. *Regulation of the European Parliament and the Council*. Brussels: European Commission, COM (2018) 392.

———. 2018b. *The CAP 2021–2027; Legislative Proposal 2018; Questions and Answers*. Brussels: European Commission, DG for Agriculture and Rural Development, Directorate C. Strategy, Simplification and Policy Analysis; C.1. Policy Perspectives.

European Court of Auditors. 2018. *Future of the CAP; Briefing Paper*. Luxembourg: European Union, March.

García Azcárate, T. 2018. *Research for AGRI Committee – The Sectoral Approach in the CAP Beyond 2020 and Possible Options to Improve the EU Food Value*

Chain. Brussels: European Parliament, Policy Department for Structural and Cohesion Policies.

Jongeneel, R., and H. Silvis. 2018. *Research for AGRI Committee – Assessing the Future Structure of Direct Payments and the Rural Development Interventions in the Light of the EU Agricultural and Environmental Challenges*. Brussels: European Parliament, Policy Department for Structural and Cohesion Policies.

Mahé, L.P., and J.-C. Bureau. 2016. *Research for Agri-Committee – CAP Reform Post 2020 – Challenges in Agriculture; Workshop Documentation*. Brussels: European Parliament, Directorate-General; for Internal Policies; Policy Department B: Structural and Cohesion Policies.

Matthews, A. 2018a. The Greening Architecture in the New CAP. Blog-Post on June 20. http://capreform.eu/the-greening-architecture-in-the-new-cap/

———. 2018b. The Article 92 Commitment to Increased Ambition with Regard to Environmental- and Climate-Related Objectives. Blog-Post on June 30. http://capreform.eu/the-article-92-commitment-to-increased-ambition-with-regard-to-environmental-and-climate-related-objectives/

———. 2019. Capping Direct Payments – A Modest Proposal. Blog-Post on May 15. http://capreform.eu/

Pe'er, G., Y. Zinngrebe, F. Moreira, R. Müller, C. Sirami, G. Passoni, D. Clough, V. Bontzorlos, P. Bezák, A. Möckel, B. Hansjürgens, A. Lomba, S. Schindler, C. Schleyer, J. Schmidt, and S. Lakner. 2017. *"Is the CAP Fit for Purpose? An Evidence-Based Fitness Check Assessment," 1824*. Leipzig: German Centre for Integrative Biodiversity Research (iDiv) Halle-Jena-Leipzig.

Petit, M. 2019. Another Reform of the CAP; What to Expect? *EuroChoices* 18 (1): 34–39.

Terluin, I., and D. Verhoog. 2018. Verdeling van de toeslagen van de eerste pijler van het GLB over landbouwbedrijven in de EU. In *Report 2018–039*. Wageningen: WUR.

Thompson, P.B. 2017. *The Spirit of the Soil: Agriculture and Environmental Ethics*. 2nd ed. New York: Routledge.

Westhoek, H., J.P. Lesschen, A. Leip, T. Rood, S. Wagner, A. De Marco, D. Murphy-Bokern, C. Pallière, C.M. Howard, O. Oenema, and M.A. Sutton. 2015. *Nitrogen on the Table: The Influence of Food Choices on Nitrogen Emissions and the European Environment (European Nitrogen Assessment Special Report on Nitrogen and Food)*. Edinburgh, UK: Centre for Ecology & Hydrology.

WEBSITES

Direct Payments explained:
http://ec.europa.eu/agriculture/markets/sfp/index_en.htm
Cross compliance explained:
https://ec.europa.eu/agriculture/direct-support/cross-compliance_en

Index[1]

[1] Note: Page numbers followed by 'n' refer to notes.

© The Author(s) 2019   229
L. Dries et al. (eds.), *EU Bioeconomy Economics and Policies: Volume I*,
Palgrave Advances in Bioeconomy: Economics and Policies,
https://doi.org/10.1007/978-3-030-28634-7

Printed by Printforce, the Netherlands